MAKE A
JOYFUL TABLE

ALSO BY JOANNA M. LUND

■ ■ ■

The Healthy Exchanges Cookbook

HELP: The Healthy Exchanges Lifetime Plan

Cooking Healthy with a Man in Mind

Cooking Healthy with the Kids in Mind

Dessert Every Night!

The Diabetic's Healthy Exchanges Cookbook

The Strong Bones Healthy Exchanges Cookbook

The Arthritis Healthy Exchanges Cookbook

The Heart Smart Healthy Exchanges Cookbook

The Best of Healthy Exchanges Food Newsletter '92 Cookbook

Letters from the Heart

It's Not a Diet, It's a Way of Life (audiotape)

MAKE A
JOYFUL TABLE

200 Recipes, Menus, and Inspiration
to Make Every Day a Celebration

JoAnna M. Lund
with Barbara Alpert

G. P. PUTNAM'S SONS

New York

Before using the recipes and advice in this book, consult your physician or health-care provider to be sure they are appropriate for you. The information in this book is not intended to take the place of any medical advice. It reflects the author's experiences, studies, research, and opinions regarding a healthy lifestyle. All material included in this publication is believed to be accurate. The publisher assumes no responsibility for any health, welfare, or subsequent damage that might be incurred from use of these materials.

G. P. Putnam's Sons
Publishers Since 1838
a member of
Penguin Putnam Inc.
375 Hudson Street
New York, NY 10014

Published simultaneously in Canada

For more information about Healthy Exchanges products, contact:

Healthy Exchanges, Inc.
P.O. Box 124
DeWitt, Iowa 52742-0124
(319) 659-8234

Diabetic Exchanges calculated by Rose Hoenig, R.D., L.D.

Library of Congress Cataloging-in-Publication Data

Lund, JoAnna M.
Make a joyful table : 200 recipes, menus, and inspiration to make every day
a celebration / by JoAnna M. Lund, with Barbara Alpert.
p.   cm.
ISBN 0-399-14527-3
1. Cookery.   I. Alpert, Barbara.   II. Healthy Exchanges, Inc.
III. Title.
TX714.L85   1999   99-17055   CIP
641.5—dc21

Printed in the United States of America
1   3   5   7   9   10   8   6   4   2

This book is printed on acid-free paper. ∞

BOOK DESIGN BY AMANDA DEWEY

As long as I'm able to create the "common folk" healthy recipes shared in my cookbooks, every one of those books will be dedicated in loving memory to my parents, Jerome and Agnes McAndrews. After all, it was at our family's kitchen table that I learned love should be served just as abundantly as food. I also inherited the ability to create my family-pleasing recipes from both of them. God has blessed me with my mother's creativity and writing talents and my father's analytical skills. When I began my quest for a commonsense approach to lifelong healthy living, He allowed their earthly abilities to flourish in me.

Even as I share this special collection with you, I know my parents are sharing the joy of this occasion in Heaven. My pleasure in offering hospitality to others was developed at an early age because of them. The coffeepot and something fresh from the oven were always waiting for unexpected company. "Welcome, come on in" is how Mom and Daddy warmly greeted guests as they ushered them into our modest home. The furnishings may have been humble, but the warmth was far beyond what money could buy.

In honor of my parents, I want to share a poem my mother wrote about just how priceless family memories really are. My hope is that my mother's words and my recipes will help stir up fond family memories for you and your loved ones for years to come.

The Old House

A new mobile trailer now stands
    where our old house used to be.
But for more than twenty-nine years,
    it was home to my family and me.

My three children played in the backyard,
    outside the kitchen door.
Now the lawn is hushed and quiet,
    for no one gathers there anymore.

The house was big and old-fashioned
    and in need of so many repairs.
But it was filled to the rafters with love
    and a family that still really cares.

Several years have passed by since
    we left that house in our hometown.
Where friends, relatives, and playmates
    so frequently gathered around.

Time and progress do not stand still,
    the years go by much too fast.
But, oh just for a day or two,
    how I would love to relive the past

When my family lived in that old house,
    so many years ago . . .
Those fond memories are the happiest
    that I believe I will ever know.

—*Agnes Carrington McAndrews*

ACKNOWLEDGMENTS

■ ■ ■

If recipes could only talk, what a history in tastes and aromas they would share! Think back to some of your favorite memories of the past. Aren't certain foods part of that memory? Well, it takes much more than thinking about recipes and cookbooks to make them become realities. For helping me share my recipes with you so that you can stir up food memories for years to come, I want to thank:

My husband and helpmate. Cliff Lund is the love of my life, but he is also the stabilizer I need so that I can continue to create my "common folk" healthy recipes day after day. He does the "behind-the-scenes" stuff so I can do the fun stuff!

My children and grandchildren. Becky and John Taylor, James and Pam Dierickx, Tom and Angie Dierickx, and the five wonderful youngsters among them that they've blessed me with so far. Whenever any or all of my clan come home to visit, the first thing I ask myself is, "What can I stir up for them that's guaranteed to make everyone smile?"

My family. Marge and Cleland Lund, Mary Benischek, Regina Reyes, Loretta Rothbart, Juanita Dithmart, and Dale Lund are all ready, willing, and able to do anything we ask of them as we continue to share recipes with the rest of the world.

My editor. John Duff has believed in my family-pleasing recipes ever since we first met, and he's done so much above and beyond the call of duty in helping me commit my recipes to paper. The highest compliment John will ever give me was when he said that my recipes remind him of the kinds of foods his mother always prepared.

My agents. Angela Miller and Coleen O'Shea are the type of agents others just dream of finding. And to think they actually help me—this "middle-aged grandma" living in the middle of the cornfields of Iowa and who writes in a "Grandma Moses" style—to plan my writing future!

My writing partner. Barbara Alpert came into my life at a time when I knew I could write, but I couldn't organize my thoughts, couldn't punctuate, and for sure couldn't spell! The best part is that not only did I gain a writing partner, I also gained a friend.

My employees. Shirley Morrow, Lori Hansen, Rita Ahlers, and everyone else at The House That Recipes Built who've helped me do what I do. I know I couldn't share what I share if I didn't have the support of everyone working on Healthy Exchanges.

My customers. Everyone who has ever used my cookbooks or newsletter to stir up nourishment and memories for their loved ones has been part of the reason my dream continues to grow. Without people continually asking for even more recipes, that dream would have stopped before it ever got started.

My medical advisors and supporters. When I have nutritional questions for Rose Hoenig, R.D., L.D., she gets the answers for me every time. I'm also especially pleased and proud that doctors, dietitians, and nutritionists agree that my recipes are indeed low enough in fats, sugars, and sodium to be healthy but just high enough to be tasty. They know that people will willingly eat my foods for the rest of their lives, not just when they're initially told they must change their diets. This is why so many recommend my recipes to their patients.

My Creator. God gives all of us talents to use for the betterment of mankind. Mine just happens to be creating "common folk" healthy recipes and sharing a commonsense approach to healthy living.

CONTENTS

■ ■ ■

MAKE A
JOYFUL TABLE

EATING HEALTHY IS A JOYFUL CHOICE

∎ ∎ ∎

"To everything there is a season,
and a time to every purpose under the heaven."
—ECCLESIASTES 3:1

WHY WE NEED TO CELEBRATE MORE, NOT LESS, AS WE GROW OLDER

Each day is precious to me, especially when I realize that the days ahead of me are probably fewer than the days behind. It's just as Frank Sinatra used to sing in "September Song": You turn around and it's summer, then you turn around and it's fall. Where did all those seasons go, and how many more will we be blessed to enjoy? None of us can know the length of our lives, so it's always been important to me to celebrate what we *do* have with the people we love.

I will always remember my grandmother's eightieth birthday, which we celebrated as we did all her birthdays, with a huge party in July, and with watermelon and homemade ice cream just like she used to serve to the folks who stayed at her boardinghouse. I can see us now, sitting under huge trees—the whole family, immediate and extended, gathered at her house for an old-time family picnic, with a table of food that seemed never-ending. My great-uncle played his violin as he always did, and it gave all of us such a feeling of comfort. If you asked me to describe one of my sweetest, most heartfelt memories, that's the scene I'd recall. Can you imagine a happier, cozier blanket of life to draw around you, surrounded by all the generations gathered together, from the little kids under five to older relatives over eighty and everyone in between? That huge, beautiful green canopy of leaves and branches seemed as if it could shelter us forever.

I'm a great believer in gathering the family around, even when life's events may have pulled you apart. Years ago, after my divorce but before Cliff and I were married, my son Tommy was about to make his first Holy Communion. I wanted everyone to be there, and I was determined to make it happen somehow.

It wasn't easy, but I took a deep breath, and then I picked up the phone. I told each of them, "This is for Tommy. I want you to be here, but you need to know that so-and-so will be coming, too. I will understand if you don't feel comfortable enough to come." Well, I was truly pleased that everyone who was important in Tommy's life chose to be there.

How wonderful it was to see my ex-mother-in-law, my future mother-in-law, and my mother, all sitting together on the couch. They sat there visiting with each other with such warmth during our celebration of this little boy they all loved, and everyone put aside thoughts of any conflict so we could all enjoy this special event. I wonder how many other households have found a way to mend fences during those times when it mattered most. I'm sure that our family is not alone in this.

Even more, because we agreed to set aside the past, at least for that day, we received a healing that we didn't expect. It left the pathway open for future celebrations, opening a door that many of us believed had been locked. It can be hard to open yourself to do something that feels awkward and difficult, but when you focus on the love instead of the pain, you may be able to make peace.

In fact, the seeds I planted at the time of Tommy's Communion bore fruit when we all gathered in the summer of 1997 for his wedding. My ex-husband joined us at the head table and was recognized during the festivities. And even though my mother didn't live to see it, I still experienced such happiness—with

Cliff beside me, and Tommy's father, his grandmother Dierickx sporting her lovely corsage, and his grandma and grandpa Lund with their flowers pinned on, all happy together because Tommy was happy.

It means everything to me, knowing that this tradition will continue into the next generation. Anytime anyone comes back for any occasion, we have a big family get-together, and now my son James is often the host. Last Thanksgiving he opened up his house and invited everyone! He and his wife, Pam, prepared all the food, and the gathering was truly multigenerational, with both sides of the family present. You can count on us never to let a year go by without those family celebrations that make wonderful memories—graduations and weddings and baptisms—a tradition that each new generation will come to treasure.

As the years pass, each of these occasions takes on even more meaning for us. Christmas Eve has always been a special night at our house, a time for just my children, Cliff, and me. Now that they've grown up and scattered around, any of my kids who can come home give me so much to be grateful for. Most recently, Tom and Angie traveled here from Arizona, James and Pam and the two boys stayed overnight, and even though Becky couldn't join us, she called, as she always does. We traditionally have a great big extended family dinner on Christmas Day, and last year we celebrated in JO's Kitchen Cafe. Finally, I had a big enough place to seat everyone around one table, and a big enough kitchen to fix all the food with ease!

Sometimes a tradition starts when you want to recapture a beloved childhood memory. When I first decided to hold my now biannual Healthy Exchanges Family Reunion Potluck Picnic, I think I really wanted to re-create what we used to have at Grandma's—and to share it with others who maybe didn't have that kind of tradition in their own families. When people tell me how comfortable they feel when they visit us here in DeWitt, I remind them that I consider them all part of my extended family—the Healthy Exchanges family—and I genuinely mean it. The notion seems to be contagious. During a recent lunchtime at the cafe, two couples who'd never met before sat together during their meal, and as they were leaving, I heard them making plans to meet again at the cafe for lunch!

I'm truly happy that I've found a way to create a place, both physical and spiritual, that gives people a real sense of belonging. I'm not a bit ashamed of being old-fashioned in that way. For me, love of family, love of country, and love of God are all part of who I am. I take comfort in knowing that, and I especially love to share what has made a joyful life possible for me. That's why I'm so pleased to be writing this celebration cookbook now.

"Serve the Lord with gladness. . . ."
—PSALM 100

MAKE THE FOOD YOU PREPARE AN EXPRESSION OF YOUR LOVE, AND YOUR FAITH IN THE FUTURE

Have you ever noticed how many people focus on food as the culprit, as the cause of ill health or excessive weight? Are you one of them? I'd like you to take a moment to consider the true power of food, which is to nourish your body and touch your soul. It's become too easy to strip food of its pleasures, of the colors and flavors that delight the eyes and mouth. In an effort to "behave," as people put it, they settle for dull, boring, bland food. They do it because they feel it's "safe," but take it from me, nothing is more dangerous to a healthy lifestyle than that!

Remember that while you are nourishing your physical body, it's important not to starve your emotions and heart. I began to create Healthy Exchanges when I first understood that myself, and it has always been my goal to bring joy and pleasure back into the process of eating. When you're eating what you like, you're smiling inside and out. You feel cared for, loved, and that sensation of self-love is amazingly powerful. Recognizing that you're of value, that you deserve to be treated well, gives you the kind of strength and self-esteem that allows you to celebrate the positive things in your life, and to build on them.

Have you ever meditated right there in the produce section of the market as you gazed at a colorful display of fresh fruit and vegetables? It's so glorious, so appealing to your senses—the juicy red tomatoes, the shiny green cucumbers, the carrots with their green leafy tops (and even a bit of earth attached!). Just looking at those vegetables can actually give you an emotional lift. Often the last thing I do at night before heading home from the office is to walk out to my gardens and take one last look, pull one last weed, take one last sniff, maybe even grab a cherry tomato or two for the road! (We don't use any pesticides here at Healthy Exchanges, so I don't even feel I have to wash my "pilfered" treasures. I know not everyone can do this at home, but you can always come visit me!)

Can you remember the last time you experienced a flood of sensual pleasure while you were out food shopping? Even if you don't have a garden or can't find a farmers' market nearby, you can still taste this feast for the senses at any grocery store: looking, smelling, touching the produce and admiring the variety of colors and textures; inhaling the wondrous scent of fresh baked bread; even enjoying the abundant variety of products on the shelves that we often take for granted (and that give visitors from other nations such joy when they visit our giant supermarkets!).

Try to allow a little extra time on your next visit if you can. Walk around your local farmers' market and visit every booth, even if you think you don't need what they're selling. Smell the fresh peaches and feel the rough texture of the red onions. Pick up a piece of the ripest fruit you can find, buy it and give it a quick rinse-off, then take a bite right there and then. As the juice dribbles just a bit down your chin, close your eyes and take in all the sensations at once. It's the closest thing to the Garden of Eden you'll ever encounter!

Practice thinking like a chef for once—don't think about what you're *supposed* to eat, but what you'd like to prepare and serve. What looks good to you? String beans? Golden ears of corn? Those beets shining like rubies will make a delectable snack when they're cooked and served cold. Sometimes you don't even know what you want until you see it, and there it is in front of you.

The proliferation of farmers' markets in this country has been such a blessing. Now we can all celebrate the harvest, eating what's just been picked hours before. Imagine serving a healthy shortcake made with freshly picked peaches and raspberries—what could be better than that?

I view the luscious abundance of fresh foods as a kind of living message from the Lord. These are His creations, and I can almost hear Him saying, "Take this, create something wonderful, and share it with those you love." So many of my best recipes were created on the spur of the moment, getting something in my hands and saying, "Now, what can I do with this to share it with others? How can I enhance the flavors it already has?" Being open to that spark of possibility will enhance your life in so many ways. Are you ready to explore your own God-given talents? See the food, close your eyes, taste it with your mind—and make up a recipe!

Isn't it time to experience your own Field of Dreams? It's up to you: you can live in the shadows of deprivation or bask in the sunshine of abundance.

"Eat only as much as you need. . . ."
—Proverbs 25:16

MAKING PEACE WITH PORTION CONTROL: YES, YOU CAN HAVE MORE OF THAT ANOTHER TIME

If you've always been a professional dieter, you already know the feeling of deprivation only too well. Either you can't have what you want (you tell yourself, or one of a myriad of diet books and programs tells you), or you can't have very much of it. Well, I'm not going to be your fairy godmother, wave a magic wand, and tell you that you can eat anything you want in whatever quantity you want. But I will joyfully wave my magic whisk and tell you that you *can* have just about anything in moderation, even foods that used to live on the "forbidden" list.

The key to making a lifelong commitment to healthy eating is learning to enjoy the foods you love in reasonable quantities, which means learning to enjoy a healthy portion size. I recently answered a letter from a woman who was worried that having to attend six weddings in only three months spelled doom for her waistline. I remember what it was like to fear those special occasions where all kinds of food were plentiful and there always seemed to be *cake* at the end! But what I reminded my concerned correspondent is that we were talking about *six—count 'em—just six pieces of wedding cake* over a twelve-week period. Now, even the richest wedding cake doesn't have the power to put ten pounds on you—unless you use it as an excuse to eat everything on the buffet table the day of the wedding, and then keep eating like that! Cake is just cake, and while sometimes it's very rich, it's still manageable as part of a healthy lifestyle. If enjoying that cake is important to her, then she could eat fruit for dessert for the rest of that weekend and maybe get in some extra exercise. That's it. It's simple, and yet it can be the hardest thing for some of us to handle.

Here's another flashback to my life as a professional dieter. Remember what it's like to have something you "shouldn't" have in the house? You tell yourself, "Guess I'd better eat it all up fast and get it out of the house. Then I will eat nothing but celery and carrots for a week, I promise."

That's a diet mentality, and *it doesn't work.* What does is learning to enjoy life on a daily basis, without those delirious peaks and depressed valleys that bingeing creates. Here's how it used to go: You've got a pint of low-fat ice cream in your freezer. You scoop out one serving, about a quarter of the container, and you eat it while watching television. When you're done, you think, "Oh, I shouldn't have eaten that. I'm just no good. Well, better finish it up and start my diet all over again tomorrow." You can be sure that whatever guilt you felt after the first serving will be multiplied when your spoon hits the bottom of the pint!

Why not consider another scenario? You bought the pint of low-fat ice cream. You enjoyed a healthy dinner, and then you sat down to dessert. You ate the half-cup serving of your favorite treat slowly and savored every bite. When you finished, you did the dishes, went for a walk with your dog, and had a relaxing evening watching your favorite sitcoms. The next day (or perhaps even the day after that) you decided to have the ice cream for dessert again. Eventually, yes, you may eat the entire pint—but when you make it part of the menu, divest it of the guilt and secrecy it used to have, it loses its power to "hurt" you and becomes what it really is: a low-fat dessert choice with calories and fat grams. Enjoyed over four evenings instead of gobbled guiltily during one, the very same pint of coffee fudge becomes part of a healthy nutrition plan.

What you're working toward is a *constant* level of enjoyment. I want deprivation to become something you used to experience but don't anymore. It's not just about food volume, either. Most of my casseroles serve you one-quarter of an 8-inch-by-8-inch baking dish. That's a pretty substantial serving, but it's not my idea of a meal *in itself*. When you're composing a meal, I'd like you to think about the different parts that comprise it. You want it to be pleasing to the eye, the flavors have to blend, the textures complement each other, and the colors coordinate. A satisfying meal is something like a beautiful flower arrangement. Any one or two of those lovely blossoms would look pretty in a vase, but when you arrange them together, you get a glorious abundance that fills the soul.

If you are used to how it feels to "live to eat," you may sometimes question the size of my portions (though most people tell me they've never eaten so much, or felt so well!). My sweet salads, for example, often serve six or eight people from an 8-inch-by-8-inch casserole dish. Why don't I give you more? Just as a composer arranges a piece of music, adding just enough piano, bass, or saxophone, I like to think I'm orchestrating a healthy meal—and that piece of salad is not planned to be eaten on its own. Sure, all by itself it may look modest on the plate, but when you team it up with your entree and a veggie side dish, you've got what my husband Cliff calls a REAL MEAL. I don't want any one portion to be out of proportion, and I hope you won't use my exchange information to cut your food intake too severely. Don't try *too hard* by putting your body in hibernation when you lower your calories too much. Try eating a truly balanced meal, enjoy it more, and see how your body responds!

We all ate those tasteless diet dinners, those spare little plates of dry tuna and a few lettuce leaves, or a three-ounce piece of chicken or turkey lying naked before you without a drop of sauce or dressing. But those days are over, when you decide to live, really live, with Healthy Exchanges! Your plate now features a nice serving of a flavorful casserole *plus* a vegetable dish *plus* a sweet or savory salad. Add a fresh roll to that, and then don't forget: dessert's coming! That's the way to enjoy eating well and living well all at once. The Lord didn't put all this abundance before us and not expect us to enjoy it—but in *moderation.* When you don't feel deprived anymore, a reasonable serving nourishes the body and truly satisfies the soul.

Think about this: What is the difference between eating to live and eating to *enjoy* living?

For me, an important part of the miracle that Healthy Exchanges has worked in my own life is that it's taught me to enjoy living as never before. I've worked hard to create a way of life that emphasizes pleasure and abundance instead of denial and deprivation. I've often said that it makes no difference how healthy a food may be; if it doesn't taste and look good, no one's going to eat it, and no one's going to say "Gee, Mom, when can we have this again?"

I've provided recipes of all kinds in this latest cookbook, and my goal is to encourage you to try as many as you can. Tasting different dishes day in and day out stimulates the pleasure centers of your brain, and enjoying a variety of foods simply keeps life interesting. This isn't "low-cal" eating as you used to know it. And this isn't a diet book that will tell you exactly what to eat and in what quantities. But it can be a healthy eating "bible" that you can turn to in moments of celebration and times of trouble, and find sustenance that does more than just provide the minimum number of calories you need to survive.

"For he satisfies the thirsty and fills the hungry with good things."
—PSALM 107:9

WHY DOING THE BEST I CAN . . . *THE BEST I CAN*, MEANS DOING A LITTLE BIT MORE

When I say that just "good enough" isn't good enough for me, I mean it with all my heart. Even one of my luscious pies isn't complete, no matter what's been layered beneath the creamy topping, until I sprinkle some nuts or mini-chips or coconut on top.

That's why I decided to share with you my philosophy of *garnishing.*

I want everything I serve to look as delectable as it tastes, and that means pleasing the eye as fully as a spoonful pleases first the tastebuds and then the tummy. Garnishing a dish is putting the period on the sentence—it's how I tell myself it's *done.* And I truly enjoy making each of my dishes special in some way.

What am I going for when I garnish?

- I want the plate to look attractive. That also means letting a dish cool on a wire rack, just enough so it doesn't run all over the plate.
- I want the people gathered round my table to smile when they contemplate the dish before them. Their satisfaction is heightened by that first look, as they murmur with wonder, *"Mmm,* that looks *good."* In this way, the eyes share what the mouth is shortly going to taste!
- I want to share whatever artistic ability I have with others. We can't all be Rembrandts, I know that, but anyone can learn to add a bit of color and crunch. It takes so little extra effort to provide a homey touch and ensure our loved ones feel cared for.
- I want to include foods in my healthy recipes that may be considered "out of bounds" so I use tiny amounts of these treats, these potentially "risky" foods, where the eye can see and enjoy them.

Garnishing is all about the *finishing touch.* It's that extra pat to your hair that your beautician gives before she tells you that you're done. It's that little extra effort your tailor provides when he presses the pleats in your favorite skirt so beautifully. There is a real difference between "good enough" and "really good," I've discovered, and my recipes are designed to remind people that they deserve *more* than just good enough. With these little touches, you can transform an ordinary meal into something extraordinary—and change the way you view this good-for-you cuisine.

These little garnishes of cheese or nuts or chocolate mean a lot, and they deliver so much more than the sum of their calories. You may only get four or five mini-chips on your piece of healthy pie, but when you bite down and get that *whoosh,* that chocolate rush, you feel satisfied by a minimal addition that doesn't feel like a little thing.

I've been asked if I have a special technique for sprinkling these little toppings so that every piece of your pie or casserole provides exactly the same serving. Truth is, your hand grows steadier with time and practice, but if you keep it "slow and steady," and don't try to be perfect, just pretty even, you'll do fine! (And if you're a little off, accept it—instead of reaching back into the bag for a little bit more. Those extra calories can add up, so stick with the measured amount.)

Because little things do mean a lot, I hope you'll make garnishing your dishes a regular habit. It could mean the difference between riding happily with me on the Health Wagon, or falling back into old habits that won't help you reach your healthy goals.

> *"Every man should eat and drink,*
> *and enjoy the good of all his labor,*
> *it is the gift of God."*
> —ECCLESIASTES 3:13

EATING ALONE, EATING TOGETHER—CREATING MEALTIME RITUALS THAT FEED THE SOUL

Everyone eats some meals alone, but that shouldn't mean standing at the sink gulping takeout food from a cardboard container or gobbling greasy fast food in your car. Whenever you eat, wherever you eat, you will truly nourish yourself as the Lord intended by taking the time to treat yourself well.

You wouldn't invite a guest for dinner and not set the table or put on some relaxing music, would you? Well, it's time to care for yourself as you care for others when it comes to meals.

Ever since I began sharing Healthy Exchanges, I've been spending more weeks on the road than I do at home. (As I write that down, I can hardly believe it—but it's true.) Yet, even when Cliff and I travel the highways and byways in our motor home, our meals are served on place mats and there's always a center-piece on our little table. The same was always true at JO's Kitchen Cafe. We didn't *have* to use pretty place mats for the guests who stopped by for the Peach Plate Special, but I *wanted to* appeal to their eyes as well as their mouths, and so we do.

Becoming aware of these little extras, these comforting rituals, may be most important for anyone eating alone. It's so easy for a single diner to scale down to the bare minimum: fewer dishes to wash if you eat out of the pan, no glasses to scrub if you drink out of a can. But I bet you won't feel satisfied after such a catch-as-catch-can meal, and that's often what triggers old, unhealthy eating behaviors.

It's vital to feed all the senses, to pause between bites and just enjoy the sen-sation of the sun spilling in through the window, or to listen to the birds outside. Even if you choose to have breakfast while you're watching the morning news, you're feeding your mind as well as your tummy. (Of course, I still sometimes have to caution myself not to gobble my food to the pace of the breaking news reports!)

When we're home, we like to sit down at our dining room table for dinner. The cozy and familiar surroundings help us relax and remember how good it feels to be home at last. True, sometimes it feels as if it takes extra effort to set the table and slow down what might ordinarily be a hurried meal, but you're worth it. Tell yourself you've got the time, and you'll be pleased to discover that you usually *do*.

I often turn on the radio for some soothing music to accompany dinner. It's a great change from the frenetic pace of the rest of the day, and I know it helps me handle stress better. I also believe that when you make the effort to eat a meal away from where you are working, whatever you eat will satisfy you much more. I read recently about a study done by an efficiency expert that said people who take a break from work to eat get more done in the long run—and feel bet-ter about what they do.

It's just too easy to become an unconscious eater if you're not paying at-tention to what you put into your mouth. At The House That Recipes Built, we created a warm and inviting "break area," because we didn't want our employ-ees eating at their desks. Instead, they can sit comfortably at tables and really "take a break" from ringing phones and piles of papers. In warm weather, they take their lunches outside in the garden at picnic tables, and in that pretty setting, surrounded by plants and flowers, the most ordinary meal tastes like a feast.

Do I always do what I suggest you do? I'm not Saint JoAnna, remember, so while I'm a believer in distinct mealtimes instead of eating on the run, I can't always manage what I know is best for me. I aim for at least 50 percent success, maybe three out of six meals eaten in a more relaxed, more enjoyable atmosphere. Sometimes I do better, and sometimes I don't, but I don't beat myself up about it. I just try to my best . . . *the best I can.*

> *"Be of good cheer, daughter; your faith has made you well."*
> —MATTHEW 9:22

HAVING FAITH IN YOURSELF— AND FAITH IN GOD

Do you remember when you first heard the word *faith*? Perhaps your parents tried to explain it to you when you were a child, or possibly you were instructed about it in Sunday school. Maybe it's something you haven't thought much about for a long time.

When I first began working on this book, I recognized that this would be a good time to share my own experiences and thoughts about faith with you. Faith is not a diet plan written down in black and white; it's not something vowed in a contract you can file in a drawer and forget about. Faith, to me, means believing in something you cannot know for certain, except in your heart.

And yet faith is more powerful than almost anything else in helping us find our life's purpose and reach our life goals. Changing your life for the better asks you for a leap of faith, especially if you've tried and failed many times before to achieve what you most want. But if you ask for God's help, and you do your part, your faith can move mountains, and what earlier seemed impossible gradually and beautifully will unfold.

In Matthew 17:20, the Bible reminds us: "If you have faith as a mustard seed, you will say to this mountain, 'Move from here to there,' and it will move; and nothing will be impossible for you."

Have you ever held a mustard seed in your hand? It's so tiny, so easy to drop and lose sight of. But from something so small, great things may come, if your faith is strong enough.

Healthy Exchanges was really an act of faith from its earliest moment of creation. I had no reason to believe that I would finally be successful in losing the 130 pounds that weighed me down both physically and psychologically; I had no evidence that the recipes I created to help me get healthy would point the way toward what became my mission in life; I had no idea that a photocopied collection of my recipes would lead me on such an amazing journey of personal and professional discovery.

All I had was a small kernel of faith in myself and in God. Each day my belief got a little stronger, and my faith began to grow, nourished by hard work and an unwillingness to "lose" what I had "gained," or gain back what I had gratefully lost.

My faith kept me going through the creation of my first cookbook, and even got me through my meetings with the New York City book publishers that led to my being published by Putnam. But the true test was when Cliff and I had to make the biggest commitment of our lives (after our decision to get married): to buy the land and build a building to house Healthy Exchanges.

Even though I knew I couldn't continue what I had started without making changes, couldn't share my message the way I wanted to if I didn't grow, I felt very apprehensive. I will always remember the moment that brought our situation to a crisis point. At that time, I was running the business from my family room, and our house isn't all that big. One day I got up very early and sat down at my desk to work. About a half hour later, one of my employees arrived to start on a rush project. Hours and hours later, when I went to bed, there were still employees working in my house. I told Cliff the very next day that we just couldn't live like this anymore.

That weekend, when we were taking a walk in the fall sunshine, we walked through a cornfield at one end of DeWitt and saw a FOR SALE sign. I said to Cliff, "I think this is where we belong." We were both scared, but we agreed that we had to do it. We no longer had a home, only a business, and it was time for a change.

We would stop by as often as possible as The House That Recipes Built was going up, and even though it seemed to take forever before the walls went up and the paths through the muddy ground were laid, we found the process more exciting than we expected. What began as a kind of impossible dream began taking shape, and now, with all that's happened for Healthy Exchanges, we've been putting up a new building a year ever since!

It took a lot of faith to build my Recipeland, USA, to take Healthy Exchanges down an unfamiliar new road. It forced me to grow along with the business, and helped me find the courage to take a leap toward where I'd never been. What kept me going is what got me started, a simple prayer that hasn't changed all that much:

> *God, help me help myself so I can help others, for Your honor and glory. Use me and Healthy Exchanges in any way You see fit, to do Your work and make me worthy.*

And now, I'm embarking on a new journey that presents entirely new challenges—choosing to step back a bit from the business that hard work and faith created, so that I can make time for the people and work that I cherish most. Each path we choose requires a fresh act of faith, but I believe that with the Lord's help, I will choose the right one.

PLANTING SEEDS AND CULTIVATING YOUR GARDEN

For me, spending time in the garden is an opportunity to commune with God, to celebrate the miracle of life, to find serenity in a world that is so often overwhelming and even chaotic, and bring more beauty into my daily existence.

There's a powerful sense of satisfaction, too, in knowing that the vegetables on your table have been nurtured in your own garden. It's a wonderful way to reinforce your commitment to living a healthy lifestyle, and a bunch of freshly cut flowers in full bloom as a centerpiece provides a true feast for the eyes just as the veggies do for your tastebuds.

When I first started dreaming about our Healthy Exchanges building, The House That Recipes Built, I wasn't only thinking about a bigger kitchen to test recipes in, or Cliff's ever-growing print shop. I knew from the very beginning that I would have a garden—and that it would start with a rhubarb patch. (When I moved off the farm into my house in DeWitt, the very first thing that came with me was my rhubarb. Want to know from the tip of your nose to the ends of your toes when spring is definitely on the way? It's when those little green leaves begin to emerge from the loamy earth and whisper that beautiful sunny days are just around the corner!)

I've always had a garden, even when all I had to plant was a tiny corner of a backyard to raise tomatoes in. Once I realized how much time I would be spending at the Healthy Exchanges offices, and that I couldn't continue to garden and get the satisfaction I treasured at home, I knew it was time to bring my garden right down here. That way, whenever I had a spare moment, I could enjoy it—and I could also get pleasure from sharing it with other people.

We now have a tomato patch (in addition to the rhubarb patch), eight elevated gardens, and four more added this year. If you're not familiar with the idea of an elevated garden, just know that they're very attractive, easier to work in, and just about the only way to keep my veggies from feeding every rabbit for miles around! They're made by stacking landscape logs about three high, then filled in with dirt. Each one is about sixty-four square feet (8 feet by 8 feet), with a beautiful grassway between the different patches so you can wander among the strawberries and rhubarb, spot cabbages and green peppers poking their heads up, get a whiff of my fresh herbs growing, and help me decide when the tomatoes are just perfect to pick!

My other great garden pleasure is my orchard of fruit trees. I have sixteen dwarf fruit trees so far, and they already give me and others so much happiness. I could have started with seeds or seedlings, but this way I get to enjoy the fruits of my labor so much sooner. And I'm not the only one—so many people have told me they found comfort and peace walking in my little orchard amid the glories of nature. City dwellers who would come here for lunch got a true feeling of being in the country. Many retired people who'd moved off their family farms loved sharing in the wonderful colors and the scents of the flowering shrubs and trees that seem to fill every foot of land!

When we first built our building, it wasn't easy to envision how beautiful the grounds would someday be. There was mud everywhere, and yet when I closed my eyes and dreamed of the future, I saw it much as it is today: with flowers everywhere, and flowering shrubs, trees for summer shade, and veggies so fresh you can nibble them right off the vine!

I often talk about making the commitment to live a healthy lifestyle, and about choosing to be good to yourself, positive instead of critical. My garden is a constant reminder of that kind of happy promise, and I celebrate my commitment by planting a few new flowering bushes or trees every year. Ever since I first owned a tiny piece of property, I've been doing it without fail—digging holes and planting trees that will show future generations that we thought about them "way back when." I want my grandchildren to know that we showed our love and shared our dreams by building a world that will be as beautiful for them as it has been for me all my life.

After all, if somebody hadn't planted trees fifty years ago, just imagine how much less joy I would find in the world around me. The trees I plant each year are for me to enjoy now, and for the generations that follow to enjoy for many years to come. I know they'll be grateful, as I was and continue to be, for the ancestors who left me a legacy of nature in their own gardens and forests.

I like to think of my garden as my way of "bringing the farm with me" no matter where I go. And when I smell the honeysuckle and lilacs, when I feast my eyes on gorgeous oriental poppies and my old-time, old-fashioned rose bushes, I feel a sweet satisfaction in my soul.

A garden is a wonderful reminder of the potential of dreams to be fulfilled, through hard work and commitment. Besides the fact that it's difficult to snack on unhealthy foods when your hands are covered in dirt, you can also apply the lesson of the garden to other aspects of your life. Just as a seed represents possibility, something that *may* happen, a vision of yourself as healthier and more energetic can be the seed of hope that keeps you on your path, that sends you in the right direction.

Even if you don't have a plot of land to grow a garden, you can still create a world of beauty on a windowsill or balcony. What more vivid commitment could there be—to yourself and those you love—than planting and nurturing the seeds of a happy future. Start planning yours today!

> *"For you shall go out with joy,*
> *And be led out with peace;*
> *The mountains and the hills*
> *Shall break forth into singing before you,*
> *And all the trees of the field shall clap their hands."*
> —ISAIAH 55:12

Dear Friends,

People often ask me why I include the same general information at the beginning of all my cookbooks. If you've seen any of my other books you'll know that my "common folk" recipes are just one part of the Healthy Exchanges picture. You know that I firmly believe—and say so whenever and wherever I can—that *Healthy Exchanges is not a diet, it's a way of life!* That's why I include the story of Healthy Exchanges in every book, because I know that the tale of my struggle to lose weight and regain my health is one that speaks to the hearts of many thousands of people. And because Healthy Exchanges is not just a collection of recipes, I always include the wisdom that I've learned from my own experiences and the knowledge of the health and cooking professionals I meet. Whether it's learning about nutrition or making shopping and cooking easier, no Healthy Exchanges book would be complete without features like "A Peek into My Pantry" or "JoAnna's Ten Commandments of Successful Cooking."

Even if you've read my other books, you might still want to skim the following chapters—you never know when I'll slip in a new bit of wisdom or suggest a new product that will make your journey to health an easier and tastier one. If you're sharing this book with a friend or family member, you'll want to make sure they read the following pages before they start stirring up the recipes.

If this is the first book of mine that you've read, I want to welcome you with all my heart to the Healthy Exchanges Family. (And, of course, I'd love to hear your comments or questions. See the back of the book for my mailing address . . . or come visit if you happen to find yourself in DeWitt, Iowa—just ask anybody for directions to Healthy Exchanges!)

Jo Anna

JOANNA M. LUND AND HEALTHY EXCHANGES

. . .

Food is the first invited guest to every special occasion in every family's memory scrapbook. From baptism to graduation, from weddings to wakes, food brings us together.

It wasn't always that way at our house. I used to eat alone, even when my family was there, because while they were dining on real food, I was nibbling at whatever my newest diet called for. In fact, for twenty-eight years, I called myself the diet queen of DeWitt, Iowa.

I tried every diet I ever came across, every one I could afford, and every one that found its way to my small town in eastern Iowa. I was willing to try anything that promised to "melt off the pounds," determined to deprive my body in every possible way in order to become thin at last.

I sent away for expensive "miracle" diet pills. I starved myself on the Cambridge Diet and the Bahama Diet. I gobbled diet candies, took thyroid pills, fiber pills, prescription and over-the-counter diet pills. I went to endless weight-loss support group meetings—but I somehow managed to turn healthy programs such as Overeaters Anonymous, Weight Watchers, and TOPS into unhealthy diets . . . diets I could never follow for more than a few months.

I was determined to discover something that worked long-term, but each new failure increased my desperation that I'd never find it.

I ate strange concoctions and rubbed on even stranger potions. I tried liquid diets. I agreed to be hypnotized. I tried reflexology and even had an acupressure device stuck in my ear!

Does my story sound a lot like yours? I'm not surprised. No wonder the weight-loss business is a billion-dollar industry!

Every new thing I tried seemed to work—at least at first. And losing that first five or ten pounds would get me so excited, I'd believe that this new miracle diet would, finally, get my weight off for keeps.

Inevitably, though, the initial excitement wore off. The diet's routine and boredom set in, and I quit. I shoved the pills to the back of the medicine chest; pushed the cans of powdered shake mix to the rear of the kitchen cabinets; slid all the program materials out of sight under my bed; and once more I felt like a failure.

Like most dieters, I quickly gained back the weight I'd lost each time, along with a few extra "souvenir" pounds that seemed always to settle around my hips. I'd done the diet-lose-weight-gain-it-all-back "yo-yo" on the average of once a year. It's no exaggeration to say that over the years I've lost 1,000 pounds—and gained back 1,150 pounds.

Finally, at the age of forty-six I weighed more than I'd ever imagined possible. I'd stopped believing that any diet could work for me. I drowned my sorrows in sacks of cake doughnuts and wondered if I'd live long enough to watch my grandchildren grow up.

Something had to change.

I had to change.

Finally, I did.

I'm over fifty now—and I'm 130 pounds less than my all-time high of close to 300 pounds. I've kept the weight off for more than seven years. I'd like to lose another ten pounds, but I'm not obsessed about it. If it takes me two or three years to accomplish it, that's okay.

What I *do* care about is never saying hello again to any of those unwanted pounds I said good-bye to!

How did I jump off the roller coaster I was on? For one thing, I finally stopped looking to food to solve my emotional problems. But what really shook me up—and got me started on the path that changed my life—was Operation Desert Storm in early 1991. I sent three children off to the Persian Gulf War— my son-in-law, Matt, a medic in Special Forces; my daughter, Becky, a full-time college student and member of a medical unit in the Army Reserve; and my son James, a member of the Inactive Army Reserve reactivated as a chemicals expert.

Somehow, knowing that my children were putting their lives on the line got me thinking about my own mortality—and I knew in my heart the last thing they needed while they were overseas was to get a letter from home saying that their mother was ill because of a food-related problem.

The day I drove the third child to the airport to leave for Saudi Arabia, something happened to me that would change my life for the better—and for-ever. I stopped praying my constant prayer as a professional dieter, which was simply "Please, God, let me lose ten pounds by Friday." Instead, I began pray-ing, "God, please help me not to be a burden to my kids and my family." I quit praying for what I wanted and started praying for what I needed—and in the process my prayers were answered. I couldn't keep the kids safe—that was out of my hands—but I could try to get healthier to better handle the stress of it. It was the least I could do on the homefront.

That quiet prayer was the beginning of the new JoAnna Lund. My initial goal was not to lose weight or create healthy recipes. I only wanted to become healthier for my kids, my husband, and myself.

Each of my children returned safely from the Persian Gulf War. But some-thing didn't come back—the 130 extra pounds I'd been lugging around for far too long. I'd finally accepted the truth after all those agonizing years of suffering through on-again, off-again dieting.

There are no "magic" cures in life.

No "miracle" potion, pill, or diet will make unwanted pounds disappear.

I found something better than magic, if you can believe it. When I turned my weight and health dilemma over to God for guidance, a new JoAnna Lund and Healthy Exchanges were born.

I discovered a new way to live my life—and uncovered an unexpected tal-ent for creating easy "common folk" healthy recipes, and sharing my common-sense approach to healthy living. I learned that I could motivate others to change their lives and adopt a positive outlook. I began publishing cookbooks and a monthly food newsletter, and speaking to groups all over the country.

I like to say, *"When life handed me a lemon, not only did I make healthy, tasty lemonade, I wrote the recipe down!"*

What I finally found was not a quick fix or a short-term diet, but a great way to live well for a lifetime.

I want to share it with you.

FOOD EXCHANGES
AND WEIGHT
LOSS CHOICES™

■ ■ ■

I f you've ever been on one of the national weight-loss programs like Weight Watchers or Diet Center, you've already been introduced to the concept of measured portions of different food groups that make up your daily food plan. If you are not familiar with such a system of weight-loss choices or exchanges, here's a brief explanation. (If you want or need more detailed information, you can write to the American Dietetic Association or the American Diabetes Association for comprehensive explanations.)

The idea of food exchanges is to divide foods into basic food groups. The foods in each group are measured in servings that have comparable values. These groups include Proteins/Meats, Breads/Starches, Vegetables, Fats, Fruits, Skim Milk, Free Foods, and Optional Calories.

Each choice or exchange included in a particular group has about the same number of calories and a similar carbohydrate, protein, and fat content as the other foods in that group. Because any food on a particular list can be "exchanged" for any other food in that group, it makes sense to call the food groups *exchanges* or *choices.*

I like to think we are also "exchanging" bad habits and food choices for good ones!

By using Weight Loss Choices or exchanges you can choose from a variety of foods without having to calculate the nutrient value of each one. This makes it easier to include a wide variety of foods in your daily menus and gives you the opportunity to tailor your choices to your unique appetite.

If you want to lose weight, you should consult your physician or other weight-control expert regarding the number of servings that would be best for you from each food group. Since men generally require more calories than women, and since the requirements for growing children and teenagers differ from those of adults, the right number of exchanges for any one person is a personal decision.

I have included a suggested plan of weight-loss choices in the pages following the exchange lists. It's a program I used to lose 130 pounds, and it's the one I still follow today.

(If you are a diabetic or have been diagnosed with heart problems, it is best to meet with your physician before using this or any other food program or recipe collection.)

FOOD GROUP WEIGHT LOSS CHOICES/EXCHANGES

Not all food group exchanges are alike. The ones that follow are for anyone who's interested in weight loss or maintenance. If you are a diabetic, you should check with your health-care provider or dietitian to get the information you need to help you plan your diet. Diabetic exchanges are calculated by the American Diabetic Association, and information about them is provided in *The Diabetic's Healthy Exchanges Cookbook* (Perigee Books).

Every Healthy Exchanges recipe provides calculations in three ways:

- Weight Loss Choices/Exchanges
- Calories, Fat, Protein, Carbohydrates, and Fiber in grams, and Sodium and Calcium in milligrams
- Diabetic Exchanges calculated for me by a registered dietitian

Healthy Exchanges recipes can help you eat well and recover your health, whatever your health concerns may be. Please take a few minutes to review the exchange lists and the suggestions that follow on how to count them. You have lots of great eating in store for you!

PROTEINS

Meat, poultry, seafood, eggs, cheese, and legumes. One exchange of Protein is approximately 60 calories. Examples of one Protein choice or exchange:

1 ounce cooked weight of lean meat, poultry, or seafood
2 ounces white fish
1½ ounces 97% fat-free ham
1 egg (limit to no more than 4 per week)
¼ cup egg substitute
3 egg whites
¾ ounce reduced-fat cheese
½ cup fat-free cottage cheese
2 ounces cooked or ¾ ounce uncooked dry beans
1 tablespoon peanut butter (also count 1 fat exchange)

BREADS

Breads, crackers, cereals, grains, and starchy vegetables. One exchange of Bread is approximately 80 calories. Examples of one Bread choice or exchange:

1 slice bread or 2 slices reduced-calorie bread (40 calories or less)
1 roll, any type (1 ounce)
½ cup cooked pasta or ¾ ounce uncooked (scant ½ cup)
½ cup cooked rice or 1 ounce uncooked (⅓ cup)
3 tablespoons flour
¾ ounce cold cereal

½ cup cooked hot cereal or ¾ ounce uncooked (2 tablespoons)

½ cup corn (kernels or cream-style) or peas

4 ounces white potato, cooked, or 5 ounces uncooked

3 ounces sweet potato, cooked, or 4 ounces uncooked

3 cups air-popped popcorn

7 fat-free crackers (¾ ounce)

3 (2½-inch squares) graham crackers

2 (¾-ounce) rice cakes or 6 mini

1 tortilla, any type (6-inch diameter)

FRUITS

All fruits and fruit juices. One exchange of Fruit is approximately 60 calories. Examples of one Fruit choice or exchange:

1 small apple or ½ cup slices

1 small orange

½ medium banana

¾ cup berries (except strawberries and cranberries)

1 cup strawberries or cranberries

½ cup canned fruit, packed in fruit juice or rinsed well

2 tablespoons raisins

1 tablespoon spreadable fruit spread

½ cup apple juice (4 fluid ounces)

½ cup orange juice (4 fluid ounces)

½ cup applesauce

SKIM MILK

Milk, buttermilk, and yogurt. One exchange of Skim Milk is approximately 90 calories. Examples of one Skim Milk choice or exchange:

1 cup skim milk

½ cup evaporated skim milk

1 cup low-fat buttermilk

¾ cup plain fat-free yogurt

⅓ cup nonfat dry milk powder

VEGETABLES

All fresh, canned, or frozen vegetables other than the starchy vegetables. One exchange of Vegetable is approximately 30 calories. Examples of one Vegetable choice or exchange:

½ cup vegetable
¼ cup tomato sauce
1 medium fresh tomato
½ cup vegetable juice

FATS

Margarine, mayonnaise, vegetable oils, salad dressings, olives, and nuts. One exchange of Fat is approximately 40 calories. Examples of one Fat choice or exchange:

1 teaspoon margarine or 2 teaspoons reduced-calorie margarine
1 teaspoon butter
1 teaspoon vegetable oil
1 teaspoon mayonnaise or 2 teaspoons reduced-calorie mayonnaise
1 teaspoon peanut butter
1 ounce olives
¼ ounce pecans or walnuts

FREE FOODS

Foods that do not provide nutritional value but are used to enhance the taste of foods are included in the Free Foods group. Examples of these are spices, herbs, extracts, vinegar, lemon juice, mustard, Worcestershire sauce, and soy sauce. Cooking sprays and artificial sweeteners used in moderation are also included in this group. However, you'll see that I include the caloric value of artificial sweeteners in the Optional Calories of the recipes.

You may occasionally see a recipe that lists "free food" as part of the portion. According to the published exchange lists, a free food contains fewer than

20 calories per serving. Two or three servings per day of free foods/drinks are usually allowed in a meal plan.

OPTIONAL CALORIES

Foods that do not fit into any other group but are used in moderation in recipes are included in Optional Calories. Foods that are counted in this way include sugar-free gelatin and puddings, fat-free mayonnaise and dressings, reduced-calorie whipped toppings, reduced-calorie syrups and jams, chocolate chips, coconut, and canned broth.

SLIDERS™

These are 80 Optional Calorie increments that do not fit into any particular category. You can choose which food group to *slide* these into. It is wise to limit this selection to approximately three to four per day to ensure the best possible nutrition for your body while still enjoying an occasional treat.

Sliders may be used in either of the following ways:

1. If you have consumed all your Protein, Bread, Fruit, or Skim Milk Weight Loss Choices for the day, and you want to eat additional foods from those food groups, you simply use a Slider. It's what I call "healthy horse trading." Remember that Sliders may not be traded for choices in the Vegetables or Fats food groups.
2. Sliders may also be deducted from your Optional Calories for the day or week. One-quarter Slider equals 20 Optional Calories; ½ Slider equals 40 Optional Calories; ¾ Slider equals 60 Optional Calories; and 1 Slider equals 80 Optional Calories.

HEALTHY EXCHANGES
WEIGHT LOSS CHOICES

My original Healthy Exchanges program of Weight Loss Choices was based on an average daily total of 1,400 to 1,600 calories per day. That was what I determined was right for my needs, and for those of most women. Because men require additional calories (about 1,600 to 1,900), here are my suggested plans for women and men. *(If you require more or fewer calories, please revise this plan to meet your individual needs.)*

Each day, women should plan to eat:

2 Skim Milk choices, 90 calories each
2 Fat choices, 40 calories each
3 Fruit choices, 60 calories each
4 Vegetable choices or more, 30 calories each
5 Protein choices, 60 calories each
5 Bread choices, 80 calories each

Each day, men should plan to eat:

2 Skim Milk choices, 90 calories each
4 Fat choices, 40 calories each
3 Fruit choices, 60 calories each
4 Vegetable choices or more, 30 calories each
6 Protein choices, 60 calories each
7 Bread choices, 80 calories each

Young people should follow the program for men but add 1 Skim Milk choice for a total of 3 servings.

You may also choose to add up to 100 Optional Calories per day, and up to 21 to 28 Sliders per week at 80 calories each. If you choose to include more Sliders in your daily or weekly totals, deduct those 80 calories from your Optional Calorie "bank."

A word about **Sliders:** These are to be counted toward your totals after you have used your allotment of choices of Skim Milk, Protein, Bread, and Fruit for the day. By "sliding" an additional choice into one of these groups, you can meet your individual needs for that day. Sliders are especially helpful when traveling, stressed-out, eating out, or for special events. I often use mine so I can enjoy my favorite Healthy Exchanges desserts. Vegetables are not to be counted as Sliders. Enjoy as many Vegetable choices as you need to feel satisfied. Because we want to limit our fat intake to moderate amounts, additional Fat choices should not be counted as Sliders. If you choose to include more fat on an *occasional* basis, count the extra choices as Optional Calories.

Keep a daily food diary of your Weight Loss Choices, checking off what you eat as you go. If, at the end of the day, your required selections are not 100 percent accounted for, but you have done the best you can, go to bed with a clear conscience. There will be days when you have ¼ Fruit or ½ Bread left over. What are you going to do—eat two slices of an orange or half a slice of bread and throw the rest out? I always say, "Nothing in life comes out exact." Just do the best you can . . . *the best you can.*

Try to drink at least eight 8-ounce glasses of water a day. Water truly is the "nectar" of good health.

As a little added insurance, I take a multivitamin each day. It's not essential, but if my day's worth of well-planned meals "bites the dust" when unexpected events intrude on my regular routine, my body still gets its vital nutrients.

The calories listed in each group of Choices are averages. Some choices within each group may be higher or lower, so it's important to select a variety of different foods instead of eating the same three or four all the time.

Use your Optional Calories! They are what I call "life's little extras." They make all the difference in how you enjoy your food and appreciate the variety available to you. Yes, we can get by without them, but do you really want to? Keep in mind that you should be using all your daily Weight Loss Choices first to ensure you are getting the basics of good nutrition. But I guarantee that Optional Calories will keep you from feeling deprived—and help you reach your weight-loss goals.

SODIUM, FAT, CHOLESTEROL, AND PROCESSED FOODS

■ ■ ■

re Healthy Exchanges ingredients really healthy?

A When I first created Healthy Exchanges, many people asked about sodium, about whether it was necessary to calculate the percentage of fat, saturated fat, and cholesterol in a healthy diet, and about my use of processed foods in many recipes. I researched these questions as I was developing my program, so you can feel confident about using the recipes and food plan.

SODIUM

Most people consume more sodium than their bodies need. The American Heart Association and the American Diabetes Association recommend limiting sodium intake to no more than 3,000 milligrams per day. If your doctor suggests you limit your sodium even more, then *you really must read labels.*

Sodium is an essential nutrient and should not be completely eliminated. It helps to regulate blood volume and is needed for normal daily muscle and nerve functions. Most of us, however, have no trouble getting "all we need" and then some.

As with everything else, moderation is my approach. I rarely ever have salt on my list as an added ingredient. But if you're especially sodium-sensitive, make the right choices for you—and save high-sodium foods such as sauerkraut for an occasional treat.

I use lots of spices to enhance flavors, so you won't notice the absence of salt In the few cases where it is used, salt is vital for the success of the recipe, so please don't omit it.

When I do use an ingredient high in sodium, I try to compensate by using low-sodium products in the remainder of the recipe. Many fat-free products are a little higher in sodium to make up for any loss of flavor that disappeared along with the fat. But when I take advantage of these fat-free, higher-sodium products, I stretch that ingredient within the recipe, lowering the amount of sodium per serving. A good example is my use of fat-free and reduced-sodium canned soups. While the suggested number of servings per can is two, I make sure my final creation serves at least four and sometimes six. So the soup's sodium has been "watered down" from one-third to one-half of the original amount.

Even if you don't have to watch your sodium intake for medical reasons, using moderation is another "healthy exchange" to make on your own journey to good health.

FAT PERCENTAGES

We've been told that 30 percent is the magic number—that we should limit fat intake to 30 percent or less of our total calories. It's good advice, and I try to have a weekly average of 15 percent to 25 percent myself. I believe any less than 15 percent is really just another restrictive diet that won't last. And more than 25 percent on a regular basis is too much of a good thing.

When I started listing fat grams along with calories in my recipes, I was tempted to include the percentage of calories from fat. After all, in the vast majority of my recipes, that percentage is well below 30 percent This even includes my pie recipes that allow you a realistic serving instead of many "diet" recipes that tell you a serving is ½ of a pie.

Figuring fat grams is easy enough. Each gram of fat equals 9 calories. Multiply fat grams by 9, then divide that number by the total calories to get the percentage of calories from fat.

So why don't I do it? After consulting four registered dietitians for advice, I decided to omit this information. They felt that it's too easy for people to become obsessed by that 30 percent figure, which is after all supposed to be a percentage of total calories over the course of a day or a week. We mustn't feel we can't include a healthy ingredient such as pecans or olives in one recipe just because, on its own, it has more than 30 percent of its calories from fat.

An example of this would be a casserole made with 90 percent lean red meat. Most of us benefit from eating red meat in moderation, as it provides iron and niacin in our diets, and it also makes life more enjoyable for us and those who eat with us. If we *only* look at the percentage of calories from fat in a serving of this one dish, which might be as high as 40 to 45 percent, we might choose not to include this recipe in our weekly food plan.

The dietitians suggested that it's important to consider the total picture when making such decisions. As long as your overall food plan keeps fat calories to 30 percent, it's all right to enjoy an occasional dish that is somewhat higher in fat content. Healthy foods I include in **MODERATION** include 90 percent lean red meat, olives, and nuts. I don't eat these foods every day, and you may not either. But occasionally, in a good recipe, they make all the difference in the world between just getting by (deprivation) and truly enjoying your food.

Remember, the goal is eating in a healthy way so you can enjoy and live well the rest of your life.

SATURATED FATS AND CHOLESTEROL

You'll see that I don't provide calculations for saturated fats or cholesterol amounts in my recipes. It's for the simple and yet not so simple reason that accurate, up-to-date, brand-specific information can be difficult to obtain from food manufacturers, especially since the way in which they produce food keeps changing rapidly. But once more I've consulted with registered dietitians and other professionals and found that, because I use only a few products that are high in saturated fat, and use them in such limited quantities, my recipes are suitable for patients concerned about controlling or lowering cholesterol. You'll also find that whenever I do use one of these ingredients *in moderation*, everything else in the recipe, and in the meals my family and I enjoy, is low in fat.

PROCESSED FOODS

Just what *is* processed food, anyway? What do I mean by the term "processed foods," and why do I use them, when the "purest" recipe developers in Recipe Land consider them "pedestrian" and won't ever use something from a box, container, or can? A letter I received and a passing statement from a stranger made me reflect on what I mean when I refer to processed foods, and helped me reaffirm why I use them in my "common folk" healthy recipes.

If you are like the vast millions who agree with me, then I'm not sharing anything new with you. And if you happen to disagree, that's okay, too.

A few months ago, a woman sent me several articles from various "whole food" publications and wrote that she was wary of processed foods, and wondered why I used them in my recipes. She then scribbled on the bottom of her note, "Just how healthy *is* Healthy Exchanges?" Then, a few weeks later, during a chance visit at a public food event with a very pleasant woman, I was struck by how we all have our own definitions of what processed foods are. She shared with me, in a somewhat self-righteous manner, that she *never* uses processed foods. She only cooks with fresh fruits and vegetables, she told me. Then later she said that she uses canned reduced-fat soups all the time! Was her definition different than mine? I wondered. Soup in a can, whether it's reduced in fat or not, still meets my definition of a processed food.

So I got out a copy of my book *HELP: Healthy Exchanges Lifetime Plan* and reread what I had written back then about processed foods. Nothing in my definition has changed since I wrote that section. I still believe that healthy processed foods, such as canned soups, prepared piecrusts, sugar-free instant puddings, fat-free sour cream, and frozen whipped topping, when used properly, all have a place as ingredients in healthy recipes.

I never use an ingredient that hasn't been approved by either the American Diabetic Association, the American Dietetic Association, or the American Heart Association. Whenever I'm in doubt, I send for their position papers, then ask knowledgeable registered dietitians to explain those papers to me in layman's language. I've been assured by all of them that the sugar- and fat-free products I use in my recipes are indeed safe.

If you don't agree, nothing I can say or write will convince you otherwise. But, if you've been using the healthy processed foods and have been concerned about the almost daily hoopla you hear about yet another product that's going to be the doom of all of us, then just stick with reason. For every product on the grocery shelves, there are those who want you to buy it and there are those who don't, *because they want you to buy their products instead.* So we have to learn to sift the fact from the fiction. Let's take sugar substitutes, for example. In making your own evaluations, you should be skeptical about any information provided by the sugar substitute manufacturers, because they have a vested interest in our buying their products. Likewise, ignore any information provided by the sugar industry, because they have a vested interest in our *not* buying sugar substitutes. Then, if you aren't sure if you can really trust the government or any of its agencies, toss out their data, too. That leaves the three associations I mentioned earlier. Do you think any of them would say a product is safe if it isn't? Or say a product isn't safe when it is? They have nothing to gain or lose, *other than their integrity,* if they intentionally try to mislead us. That's why I go to only these associations for information concerning healthy processed foods.

I certainly don't recommend that everything we eat should come from a can, box, or jar. I think the best of all possible worlds is to start with the basics: grains such as rice, pasta, or corn. Then, for example, add some raw vegetables and extra-lean meat such as poultry, fish, beef, or pork. Stir in some healthy canned soup or tomato sauce, and you'll end up with something that is not only healthy but tastes so good, everyone from toddlers to great-grandparents will want to eat it!

I've never been in favor of spraying everything we eat with chemicals, and I don't believe that all our foods should come out of packages. But I do think we should use the best available healthy processed foods to make cooking easier and food taste better. I take advantage of the good-tasting low-fat and low-sugar products found in any grocery store. My recipes are created for busy people like me, people who want to eat healthily and economically but who still want the food to satisfy their tastebuds. I don't expect anyone to visit out-of-the-way health-food stores or find the time to cook beans from scratch—*because I don't!* Most of you can't grow fresh food in the backyard, and many of you may not have access to farmers' markets or large supermarkets. I want to help you figure out realistic ways to make healthy eating a reality *wherever you live,* or you will not stick to a healthy lifestyle for long.

So if you've been swayed (by individuals or companies with vested interests or hidden agendas) into thinking that all processed foods are bad for you, you may want to reconsider your position. Or if you've been fooling yourself into believing that you *never* use processed foods but regularly reach for that healthy canned soup, stop playing games with yourself—you are using processed foods in a healthy way. And, if you're like me and use healthy processed foods in *moderation*, don't let anyone make you feel ashamed about including these products in your healthy lifestyle. Only *you* can decide what's best for *you* and your family's needs.

Part of living a healthy lifestyle is making those decisions and then getting on with life. Congratulations on choosing to live a healthy lifestyle, and let's celebrate together by sharing a piece of Healthy Exchanges pie that I've garnished with Cool Whip Lite!

JOANNA'S TEN COMMANDMENTS OF SUCCESSFUL COOKING

■ ■ ■

A very important part of any journey is knowing where you are going and the best way to get there. If you plan and prepare before you start to cook, you should reach mealtime with foods to write home about!

1. **Read the entire recipe from start to finish** and be sure you understand the process involved. Check that you have all the equipment you will need *before* you begin.
2. **Check the ingredient list** and be sure you have *everything* and in the amounts required. Keep cooking sprays handy—while they're not listed as ingredients, I use them all the time (just a quick squirt!).
3. **Set out *all* the ingredients and equipment needed** to prepare the recipe on the counter near you *before* you start. Remember that old saying *A stitch in time saves nine*? It applies in the kitchen, too.

4. **Do as much advance preparation as possible** before actually cooking. Chop, cut, grate, or do whatever is needed to prepare the ingredients and have them ready before you start to mix. Turn the oven on at least ten minutes before putting food in to bake, to allow the oven to preheat to the proper temperature.

5. **Use a kitchen timer** to tell you when the cooking or baking time is up. Because stove temperatures vary slightly by manufacturer, you may want to set your timer for five minutes less than the suggested time just to prevent overcooking. Check the progress of your dish at that time, then decide if you need the additional minutes or not.

6. **Measure carefully.** Use glass measures for liquids and metal or plastic cups for dry ingredients. My recipes are based on standard measurements. Unless I tell you it's a scant or full cup, measure the cup level.

7. **For best results, follow the recipe instructions exactly.** Feel free to substitute ingredients that *don't tamper* with the basic chemistry of the recipe, but be sure to leave key ingredients alone. For example, you could substitute sugar-free instant chocolate pudding for sugar-free instant butterscotch pudding, but if you used a six-serving package when a four-serving package was listed in the ingredients, or you used instant when cook-and-serve is required, you won't get the right result.

8. **Clean up as you go.** It is much easier to wash a few items at a time than to face a whole counter of dirty dishes later. The same is true for spills on the counter or floor.

9. **Be careful about doubling or halving a recipe.** Though many recipes can be altered successfully to serve more or fewer people, *many cannot.* This is especially true when it comes to spices and liquids. If you try to double a recipe that calls for 1 teaspoon pumpkin-pie spice, for example, and you double the spice, you may end up with a too-spicy taste. I usually suggest increasing spices or liquid by 1½ times when doubling a recipe. If it tastes a little bland to you, you can increase the spice to 1¾ times the original amount the next time you prepare the dish. Remember: You can always add more, but you can't take it out after it's stirred in.

The same is true with liquid ingredients. If you wanted to **triple** a recipe like my **Pizza Rice Skillet** because you were planning to serve a crowd, you might think you should use three times as much of every ingredient. Don't, or you could end up with Pizza Rice Skillet Soup! The original recipe calls for 1 cup tomato sauce, so I'd suggest using 2 cups when you **triple** the recipe (or 1½ cups if you **double** it). You'll still have a good-tasting dish that won't run all over the plate.

10. **Write your reactions next to each recipe once you've served it.**
Yes, that's right, I'm giving you permission to write in this book. It's yours, after all. Ask yourself: Did everyone like it? Did you have to add another half teaspoon of chili seasoning to please your family, who like to live on the spicier side of the street? You may even want to rate the recipe on a scale of 1★ to 4★, depending on what you thought of it. (Four stars would be the top rating—and I hope you'll feel that way about many of my recipes.) Jotting down your comments while they are fresh in your mind will help you personalize the recipe to your own taste the next time you prepare it.

MY BEST HEALTHY EXCHANGES TIPS AND TIDBITS

■ ■ ■

MEASUREMENTS, GENERAL COOKING TIPS, AND BASIC INGREDIENTS

The word *moderation* best describes **my use of fats, sugar substitutes,** and **sodium** in these recipes. Wherever possible, I've used cooking spray for sautéing and for browning meats and vegetables. I also use reduced-calorie margarine and fat-free mayonnaise and salad dressings. Lean ground turkey *or* ground beef can be used in the recipes. Just be sure whatever you choose is at least *90 percent lean.*

SUGAR SUBSTITUTES

I've also included **small amounts of sugar substitutes as the sweetening agent** in many of the recipes. I don't drink a hundred cans of soda a day or eat enough artificially sweetened foods in a 24-hour time period to be troubled by sugar substitutes. But if this is a concern of yours and you *do not* need to watch your sugar intake, you can always replace the sugar substitutes with processed sugar and the sugar-free products with regular ones.

I created my recipes knowing they would also be used by hypoglycemics, diabetics, and those concerned about triglycerides. If you choose to use sugar instead, be sure to count the additional calories.

A word of caution when cooking with **sugar substitutes:** Use **saccharin**-based sweeteners when **heating or baking.** In recipes that **don't require heat, aspartame** (known as NutraSweet) works well in uncooked dishes but leaves an aftertaste in baked products.

Sugar Twin is my first choice for a sugar substitute. If you can't find that, use **Sprinkle Sweet.** They measure like sugar, you can cook and bake with them, they're inexpensive, and they are easily poured from their boxes.

Many of my recipes for quick breads, muffins, and cakes include a package of sugar-free instant pudding mix, which is sweetened with NutraSweet. Yet we've been told that NutraSweet breaks down under heat. I've tested my recipes again and again, and here's what I've found: baking with a NutraSweet product sold for home sweetening doesn't work, but baking with NutraSweet-sweetened instant pudding mixes turns out great. I choose not to question why this is, but continue to use these products in creating my Healthy Exchanges recipes.

How much sweetener is the right amount? I use pourable Sugar Twin, Brown Sugar Twin, and Sprinkle Sweet in my recipes because they measure just like sugar. What could be easier? I also use them because they work wonderfully in cooked and baked products.

If you are using a brand other than these, you need to check the package to figure out how much of your sweetener will equal what's called for in the recipe.

If you choose to use real sugar or brown sugar, then you would use the same amount the recipe lists for pourable Sugar Twin or Brown Sugar Twin.

You'll see that I list only the specific brands when the recipe preparation involves heat. In a salad or other recipe that doesn't require cooking, I will list the ingredient as "sugar substitute to equal 2 tablespoons sugar." You can then use any sweetener you choose—Equal, Sweet'n Low, Sweet Ten, or any other aspartame-based sugar substitute. Just check the label so you'll be using the right amount to equal those 2 tablespoons of sugar. Or, if you choose, you can use regular sugar.

With Healthy Exchanges recipes, the "sweet life" is the only life for me!

PAN SIZES

I'm often asked why I use an **8-by-8-inch baking dish** in my recipes. It's for portion control. If the recipe says it serves 4, just cut down the center, turn the dish, and cut again. Like magic, there's your serving. Also, if this is the only recipe you are preparing requiring an oven, the square dish fits into a tabletop toaster oven easily and energy can be conserved.

While many of my recipes call for an 8-by-8-inch baking dish, others ask for a 9-by-9-inch cake pan. If you don't have a 9-inch square pan, is it all right to use your 8-inch dish instead? In most cases, the small difference in the size of these two pans won't significantly affect the finished product, so until you can get your hands on the right-size pan, go ahead and use your baking dish.

However, since the 8-inch dish is usually made of glass and the 9-inch cake pan is made of metal, you will want to adjust the baking temperature. If you're using a glass baking dish in a recipe that calls for a 9-inch pan, be sure to lower your baking temperature by 15 degrees *or* check your finished product at least 6 to 8 minutes before the specified baking time is over.

But it really is worthwhile to add a 9-by-9-inch pan to your collection, and if you're going to be baking lots of my Healthy Exchanges cakes, you'll definitely use it frequently. A cake baked in this pan will have a better texture, and the servings will be a little larger. Just think of it—an 8-by-8-inch pan produces 64 square inches of dessert, while a 9-by-9-inch pan delivers 81 square inches. Those 17 extra inches are too tasty to lose!

To make life even easier, **whenever a recipe calls for ounce measurements** (other than raw meats) I've included the closest cup equivalent. I need to use my scale daily when creating recipes, so I've measured for you at the same time.

Most of the recipes are for **4 to 8 servings.** If you don't have that many to feed, do what I do: freeze individual portions. Then all you have to do is choose something from the freezer and take it to work for lunch or have your evening meals prepared in advance for the week. In this way, I always have something on hand that is both good to eat and good for me.

Unless a recipe includes hard-boiled eggs, cream cheese, mayonnaise, or a raw vegetable or fruit, **the leftovers should freeze well**. (I've marked recipes that freeze well with the symbol of a **snowflake** ❆.) This includes most of the cream pies. Divide any recipe up into individual servings and freeze for your own "TV" dinners.

Another good idea is **cutting leftover pie into individual pieces and freezing each one separately** in a small Ziploc freezer bag. Once you've cut the pie into portions, place them on a cookie sheet and put it in the freezer for 15 minutes. That way, the creamy topping won't get smashed and your pie will keep its shape.

When you want to thaw a piece of pie for yourself, you don't have to thaw the whole pie. You can practice portion control at the same time, and it works really well for brown-bag lunches. Just pull a piece out of the freezer on your way to work, and by lunchtime you will have a wonderful dessert waiting for you.

Why do I so often recommend freezing leftover desserts? One reason is that if you leave baked goods made with sugar substitute out on the counter for more than a day or two, they get moldy. Sugar is a preservative and retards the molding process. It's actually what's called an antimicrobial agent, meaning it works against microbes such as molds, bacteria, fungi, and yeasts that grow in foods and can cause food poisoning. Both sugar and salt work as antimicrobial agents to withdraw water from food. Since microbes can't grow without water, food protected in this way doesn't spoil.

So what do we do if we don't want our muffins to turn moldy, but we also don't want to use sugar because of the excess carbohydrates and calories? Freeze them! Just place each muffin or individually sliced bread serving into a Ziploc sandwich bag, seal, and toss into your freezer. Then, whenever you want one for a snack or a meal, you can choose to let it thaw naturally or "zap" it in the microwave. If you know that baked goods will be eaten within a day or two, packaging them in a sealed plastic container and storing in the refrigerator will do the trick.

Unless I specify **"covered" for simmering or baking,** prepare my recipes **uncovered.** Occasionally you will read a recipe that asks you to cover a dish for a time, then to uncover, so read the directions carefully to avoid confusion—and to get the best results.

COOKING SPRAY

Low-fat cooking spray is another blessing in a Healthy Exchanges kitchen. It's currently available in three flavors . . .

- **OLIVE OIL FLAVORED** when cooking Mexican, Italian, or Greek dishes
- **BUTTER FLAVORED** when the hint of butter is desired
- **REGULAR** for everything else

A quick spray of butter flavored makes air-popped popcorn a low-fat taste treat, or try it as a butter substitute on steaming hot corn on the cob. One light spray of the skillet when browning meat will convince you that you're using "old-fashioned fat," and a quick coating of the casserole dish before you add the ingredients will make serving easier and cleanup quicker.

BAKING TIMES

Sometimes I give you a range as a **baking time,** such as 22 to 28 minutes. Why? Because every kitchen, every stove, and every chef's cooking technique is slightly different. On a hot and humid day in Iowa, the optimum cooking time won't be the same as on a cold, dry day. Some stoves bake hotter than the temperature setting indicates; other stoves bake cooler. Electric ovens usually are more temperamental than gas ovens. If you place your baking pan on a lower shelf, the temperature is warmer than if you place it on a higher shelf. If you stir the mixture more vigorously than I do, you could affect the required baking time by a minute or more.

The best way to gauge the heat of your particular oven is to purchase an oven temperature gauge that hangs in the oven. These can be found in any discount store or kitchen equipment store, and if you're going to be cooking and baking regularly, it's a good idea to own one. Set the oven to 350 degrees and when the oven indicates that it has reached that temperature, check the reading on the gauge. If it's less than 350 degrees, you know your oven cooks cooler, and you need to add a few minutes to the cooking time *or* set your oven at a higher temperature. If it's more than 350 degrees, then your oven is warmer and you need to subtract a few minutes from the cooking time. In any event, always treat the suggested baking time as approximate. Check on your baked product at the earliest suggested time. You can always continue baking a few minutes more if needed, but you can't unbake it once you've cooked it too long.

MISCELLANEOUS INGREDIENTS

I use reduced-sodium **canned chicken broth** in place of dry bouillon to lower the sodium content. The intended flavor is still present in the prepared dish. As a reduced-sodium beef broth is not currently available (at least not in DeWitt, Iowa), I use the canned regular beef broth. The sodium content is still lower than regular dry bouillon.

Whenever **cooked rice or pasta** is an ingredient, follow the package directions, but eliminate the salt and/or margarine called for. This helps lower the sodium and fat content. It tastes just fine; trust me on this.

Here's another tip: When **cooking rice or noodles,** why not cook extra "for the pot"? After you use what you need, store leftover rice in a covered container (where it will keep for a couple of days). With noodles like spaghetti or macaroni, first rinse and drain as usual, then measure out what you need. Put the leftovers in a bowl covered with water, then store in the refrigerator, covered, until they're needed. Then, measure out what you need, rinse and drain them, and they're ready to go.

Does your **pita bread** often tear before you can make a sandwich? Here's my tip to make them open easily: cut the bread in half, put the halves in the microwave for about 15 seconds, and they will open up by themselves. *Voilà!*

When **chunky salsa** is listed as an ingredient, I leave the degree of "heat" up to your personal taste. In our house, I'm considered a wimp. I go for the "mild" while Cliff prefers "extra-hot." How do we compromise? I prepare the recipe with mild salsa because he can always add a spoonful or two of the hotter version to his serving, but I can't enjoy the dish if it's too spicy for me.

MILK, YOGURT, AND MORE

Take it from me—nonfat dry milk powder is great! I *do not* use it for drinking, but I *do* use it for cooking. Three good reasons why:

1. It is very **inexpensive.**
2. It does not **sour** because you use it only as needed. Store the box in your refrigerator or freezer and it will keep almost forever.
3. You can easily **add extra calcium** to just about any recipe without added liquid.

I consider nonfat dry milk powder one of Mother Nature's modern-day miracles of convenience. But do purchase a good national name brand (I like Carnation), and keep it fresh by proper storage.

I've said many times, "Give me my mixing bowl, my wire whisk, and a box of nonfat dry milk powder, and I can conquer the world!" Here are some of my favorite ways to use dry milk powder:

1. You can make a **pudding** with the nutrients of 2 cups skim milk, but the liquid of only 1¼ to 1½ cups by using ⅔ cup nonfat dry milk powder, a 4-serving package of sugar-free instant pudding, and the lesser amount of water. This makes the pudding taste much creamier and more like homemade. Also, pie filling made my way will set up in minutes. If company is knocking at your door, you can prepare a pie for them almost as fast as you can open the door and invite them in. And if by chance you have leftovers, the filling will not separate the way it does when you use the 2 cups skim milk suggested on the package. (If you absolutely refuse to use this handy powdered milk, you can substitute skim milk in the amount of water I call for. Your pie won't be as creamy, and will likely get runny if you have leftovers.)

2. You can make your own **"sour cream"** by combining ¾ cup plain fat-free yogurt with ⅓ cup nonfat dry milk powder. What you did by doing this is fourfold: (1) The dry milk stabilizes the yogurt and keeps the whey from separating; (2) the dry milk slightly helps to cut the tartness of the yogurt; (3) it's still virtually fat-free; and (4) the calcium has been increased by 100 percent. Isn't it great how we can make that distant rel-

ative of sour cream a first kissin' cousin by adding the nonfat dry milk powder? Or, if you place 1 cup plain fat-free yogurt in a sieve lined with a coffee filter, and place the sieve over a small bowl and refrigerate for about 6 hours, you will end up with a very good alternative for sour cream. To **stabilize yogurt** when cooking or baking with it, just add 1 teaspoon cornstarch to every ¾ cup yogurt.

3. You can make **evaporated skim milk** by using ⅓ cup nonfat dry milk powder and ½ cup water for every ½ cup evaporated skim milk you need. This is handy to know when you want to prepare a recipe calling for evaporated skim milk and you don't have any in the cupboard. And if you are using a recipe that requires only 1 cup evaporated skim milk, you don't have to worry about what to do with the leftover milk in the can.

4. You can make **sugar-free and fat-free sweetened condensed milk** by using 1⅓ cups nonfat dry milk powder mixed with ½ cup cold water, microwaved on HIGH until the mixture is hot but not boiling. Then stir in ½ cup Sprinkle Sweet or pourable Sugar Twin. Cover and chill at least 4 hours.

5. For any recipe that calls for **buttermilk,** you might want to try **JO's Buttermilk:** Blend 1 cup water and ⅔ cup dry milk powder (the nutrients of 2 cups of skim milk). It'll be thicker than this mixed-up milk usually is, because it's doubled. Add 1 teaspoon white vinegar and stir, then let it sit for at least 10 minutes.

What else? Nonfat dry milk powder adds calcium without fuss to many recipes, and it can be stored for months in your refrigerator or freezer.

SOUP SUBSTITUTES

One of my subscribers was looking for a way to further restrict salt intake and needed a substitute for **cream of mushroom soup.** For many of my recipes, I use Healthy Request Cream of Mushroom Soup, as it is a reduced-sodium product. The label suggests two servings per can, but I usually incorporate the soup into a recipe serving at least four. By doing this, I've reduced the sodium in the soup by half again.

But if you must restrict your sodium even more, try making my Healthy Exchanges **Creamy Mushroom Sauce.** Place 1½ cups evaporated skim milk and 3 tablespoons flour in a covered jar. Shake well and pour the mixture into a medium saucepan sprayed with butter-flavored cooking spray. Add ½ cup canned sliced mushrooms, rinsed and drained. Cook over medium heat, stirring often, until mixture thickens. Add any seasonings of your choice. You can use this sauce in any recipe that calls for one 10¾-ounce can of cream of mushroom soup.

Why did I choose these proportions and ingredients?

- 1½ cups evaporated skim milk is the amount in one can.
- It's equal to three Skim Milk choices or exchanges.
- It's the perfect amount of liquid and flour for a medium cream sauce.
- 3 tablespoons flour is equal to one Bread/Starch choice or exchange.
- Any leftovers will reheat beautifully with a flour based sauce, but not with a cornstarch base.
- The mushrooms are one Vegetable choice or exchange.
- This sauce is virtually fat-free, sugar-free, and sodium-free.

PROTEINS

Eggs

I use eggs in moderation. I enjoy the real thing on an average of three to four times a week. So, my recipes are calculated on using whole eggs. However, if you choose to use egg substitute in place of the egg, the finished product will turn out just fine and the fat grams per serving will be even lower than those listed.

If you like the look, taste, and feel of **hard-boiled eggs** in salads but haven't been using them because of the cholesterol in the yolk, I have a couple of alternatives for you. (1) Pour an 8-ounce carton of egg substitute into a medium skillet sprayed with cooking spray. Cover the skillet tightly and cook over low heat until substitute is just set, about 10 minutes. Remove from heat and let set, still covered, for 10 minutes more. Uncover and cool completely. Chop the set mixture. This will make about 1 cup of chopped egg. (2) Even easier is to hard-boil "real eggs," toss the yolk away, and chop the white. Either way, you don't deprive yourself of the pleasure of egg in your salad.

In most recipes calling for **egg substitutes,** you can use 2 egg whites in

place of the equivalent of 1 egg substitute. Just break the eggs open and toss the yolks away. I can hear some of you already saying, "But that's wasteful!" Well, take a look at the price on the egg substitute package (which usually has the equivalent of 4 eggs in it), then look at the price of a dozen eggs, from which you'd get the equivalent of 6 egg substitutes. Now, what's wasteful about that?

MEATS

Whenever I include **cooked chicken** in a recipe, I use roasted white meat without skin. Whenever I include **roast beef or pork** in a recipe, I use the loin cuts because they are much leaner. However, most of the time, I do my roasting of all these meats at the local deli. I just ask for a chunk of their lean roasted meat, 6 or 8 ounces, and ask them not to slice it. When I get home, I cube or dice the meat and am ready to use it in my recipe. The reason I do this is threefold: (1) I'm getting just the amount I need without leftovers; (2) I don't have the expense of heating the oven; and (3) I'm not throwing away the bone, gristle, and fat I'd be cutting off the meat. Overall, it is probably cheaper to "roast" it the way I do.

Did you know that you can make an acceptable **meatloaf** without using egg for the binding? Just replace every egg with ¼ cup of liquid. You could use beef broth, tomato sauce, even applesauce, to name just a few. For a meatloaf to serve 6, I always use 1 pound of extra-lean ground beef or turkey, 6 tablespoons of dried fine bread crumbs, and ¼ cup of the liquid, plus anything else healthy that strikes my fancy at the time. I mix well and place the mixture in an 8-by-8-inch baking dish or 9-by-5-inch loaf pan sprayed with cooking spray. Bake uncovered at 350 degrees for 35 to 50 minutes (depending on the added ingredients). You will never miss the egg.

Any time you are **browning ground meat** for a casserole and want to get rid of almost all the excess fat, just place the uncooked meat loosely in a plastic colander. Set the colander in a glass pie plate. Place in microwave and cook on HIGH for 3 to 6 minutes (depending on the amount being browned), stirring often. Use as you would for any casserole. You can also chop up onions and brown them with the meat if you want.

GRAVY

For **gravy** with all the "old time" flavor but without the extra fat, try this almost effortless way to prepare it. (It's almost as easy as opening up a store-bought jar.) Pour the juice off your roasted meat, then set the roast aside to "rest" for about 20 minutes. Place the juice in an uncovered cake pan or other large flat pan (we want the large air surface to speed up the cooling process) and put in the freezer until the fat congeals on top and you can skim it off. Or, if you prefer, use a skimming pitcher purchased at your kitchen gadget store. Either way, measure about 1½ cups skimmed broth and pour into a medium saucepan. Cook over medium heat until heated through, about 5 minutes. In a covered jar, combine ½ cup water or cooled potato broth with 3 tablespoons flour. Shake well. Pour the flour mixture into the warmed juice. Combine well using a wire whisk. Continue cooking until the gravy thickens, about 5 minutes. Season with salt and pepper to taste.

Why did I use flour instead of cornstarch? Because any leftovers will reheat nicely with the flour base and would not with a cornstarch base. Also, 3 tablespoons of flour works out to 1 Bread/Starch exchange. This virtually fat-free gravy makes about 2 cups, so you could spoon about ½ cup gravy on your low-fat mashed potatoes and only have to count your gravy as ¼ Bread/Starch exchange.

FRUITS AND VEGETABLES

If you want to enjoy a **"fruit shake"** with some pizazz, just combine soda water and unsweetened fruit juice in a blender. Add crushed ice. Blend on HIGH until thick. Refreshment without guilt.

You'll see that many recipes use ordinary **canned vegetables.** They're much cheaper than reduced-sodium versions, and once you rinse and drain them, the sodium is reduced anyway. I believe in saving money wherever possible so we can afford the best fat-free and sugar-free products as they come onto the market.

All three kinds of **vegetables—fresh, frozen, and canned**—have their place in a healthy diet. My husband, Cliff, hates the taste of frozen or fresh green beans, thinks the texture is all wrong, so I use canned green beans instead. In this case, canned vegetables have their proper place when I'm feeding my husband. If someone in your family has a similar concern, it's important to respond to it so everyone can be happy and enjoy the meal.

When I use **fruits or vegetables** like apples, cucumbers, and zucchini, I wash them really well and **leave the skin on.** It provides added color, fiber, and attractiveness to any dish. And, because I use processed flour in my cooking, I like to increase the fiber in my diet by eating my fruits and vegetables in their closest-to-natural state.

To help keep **fresh fruits and veggies fresh,** just give them a quick "shower" with lemon juice. The easiest way to do this is to pour purchased lemon juice into a kitchen spray bottle and store in the refrigerator. Then, every time you use fresh fruits or vegetables in a salad or dessert, simply give them a quick spray with your "lemon spritzer." You just might be amazed by how this little trick keeps your produce from turning brown so fast.

The next time you warm canned vegetables such as carrots or green beans, drain and heat the vegetables in ¼ cup beef or chicken broth. It gives a nice variation to an old standby. Here's a simple **white sauce** for vegetables and casseroles without using added fat that can be made by spraying a medium saucepan with butter-flavored cooking spray. Place 1½ cups evaporated skim milk and 3 tablespoons flour in a covered jar. Shake well. Pour into the sprayed saucepan and cook over medium heat until thick, stirring constantly. Add salt and pepper to taste. You can also add ½ cup canned drained mushrooms and/or 3 ounces (¾ cup) shredded reduced-fat cheese. Continue cooking until the cheese melts.

Zip up canned or frozen green beans with **chunky salsa:** ½ cup to 2 cups beans. Heat thoroughly. Chunky salsa also makes a wonderful dressing on lettuce salads. It only counts as a vegetable, so enjoy.

Another wonderful **south-of-the-border** dressing can be stirred up by using ½ cup of chunky salsa and ¼ cup fat-free ranch dressing. Cover and store in your refrigerator. Use as a dressing for salads or as a topping for baked potatoes.

DELIGHTFUL DESSERT IDEAS

For a special treat that tastes anything but "diet," try placing **spreadable fruit** in a container and microwave for about 15 seconds. Then pour the melted fruit spread over a serving of nonfat ice cream or frozen yogurt. One tablespoon of spreadable fruit is equal to 1 Fruit choice or exchange. Some combinations to get you started are apricot over chocolate ice cream, strawberry over strawberry ice cream, or any flavor over vanilla.

Another way I use spreadable fruit is to make a delicious **topping for a**

cheesecake or angel food cake. I take ½ cup of fruit and ½ cup Cool Whip Lite and blend the two together with a teaspoon of coconut extract.

Here's a really **good topping** for the fall of the year. Place 1½ cups unsweetened applesauce in a medium saucepan or 4-cup glass measure. Stir in 2 tablespoons raisins, 1 teaspoon apple pie spice, and 2 tablespoons Cary's Sugar Free Maple Syrup. Cook over medium heat on the stove or process on HIGH in microwave until warm. Then spoon about ½ cup of the warm mixture over pancakes, French toast, or sugar-free and fat-free vanilla ice cream. It's as close as you will get to guilt-free apple pie!

Do you love hot fudge sundaes as much as I do? Here's my secret for making **Almost Sinless Hot Fudge Sauce.** Just combine the contents of a 4-serving package of JELL-O sugar-free chocolate cook-and-serve pudding with ⅔ cup Carnation Nonfat Dry Milk Powder in a medium saucepan. Add 1¼ cups water. Cook over medium heat, stirring constantly with a wire whisk, until the mixture thickens and starts to boil. Remove from heat and stir in 1 teaspoon vanilla extract, 2 teaspoons reduced-calorie margarine, and ½ cup miniature marshmallows. This makes six ¼-cup servings. Any leftovers can be refrigerated and reheated later in the microwave. Yes, you can buy fat-free chocolate syrup nowadays, but have you checked the sugar content? For a ¼-cup serving of store-bought syrup (and you show me any true hot fudge sundae lover who would settle for less than ¼ cup) it clocks in at over 150 calories with 39 grams of sugar! Hershey's Lite Syrup, while better, still has 100 calories and 10 grams of sugar. But this "homemade" version costs you only 60 calories, less than ½ gram of fat, and just 6 grams of sugar for the same ¼-cup serving. For an occasional squirt on something where 1 teaspoon is enough, I'll use Hershey's Lite Syrup. But when I crave a hot fudge sundae, I scoop out some sugar- and fat-free ice cream, then spoon my Almost Sinless Hot Fudge Sauce over the top and smile with pleasure.

A quick yet tasty way to prepare **strawberries for shortcake** is to place about ¾ cup sliced strawberries, 2 tablespoons Diet Mountain Dew, and sugar substitute to equal ¼ cup sugar in a blender container. Process on BLEND until mixture is smooth. Pour the mixture into bowl. Add 1¼ cups sliced strawberries and mix well. Cover and refrigerate until ready to serve with shortcakes. This tastes just like the strawberry sauce I remember my mother making when I was a child.

Have you tried **thawing Cool Whip Lite** by stirring it? Don't! You'll get a runny mess and ruin the look and taste of your dessert. You can *never* treat Cool Whip Lite the same way you did regular Cool Whip because the "lite" version just doesn't contain enough fat. Thaw your Cool Whip Lite by placing it in your refrigerator at least two hours before you need to use it. When they took the excess fat out of Cool Whip to make it "lite," they replaced it with air. When you stir the living daylights out of it to hurry up the thawing, you also stir out the air. You also can't thaw your Cool Whip Lite in the microwave, or you'll end up with Cool Whip Soup!

Always have a thawed container of Cool Whip Lite in your refrigerator, as it keeps well for up to two weeks. It actually freezes and thaws and freezes and thaws again quite well, so if you won't be using it soon, you could refreeze your leftovers. Just remember to take it out a few hours before you need it, so it'll be creamy and soft and ready to use.

Remember, anytime you see the words "fat-free" or "reduced-fat" on the labels of cream cheese, sour cream, or whipped topping, handle it gently. The fat has been replaced by air or water, and the product has to be treated with special care.

How can you **frost an entire pie with just ½ cup of whipped topping?** First, don't use an inexpensive brand. I use Cool Whip Lite or La Creme Lite. Make sure the topping is fully thawed. Always spread from the center to the sides using a rubber spatula. This way, ½ cup topping will cover an entire pie. Remember, the operative word is *frost,* not pile the entire container on top of the pie!

Another trick I often use is to include tiny amounts of "real people" food, such as coconut, but extend the flavor by using extracts. Try it—you will be surprised by how little of the real thing you can use and still feel you are not being deprived.

If you are preparing a pie filling that has ample moisture, just line the bottom of a 9-by-9-inch cake pan with **graham crackers.** Pour the filling over the top of the crackers. Cover and refrigerate until the moisture has enough time to soften the crackers. Overnight is best. This eliminates the added **fats and sugars** of a piecrust.

One of my readers provided a smart and easy way to enjoy a **two-crust pie** without all the fat that usually comes along with those two crusts. Just use one Pillsbury refrigerated piecrust. Let it set at room temperature for about 20 minutes. Cut the crust in half on the folded line. Gently roll each half into a ball. Wipe your counter with a wet cloth and place a sheet of wax paper on it. Put one of the balls on the wax paper, then cover with another piece of wax paper, and roll it out with your rolling pin. Carefully remove the wax paper on one side and place that side into your 8- or 9-inch pie plate. Fill with your usual pie filling, then repeat the process for the top crust. Bake as usual. Enjoy!

When you are preparing a pie that uses a purchased piecrust, simply tear out the paper label on the plastic cover (but do check it for a coupon good on a future purchase) and turn the cover upside down over the prepared pie. You now have a cover that protects your beautifully garnished pie from having anything fall on top of it. It makes the pie very portable when it's your turn to bring dessert to a get-together.

Did you know you can make your own **fruit-flavored yogurt?** Mix 1 tablespoon of any flavor of spreadable fruit spread with ¾ cup plain yogurt. It's every bit as tasty and much cheaper. You can also make your own **lemon yogurt** by combining 3 cups plain fat-free yogurt with 1 tub Crystal Light lemonade powder. Mix well, cover, and store in the refrigerator. I think you will be pleasantly surprised by the ease, cost, and flavor of this "made from scratch" calcium-rich treat. P.S.: You can make any flavor you like by using any of the Crystal Light mixes   Cranberry? Iced Tea? You decide.

OTHER SMART SUBSTITUTIONS

Many people have inquired about **substituting applesauce and artificial sweetener for butter and sugar,** but what if you aren't satisfied with the result? One woman wrote to me about a recipe for her grandmother's cookies that called for 1 cup of butter and 1½ cups of sugar. Well, any recipe that depends on as much butter and sugar as this one does is generally not a good candidate for "healthy exchanges." The original recipe needed a large quantity of fat to produce a crisp cookie just like Grandma made.

Applesauce can often be used instead of vegetable oil but generally doesn't work well as a replacement for butter, margarine, or lard. If a recipe calls for ½ cup of vegetable oil or less and your recipe is for a bar cookie, quick bread, muffin, or cake mix, you can try substituting an equal amount of unsweetened applesauce. If the recipe calls for more, try using ½ cup applesauce and the rest oil. You're cutting down the fat but shouldn't end up with a taste disaster! This "applesauce shortening" works great in many recipes, but so far I haven't been able to figure out a way to deep-fat fry with it!

Another rule for healthy substitution: Up to ½ cup sugar or less can be replaced by *an artificial sweetener that can withstand the heat of baking,* like pourable Sugar Twin or Sprinkle Sweet. If it requires more than ½ cup sugar, cut the amount needed by 75 percent and use ½ cup sugar substitute and sugar for the rest. Other options: Reduce the butter and sugar by 25 percent and see if the finished product still satisfies you in taste and appearance. Or, make the cookies just like Grandma did, realizing they are part of your family's holiday tradition. Enjoy a *moderate* serving of a couple of cookies once or twice during the season, and just forget about them the rest of the year.

Did you know that you can replace the fat in many quick breads, muffins, and shortcakes with **fat-free mayonnaise** or **fat-free sour cream?** This can work if the original recipe doesn't call for a lot of fat *and* sugar. If the recipe is truly fat and sugar dependent, such as traditional sugar cookies, cupcakes, or pastries, it won't work. Those recipes require the large amounts of sugar and fat to make love in the dark of the oven to produce a tender finished product. But if you have a favorite quick bread that doesn't call for a lot of sugar or fat, why don't you give one of these substitutes a try?

If you enjoy beverage mixes like those from Alba, here are my Healthy Exchanges versions:

For **chocolate flavored,** use ⅓ cup nonfat dry milk powder and 2 tablespoons Nestlé Sugar-Free Chocolate Flavored Quik. Mix well and use as usual. Or, use ⅓ cup nonfat dry milk powder, 1 teaspoon unsweetened cocoa, and sugar substitute to equal 3 tablespoons sugar. Mix well and use as usual.

For **vanilla flavored,** use ⅓ cup nonfat dry milk powder, sugar substitute to equal 2 tablespoons sugar, and add 1 teaspoon vanilla extract when adding liquid.

For **strawberry flavored,** use ⅓ cup nonfat dry milk powder, sugar substitute to equal 2 tablespoons sugar, and add 1 teaspoon strawberry extract and 3–4 drops red food coloring when adding liquid.

Each of these makes one packet of drink mix. If you need to double the recipe, double everything but the extract. Use 1½ teaspoons of extract or it will be too strong. Use 1 cup cold water with one recipe mix to make a glass of flavored milk. If you want to make a shake, combine the mix, water, and 3–4 ice cubes in your blender, then process on BLEND till smooth.

A handy tip when making **healthy punch** for a party: Prepare a few extra cups of your chosen drink, freeze it in cubes in a couple of ice trays, then keep your punch from "watering down" by cooling it with punch cubes instead of ice cubes.

What should you do if you can't find the product listed in a Healthy Exchanges recipe? You can substitute in some cases—use Lemon JELL-O if you can't find Hawaiian Pineapple, for example. But if you're determined to track down the product you need, and your own store manager hasn't been able to order it for you, why not use one of the new online grocers and order exactly what you need, no matter where you live. Try **http://www.netgrocer.com**.

Not all low-fat cooking products are interchangeable, as one of my readers recently discovered when she tried to cook pancakes on her griddle using I Can't Believe It's Not Butter! spray—and they stuck! This butter-flavored spray is wonderful for a quick squirt on air-popped popcorn or corn on the cob, and it's great for topping your pancakes once they're cooked. In fact, my tastebuds have to check twice because it tastes so much like real butter! (And this is high praise from someone who once thought butter was the most perfect food ever created.)

But I Can't Believe It's Not Butter! doesn't work well for sautéing or browning. After trying to fry an egg with it and cooking up a disaster, I knew this product had its limitations. So I decided to continue using Pam or Weight Watchers butter-flavored cooking spray whenever I'm browning anything in a skillet or on a griddle.

Many of my readers have reported difficulty finding a product I use in many recipes: JELL-O cook-and-serve puddings. I have three suggestions for those of you with this problem:

1. **Work with your grocery store manager to get this product into your store,** and then make sure you and everyone you know buys it by the bagful! Products that sell well are reordered and kept in stock, especially with today's computerized cash registers that record what's purchased. You may also want to write or call Kraft General Foods and ask for their help. They can be reached at (800) 431-1001 weekdays from 9 A.M. to 4 P.M. (EST).

2. **You can prepare a recipe that calls for cook-and-serve pudding by using instant pudding of the same flavor.** Yes, that's right, you **can** cook with the instant when making my recipes. The finished product won't be quite as wonderful, but still at least a 3 on a 4-star scale. You can never do the opposite—never use cook-and-serve in a recipe that calls for instant! One time at a cooking demonstration, I could not understand why my Blueberry Mountain Cheesecake never did set up. Then I spotted the box in the trash and noticed I'd picked the wrong type of pudding mix. Be careful—the boxes are both blue, but the instant has pudding on a silver spoon, and the cook-and-serve has a stream of milk running down the front into a bowl with a wooden spoon.

3. **You can make JO's Sugar-Free Vanilla Cook-and-Serve Pudding Mix instead of using JELL-O's.** Here's my recipe: 2 tablespoons corn-

starch, ½ cup pourable Sugar Twin or Sprinkle Sweet, ⅔ cup Carnation Nonfat Dry Milk Powder, 1½ cups water, 2 teaspoons vanilla extract, and 4 to 5 drops yellow food coloring. Combine all this in a medium saucepan and cook over medium heat, stirring constantly, until the mixture comes to a full boil and thickens. This is for basic cooked vanilla sugar-free pudding. For a chocolate version, the recipe is 2 tablespoons cornstarch, ¼ cup pourable Sugar Twin or Sprinkle Sweet, 2 tablespoons sugar-free chocolate-flavored Nestlé's Quik, 1½ cups water, and 1 teaspoon vanilla extract. Follow the same cooking instructions as for the vanilla.

If you're preparing this as part of a recipe that also calls for adding a package of gelatin, just stir that into the mix.

Adapting a favorite family cake recipe? Here's something to try: Replace an egg and oil in the original with ⅓ cup fat-free yogurt and ¼ cup fat-free mayonnaise. Blend these two ingredients with your liquids in a separate bowl, then add the yogurt mixture to the flour mixture and mix gently just to combine. (You don't want to overmix or you'll release the gluten in the batter and end up with a tough batter.)

Want a tasty coffee creamer without all the fat? You could use Carnation's Fat Free Coffee-mate, which is 10 calories per teaspoon, but if you drink several cups a day with several teaspoons each, that adds up quickly to nearly 100 calories a day! Why not try my version? It's not quite as creamy, but it *is* good. Simply combine ⅓ cup Carnation Nonfat Dry Milk Powder and ¼ cup pourable Sugar Twin. Cover and store in your cupboard or refrigerator. At 3 calories per teaspoon, you can enjoy three teaspoons for less than the calories of one teaspoon of the purchased variety.

SOME HELPFUL HINTS

Sugar-free puddings and gelatins are important to many of my recipes, but if you prefer to avoid sugar substitutes, you could still prepare the recipes with regular puddings or gelatins. The calories would be higher, but you would still be cooking low-fat.

When a recipe calls for **chopped nuts** (and you only have whole ones), who wants to dirty the food processor just for a couple of tablespoonsful? You could try to chop them using your cutting board, but be prepared for bits and pieces to fly all over the kitchen. I use "Grandma's food processor." I take the biggest nuts I can find, put them in a small glass bowl, and chop them into chunks just the right size using a metal biscuit cutter.

A quick hint about **reduced-fat peanut butter:** Don't store it in the refrigerator. Because the fat has been reduced, it won't spread as easily when it's cold. Keep it in your cupboard and a little will spread a lot further.

Crushing **graham crackers** for topping? A self-seal sandwich bag works great!

If you have a **leftover muffin** and are looking for something a little differ-ent for breakfast, you can make **a "breakfast sundae."** Crumble the muffin into a cereal bowl. Sprinkle a serving of fresh fruit over it and top with a couple of tablespoons of plain fat-free yogurt sweetened with sugar substitute and your choice of extract. The thought of it just might make you jump out of bed with a smile on your face. (Speaking of muffins, did you know that if you fill the unused muffin wells with water when baking muffins, you help ensure more even baking and protect the muffin pan at the same time?) Another muffin hint: Lightly spray the inside of paper baking cups with butter-flavored cooking spray before spooning the muffin batter into them. Then you won't end up with paper clinging to your fresh-baked muffins.

The secret of making **good meringues** without sugar is to use 1 table-spoon of Sprinkle Sweet or pourable Sugar Twin for every egg white, and a small amount of extract. Use ½ to 1 teaspoon for the batch. Almond, vanilla, and coconut are all good choices. Use the same amount of cream of tartar you usually do. Bake the meringue in the same old way. Even if you can't eat sugar, you can enjoy a healthy meringue pie when it's prepared *The Healthy Exchanges Way.* (Remember that egg whites whip up best at room temp-erature.)

Try **storing your Bisquick Reduced Fat Baking Mix** in the freezer. It won't freeze, and it *will* stay fresh much longer. (It works for coffee, doesn't it?)

If you've ever wondered about **changing ingredients** in one of my recipes, the answer is that some things can be changed to suit your family's tastes, but others should not be tampered with. **Don't change:** the amount of flour, bread crumbs, reduced-fat baking mix, baking soda, baking powder, or liquid or dry milk powder. And if I include a small amount of salt, it's necessary for the recipe to turn out correctly. **What you can change:** an extract flavor (if you don't like coconut, choose vanilla or almond instead); a spreadable fruit fla-vor; the type of fruit in a pie filling (but be careful about substituting fresh for frozen and vice versa—sometimes it works, but it may not); the flavor of pud-ding or gelatin. As long as package sizes and amounts are the same, go for it. It will never hurt my feelings if you change a recipe, so please your family—don't worry about me!

Because I always say that "good enough" isn't good enough for me anymore, here's a way to make your cup of **fat-free and sugar-free hot cocoa** more special. After combining the hot chocolate mix and hot water, stir in ½ teaspoon vanilla extract and a light sprinkle of cinnamon. If you really want to feel decadent, add a tablespoon of Cool Whip Lite. Isn't life grand?

If you must limit your sugar intake, but you love the idea of sprinkling **powdered sugar** on dessert crepes or burritos, here's a pretty good substitute: Place 1 cup Sprinkle Sweet or pourable Sugar Twin and 1 teaspoon cornstarch in a blender container, then cover and process on HIGH until the mixture resembles powdered sugar in texture, about 45 to 60 seconds. Store in an airtight container and use whenever you want a dusting of "powdered sugar" on any dessert.

Want my "almost instant" pies to set up even more quickly? Do as one of my readers does: freeze your Keebler piecrusts. Then, when you stir up one of my pies and pour the filling into the frozen crust, it sets up within seconds.

Some of my "island-inspired" recipes call for **rum or brandy extracts,** which provide the "essence" of liquor without the real thing. I'm a teetotaler by choice, so I choose not to include real liquor in any of my recipes. They're cheaper than liquor and you won't feel the need to shoo your kids away from the goodies. If you prefer not to use liquor extracts in your cooking, you can always substitute vanilla extract.

SOME HEALTHY COOKING CHALLENGES AND HOW I SOLVED 'EM

When you stir up one of my pie fillings, do you ever have a problem with **lumps?** Here's an easy solution for all of you "careful" cooks out there. Lumps occur when the pudding starts to set up before you can get the dry milk powder incorporated into the mixture. I always advise you to dump, pour, and stir fast with that wire whisk, letting no more than 30 seconds elapse from beginning to end.

But if you are still having problems, you can always combine the dry milk powder and the water in a separate bowl before adding the pudding mix and whisking quickly. Why don't I suggest this right from the beginning? Because that would mean an extra dish to wash every time—and you know I hate to wash dishes!

With a little practice and a light touch, you should soon get the hang of my original method. But now you've got an alternative way to lose those lumps!

I love the chemistry of foods, and so I've gotten great pleasure from analyzing what makes fat-free products tick. By dissecting these "miracle" products, I've learned how to make them work best. They require different handling than the high-fat products we're used to, but if treated properly, these slimmed-down versions can produce delicious results!

Fat-free sour cream: This product is wonderful on a hot baked potato, but have you noticed that it tends to be much gummier than regular sour cream? If you want to use it in a stroganoff dish or baked product, you must stir a tablespoon or two of skim milk into the fat-free sour cream before adding it to other ingredients.

Cool Whip Free: When the fat went out of the formula, air was stirred in to fill the void. So, if you stir it too vigorously, you release the air and *decrease* the volume. Handle it with kid gloves—gently. Since the manufacturer forgot to ask for my input, I'll share with you how to make it taste almost the same as it used to. Let the container thaw in the refrigerator, then ever so gently stir in 1 teaspoon vanilla extract. Now, put the lid back on and enjoy it a tablespoon at a time, the same way you did Cool Whip Lite.

Fat-free cream cheese: When the fat was removed from this product, water replaced it. So don't ever use an electric mixer on the fat-free version, or you risk releasing the water and having your finished product look more like dip than cheesecake! Stirring it gently with a sturdy spoon in a glass bowl with a handle will soften it just as much as it needs to be. (A glass bowl with a handle lets you see what's going on; the handle gives you control as you stir. This "user-friendly" method is good for tired cooks, young cooks, and cooks with arthritis.) And don't be alarmed if the cream cheese gets caught in your wire whisk when you start combining the pudding mix and other ingredients. Just keep knocking it back down into the bowl by hitting the whisk against the rim of the bowl, and as you continue blending, it will soften even more and drop off the whisk. When it's time to pour the filling into your crust, your whisk shouldn't have anything much clinging to it.

Reduced-fat margarine: Again, the fat was replaced by water. If you try to use the reduced-fat kind in your cookie recipe spoon for spoon, you will end up with a cakelike cookie instead of the crisp kind most of us enjoy. You have to take into consideration that some water will be released as the product bakes. Use less liquid than the recipe calls for (when re-creating family recipes *only*— I've figured that into Healthy Exchanges recipes). And never, never, never use fat-*free* margarine and expect anyone to ask for seconds!

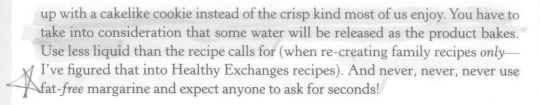

HOMEMADE OR STORE-BOUGHT?

I've been asked which is better for you: homemade from scratch, or purchased foods. My answer is *both!* Each has a place in a healthy lifestyle, and what that place is has everything to do with you.

Take **piecrusts,** for instance. If you love spending your spare time in the kitchen preparing foods, and you're using low-fat, low-sugar, and reasonably low-sodium ingredients, go for it! But if, like so many people, your time is limited and you've learned to read labels, you could be better off using purchased foods.

I know that when I prepare a pie (and I experiment with a couple of pies each week, because this is Cliff's favorite dessert), I use a purchased crust. Why? Mainly because I can't make a good-tasting piecrust that is lower in fat than the brands I use. Also, purchased piecrusts fit my rule of "If it takes longer to fix than to eat, forget it!"

I've checked the nutrient information for the purchased piecrusts against recipes for traditional and "diet" piecrusts, using my computer software program. The purchased crust calculated lower in both fat and calories! I have tried some low-fat and low-sugar recipes, but they just didn't spark my tastebuds, or were so complicated you needed an engineering degree just to get the crust in the pie plate.

I'm very happy with the purchased piecrusts in my recipes, because the finished product rarely, if ever, has more than 30 percent of total calories coming from fats. I also believe that we have to prepare foods our families and friends will eat with us on a regular basis and not feel deprived, or we've wasted time, energy, and money.

I could use a purchased "lite" **pie filling,** but instead I make my own. Here I can save both fat and sugar, and still make the filling almost as fast as opening a can. The bottom line: Know what you have to spend when it comes to both time and fat/sugar calories, then make the best decision you can for you and your family. And don't go without an occasional piece of pie because you think it isn't *necessary*. A delicious pie prepared in a healthy way is one of the simple pleasures of life. It's a little thing, but it can make all the difference between just getting by with the bare minimum and living a full and healthy lifestyle.

I'm sure you'll add to this list of cooking tips as you begin preparing Healthy Exchanges recipes and discover how easy it can be to adapt your own favorite recipes using these ideas and your own common sense.

A PEEK INTO MY PANTRY AND MY FAVORITE BRANDS

. . .

Everyone asks me what foods I keep on hand and what brands I use. There are lots of good products on the grocery shelves today—many more than we dreamed about even a year or two ago. And I can't wait to see what's out there twelve months from now. The following are my staples and, where appropriate, my favorites *at this time.* I feel these products are healthier, tastier, easy to get—and deliver the most flavor for the least amount of fat, sugar, or calories. If you find others you like as well *or better,* please use them. This is only a guide to make your grocery shopping and cooking easier.

Fat-free plain yogurt (*Yoplait or Dannon*)
Nonfat dry milk powder (*Carnation*)
Evaporated skim milk (*Carnation*)

Skim milk
Fat-free cottage cheese
Fat-free cream cheese (*Philadelphia*)
Fat-free mayonnaise (*Kraft*)
Fat-free salad dressings (*Kraft*)
Fat-free sour cream (*Land O Lakes*)
Reduced-calorie margarine (*Weight Watchers, Promise, or Smart Beat*)
Cooking spray
   Olive oil flavored and regular (*Pam*)
   Butter flavored for sautéing (*Pam or Weight Watchers*)
   Butter flavored for spritzing *after* cooking (*I Can't Believe It's Not Butter!*)
Vegetable oil (*Puritan Canola Oil*)
Reduced-calorie whipped topping (*Cool Whip Lite or Cool Whip Free*)
Sugar substitute
   if no heating is involved (*Equal*)
   if heating is required
      white (*pourable Sugar Twin or Sprinkle Sweet*)
      brown (*Brown Sugar Twin*)
Sugar-free gelatin and pudding mixes (*JELL-O*)
Baking mix (*Bisquick Reduced Fat*)
Pancake mix (*Aunt Jemima Reduced Calorie*)
Reduced-calorie pancake syrup (*Cary's Sugar Free*)
Parmesan cheese (*Kraft fat-free*)
Reduced-fat cheese (*Kraft 2% Reduced Fat*)
Shredded frozen potatoes (*Mr. Dell's*)
Spreadable fruit spread (*Smucker's, Welch's or Knott's Berry Farm*)
Peanut butter (*Peter Pan reduced-fat, Jif reduced-fat, or Skippy reduced-fat*)
Chicken broth (*Healthy Request*)
Beef broth (*Swanson*)
Tomato sauce (*Hunt's—plain, Italian, or chili*)
Canned soups (*Healthy Request*)
Tomato juice (*Campbell's Reduced-Sodium*)
Ketchup (*Heinz Light Harvest or Healthy Choice*)
Purchased piecrust
   unbaked (*Pillsbury—from dairy case*)
   graham cracker, butter flavored, or chocolate flavored (*Keebler*)
Crescent rolls (*Pillsbury Reduced Fat*)

Pastrami and corned beef (*Carl Buddig Lean*)

Luncheon meats (*Healthy Choice or Oscar Mayer*)

Ham (*Dubuque 97% fat-free and reduced-sodium or Healthy Choice*)

Frankfurters and kielbasa sausage (*Healthy Choice*)

Canned white chicken, packed in water (*Swanson*)

Canned tuna, packed in water (*Starkist or Chicken of the Sea*)

90–95 percent lean ground turkey and beef

Soda crackers (*Nabisco Fat-Free*)

Reduced-calorie bread—40 calories per slice or less

Hamburger buns—80 calories each (*Less*)

Rice—instant, regular, brown, and wild

Instant potato flakes (*Betty Crocker Potato Buds*)

Noodles, spaghetti, and macaroni

Salsa (*Chi Chi's Mild Chunky*)

Pickle relish—dill, sweet, and hot dog

Mustard—Dijon, prepared, and spicy

Unsweetened apple juice

Unsweetened applesauce

Fruit—fresh, frozen (no sugar added), or canned in juice

Vegetables—fresh, frozen, or canned

Spices—JO's Spices

Lemon and lime juice (in small plastic fruit-shaped bottles found
    in the produce section)

Instant fruit beverage mixes (*Crystal Light*)

Dry dairy beverage mixes (*Nestlé Quik*)

Ice Cream—*Wells' Blue Bunny sugar- and fat-free*

The items on my shopping list are everyday foods found in just about any grocery store in America. But all are as low in fat, sugar, calories, and sodium as I can find—and still taste good! I can make any recipe in my cookbooks and newsletters as long as I have my cupboards and refrigerator stocked with these items. Whenever I use the last of any one item, I just make sure I pick up another supply the next time I'm at the store.

If your grocer does not stock these items, why not ask if they can be ordered on a trial basis? If the store agrees to do so, be sure to tell your friends to stop by, so that sales are good enough to warrant restocking the new products. Competition for shelf space is fierce, so only products that sell well stay around.

SHOPPING
"THE HEALTHY
EXCHANGES WAY"

■ ■ ■

Sometimes, as part of a cooking demonstration, I take the group on a field trip to the nearest supermarket. There's no better place to share my discoveries about which healthy products taste best, which are best for you, and which healthy products don't deliver enough taste to include in my recipes.

While I'd certainly enjoy accompanying you to your neighborhood store, we'll have to settle for a field trip *on paper*. I've tasted and tried just about every fat- and sugar-free product on the market, but so many new ones keep coming all the time, you're going to have to learn to play detective on your own. I've turned label reading into an art, but often the label doesn't tell me everything I need to know.

Sometimes you'll find, as I have, that the product with *no* fat doesn't provide the taste satisfaction you require; other times, a no-fat or low-fat product just doesn't cook up the same way as the original product. And some foods, including even the leanest meats, can't eliminate *all* the fat. That's okay, though—a healthy diet should include anywhere from 15 to 25 percent of total calories from fat on any given day.

Take my word for it—your supermarket is filled with lots of delicious foods that can and should be part of your healthy diet for life. Come, join me as we check it out on the way to the checkout!

Before I buy anything at the store, I read the label carefully: I check the total fat plus the saturated fat; I look to see how many calories are in a realistic serving, and I say to myself, Would I eat that much—or would I eat more? I look at the sodium and I look at the total carbohydrates. I like to check those ingredients because I'm cooking for diabetics and heart patients too. And I check the total calories from fat.

Remember that 1 fat gram equals 9 calories, while 1 protein or 1 carbohydrate gram equals 4 calories.

A wonderful new product is I Can't Believe It's Not Butter! spray, with zero calories and zero grams of fat in five squirts. It's great for your air-popped popcorn. As for **light margarine spread,** beware—most of the fat-free brands don't melt on toast, and they don't taste very good either, so I just leave them on the shelf. For the few times I do use a light margarine I tend to buy Smart Beat Ultra, Promise Ultra, or Weight Watchers Light Ultra. The number-one ingredient in them is water. I occasionally use the light margarine in cooking, but I don't really put margarine on my toast anymore. I use apple butter or make a spread with fat-free cream cheese mixed with a little spreadable fruit instead.

So far, Pillsbury hasn't released a reduced-fat **crescent roll,** so you'll only get one crescent roll per serving from me. I usually make eight of the rolls serve twelve by using them for a crust. The house brands may be lower in fat, but they're usually not as good flavorwise—and they don't quite cover the pan when you use them to make a crust. If you're going to use crescent rolls with lots of other stuff on top, then a house brand might be fine.

The Pillsbury French Loaf makes a wonderful **pizza crust** and fills a giant jelly roll pan. One fifth of this package "costs" you only 1 gram of fat (and I don't even let you have that much!). Once you use this for your pizza crust, you will never go back to anything else instead. I use it to make calzones, too.

I only use Philadelphia fat-free **cream cheese** because it has the best consistency. I've tried other brands, but I wasn't happy with them. Healthy Choice makes lots of great products, but their cream cheese just doesn't work as well with my recipes.

Let's move to the **cheese** aisle. My preferred brand is Kraft 2% Reduced Fat Shredded Cheeses. I will not use the fat-free versions because *they don't melt.* I would gladly give up sugar and fat, but I will not give up flavor. This is a happy compromise. I use the reduced-fat version, I use less, and I use it where your eyes "eat" it, on top of the recipe. So you walk away satisfied and with a finished product that's very low in fat. If you want to make grilled-cheese sandwiches for your kids, use the Kraft reduced-fat cheese slices, and it'll taste exactly like the ones they're used to. The fat-free will not.

Dubuque's Extra-Lean Reduced-Sodium **ham** tastes wonderful, reduces the sodium as well as the fat, and gives you a larger serving. Don't be fooled by products called turkey ham; they may *not* be lower in fat than a very lean pork product. Here's one label as an example: I checked a brand of turkey ham called Genoa. It gives you a 2-ounce serving for 70 calories and 3½ grams of fat. The Dubuque extra-lean ham, made from pork, gives you a 3-ounce serving for 90 calories, but only 2½ grams of fat. *You get more food and less fat.*

Frozen dinners can be expensive and high in sodium, but it's smart to have two or three in the freezer as a backup when your best-laid plans go awry and you need to grab something on the run. It's not a good idea to rely on them too much—what if you can't get to the store to get them, or you're short on cash? The sodium can be high in some of them because they often replace the fat with salt, so be sure to read the labels. Also ask yourself if the serving is enough to satisfy you; for many of us, it's not.

Egg substitute is expensive, and probably not necessary unless you're cooking for someone who has to worry about every bit of cholesterol in his or her diet. If you occasionally have a fried egg or an omelet, *use the real egg.* For cooking, you can usually substitute two egg whites for one whole egg. Most of the time it won't make any difference, but check your recipe carefully.

Healthy frozen desserts are hard to find except for the Weight Watchers brands. I've always felt that their portions are so small, and for their size still pretty high in fat and sugar. (This is one of the reasons I think I'll be successful marketing my frozen desserts someday. After Cliff tasted one of my earliest healthy pies—and licked the plate clean—he remarked that if I ever opened a restaurant, people would keep coming back for my desserts alone!) Keep an eye out for fat-free or very low fat frozen yogurt or sorbet products. Even Häagen-Dazs, which makes some of the highest-fat-content ice cream, now has a fat-free fruit sorbet pop out that's pretty good. I'm sure there will be more before too long.

You have to be realistic: What are you willing to do, and what are you *not* willing to do? Let's take bread, for example. Some people just have to have the real thing—rye bread with caraway seeds or a whole-wheat version with bits of bran in it.

I prefer to use reduced-calorie **bread** because I like a *real* sandwich. This way, I can have two slices of bread and it counts as only one Bread/Starch exchange.

HOW I SHOP FOR MYSELF

I always keep my kitchen stocked with my basic staples; that way, I can go to the cupboard and create new recipes anytime I'm inspired. I hope you will take the time (and allot the money) to stock your cupboards with items from the staples list, so you can enjoy developing your own healthy versions of family favorites without making extra trips to the market.

I'm always on the lookout for new products sitting on the grocery shelf. When I spot something I haven't seen before, I'll usually grab it, glance at the front, then turn it around and read the label carefully. I call it looking at the "promises" (the "come-on" on the front of the package) and then at the "warranty" (the ingredients list and the label on the back).

If it looks as good on the back as it does on the front, I'll say okay and either create a recipe on the spot or take it home for when I do think of something to do with it. Picking up a new product is just about the only time I buy something not on my list.

The items on my shopping list are normal, everyday foods, but as low-fat and low-sugar (*while still tasting good*) as I can find. I can make any recipe in this book as long as these staples are on my shelves. After using these products for a couple of weeks, you will find it becomes routine to have them on hand. And I promise you, I really don't spend any more at the store now than I did a few years ago when I told myself I couldn't afford some of these items. Back then, of course, plenty of unhealthy, high-priced snacks I really didn't need somehow made the magic leap from the grocery shelves into my cart. Who was I kidding?

Yes, you often have to pay a little more for fat-free or low-fat products, including meats. But since I frequently use a half pound of meat to serve four to six people, your cost per serving will be much lower.

Try adding up what you were spending before on chips and cookies, premium brand ice cream, and fatty cuts of meat, and you'll soon see that we've *streamlined* your shopping cart, and taken the weight off your pocketbook as well as your hips!

Remember, your good health is *your* business—but it's big business too. Write to the manufacturers of products you and your family enjoy but feel are just too high in fat, sugar, or sodium to be part of your new healthy lifestyle. Companies are spending millions of dollars to respond to consumers' concerns about food products, and I bet that in the next few years, you'll discover fat-free and low-fat versions of nearly every product piled high on your supermarket shelves!

THE JOYFUL
TABLE HEALTHY
EXCHANGES KITCHEN

...

You might be surprised to discover I still don't have a massive test kitchen stocked with every modern appliance and handy gadget ever made. The tiny galley kitchen where I first launched Healthy Exchanges has room for only one person at a time, but it never stopped me from feeling the sky's the limit when it comes to seeking out great healthy taste!

Because storage is at such a premium in my kitchen, I don't waste space with equipment I don't really need. Here's a list of what I consider worth having. If you notice serious gaps in your equipment, you can probably find most of what you need at a local discount store or garage sale. If your kitchen is equipped with more sophisticated appliances, don't feel guilty about using them. Enjoy every appliance you can find room for or that you can afford. Just be assured that healthy, quick, and delicious food can be prepared with the "basics."

A HEALTHY EXCHANGES
KITCHEN EQUIPMENT LIST

Good-quality nonstick skillets (medium, large)

Good-quality saucepans (small, medium, large)

Glass mixing bowls (small, medium, large)

Glass measures (1-cup, 2-cup, 4-cup, 8-cup)

Sharp knives (paring, chef, butcher)

Rubber spatulas

Wire whisks

Measuring spoons

Measuring cups

Large mixing spoons

Egg separator

Covered jar

Vegetable parer

Grater

Potato masher

Electric mixer

Electric blender

Electric skillet

Cooking timer

Slow cooker

Air popper for popcorn

Kitchen scales (unless you *always* use my recipes)

Wire racks for cooling baked goods

Electric toaster oven (to conserve energy for those times when only one item is being baked or for a recipe that requires a short baking time)

4-inch round custard dishes

Glass pie plates

8-by-8-inch glass baking dishes

Cake pans (9-by-9-inch, 9-by-13-inch)

10¾-by-7-by-1½-inch biscuit pan

Cookie sheets (good nonstick ones)

Jelly-roll pan

Muffin tins

5-by-9-inch bread pan

Plastic colander

Cutting board

Pie wedge server

Square-shaped server

Can opener (I prefer manual)

Rolling pin

A FEW COOKING
TERMS TO EASE
THE WAY

▪ ▪ ▪

Everyone can learn to cook *The Healthy Exchanges Way*. It's simple, it's quick, and the results are delicious! If you've tended to avoid the kitchen because you find recipe instructions confusing or complicated, I hope I can help you feel more confident. I'm not offering a full cooking course here, just some terms I use often that I know you'll want to understand.

Bake: To cook food in the oven; sometimes called roasting

Beat: To mix very fast with a spoon, wire whisk, or electric mixer

Blend: To mix two or more ingredients together thoroughly so that the mixture is smooth

Boil: To cook in liquid until bubbles form

Brown:	To cook at low to medium-low heat until ingredients turn brown
Chop:	To cut food into small pieces with a knife, blender, or food processor
Cool:	To let stand at room temperature until food is no longer hot to the touch
Combine:	To mix ingredients together with a spoon
Dice:	To chop into small, even-sized pieces
Drain:	To pour off liquid. Sometimes you will need to reserve the liquid to use in the recipe, so please read carefully.
Drizzle:	To sprinkle drops of liquid (for example, chocolate syrup) lightly over the top of food
Fold in:	To combine delicate ingredients with other foods by using a gentle, circular motion. Example: adding Cool Whip Lite to an already stirred-up bowl of pudding.
Preheat:	To heat your oven to the desired temperature, usually about 10 minutes before you put your food in to bake
Sauté:	To cook in a skillet or frying pan until the food is soft
Simmer:	To cook in a small amount of liquid over low heat; this lets the flavors blend without too much liquid evaporating.
Whisk:	To beat with a wire whisk until mixture is well mixed. Don't worry about finesse here; just use some elbow grease!

HOW TO MEASURE

I try to make it as easy as possible by providing more than one measurement for many ingredients in my recipes—both the weight in ounces and the amount measured by a measuring cup, for example. Just remember:

- You measure **solids** (flour, Cool Whip Lite, yogurt, nonfat dry milk powder) in your set of separate measuring cups (¼, ⅓, ½, 1 cup)

- You measure **liquids** (Diet Mountain Dew, water, juice) in the clear glass or plastic measuring cups that measure ounces, cups, and pints. Set the cup on a level surface and pour the liquid into it, or you may get too much.

• You can use your measuring spoon set for liquids or solids. **Note:** Don't pour a liquid like an extract into a measuring spoon held over the bowl in case you overpour; instead, do it over the sink.

Here are a few handy equivalents:

3 teaspoons	equals	1 tablespoon
4 tablespoons	equals	¼ cup
5⅓ tablespoons	equals	⅓ cup
8 tablespoons	equals	½ cup
10⅔ tablespoons	equals	⅔ cup
12 tablespoons	equals	¾ cup
16 tablespoons	equals	1 cup
2 cups	equals	1 pint
4 cups	equals	1 quart
8 ounces liquid	equals	1 fluid cup

That's it. Now, ready, set, cook!

A YEAR AT THE JOYFUL TABLE

■ ■ ■

So many people have asked me for help in creating celebration menus for entertaining dear family members and beloved friends. I decided to make a year's worth of festive Healthy Exchanges meals a special feature of this book that is so close to my heart. This year, and in all the years to come, celebrate more, and celebrate often—bringing your loved ones together for a dozen joyful occasions!

"FORGET YOUR RESOLUTIONS, JUST LIVE HEALTHY" DINNER PARTY

■ ■ ■

Ever since I changed my prayer from losing weight to living healthy, January 4 has been my "Living Healthy Anniversary." Each year, I thank the Lord for helping me help myself and others, and I rededicate myself to doing the best I can . . . *the best I can!* Join me at the table and on a wonderful journey to good health.

Creamy Stroganoff Soup (103) 8
Broccoli Party Casserole (158) 5
Baked Chicken in Mushroom Sauce (189) 3
White Chocolate–Covered Cherry Cheesecake (258) 7
Chocolate Brandy Alexander (308) 1

(24) FG   (20)   972 Cal.

JUST TO SAY "I LOVE YOU" SUPPER FOR TWO

■ ■ ■

You can show your love in so many ways, and on so many occasions throughout the year, but Valentine's Day has always been a sweet time for husbands and wives to make a special declaration of love. Cliff has helped me make so many dreams come true, and he has given me support and friendship as well as his love. Pleasing Cliff's tastebuds is one of my favorite occupations, and never more of a pleasure than on a day that celebrates a love that lasts.

Honey Dijon Sweet Potato Salad (141) 3
Peas Lorraine (165) 1
Stuffed Beef Rounds (214) 7
Layered Cherry Almond Pie (254) 8
Berry Bash Slush (307) 0

 (19) FG   (15)   811 Cal.

"WELCOME SPRING" FAMILY
SUNDAY BRUNCH

■ ■ ■

Winters in Iowa can be long and cold, and sometimes I gaze out my window and wonder if I will ever see my garden in bloom again! But I've learned to have faith that new life is just beneath the surface, and I know my patience will be rewarded come spring. Here's a fun way to greet the arrival of the season that promises renewal for all living things!

Banana Split Gelatin Salad (112) 4 *(14)*
Bacon and Egg Pizza (286) 8
Pumpkin Chocolate Chip Muffins (290) 4
Cranberry Orange Bread (294) 3
Black Forest Cake Roll (265) 5

24 FG   8 76 Cal.

A GATHERING OF
GENERATIONS BABY SHOWER
OR CHRISTENING SUPPER

■ ■ ■

Sometimes blessings come more than one at a time, filling your life with so much joy you think you may just explode with happiness! This past year has been like that for me, with the arrival of not one, not two, but three little miracles in the Lund family! Join me in welcoming Aaron (James and Pam's son), Cheyanne (Tommy and Angie's daughter), and Spencer (Becky and John's son). What better time than spring to gather your loved ones close and revel in the spiritual gifts each generation offers the next.

Tropical Ambrosia Salad (117) 0 *(15)*
Springtime Potato Salad (140) 0
Baked Carrot Croquettes with Creamed Pea Sauce (162) 2
Rio Bravo Pork Tenders (217) 7
Heavenly Chocolate and Raspberry Dream Dessert (243) 2

11 FG   8 47 Cal.

"CINCO DE MAYO"
FIESTA DINNER

■ ■ ■

If you're lucky enough to be vacationing in Mexico come May 5, you might be astonished by the enthusiastic celebrations everywhere you turn! But you don't need a plane ticket to make merry in the month of May—just a little salsa, a little imagination, and some Healthy Exchanges recipes that take their inspiration from our lively next-door neighbor to the south!

Mexican Onion Soup (91) 4
Chili Corn Salad (136) 0
South-of-the-Border Chicken Breasts (191) 2
Apple Dessert Enchiladas (273) 2
Mexican Mocha Float (306) 1

A UNION OF SPIRITS
UNDER THE STARS

■ ■ ■

I love June for so many reasons: strawberries are ripe, flowers are in bloom, and there's usually some festive family event—a wedding, an anniversary, a graduation. Just as a bride and groom seek to join their lives and create something brand-new, something greater than the sum of its parts, I've chosen dishes that are special served on their own, but presented together provide a truly memorable meal.

Hawaiian Strawberry Salad (111) 0
Layered Summer Salad Pie (142) 9
Chicken Pot Pie Sauce with Noodles (194) 7
Island Shrimp and Rice (186) 1
Ice Cream Mince Pie (253) 6

FUN TIMES FINGER-LICKIN' KIDS' NIGHT COOKOUT

■ ■ ■

School's out (hurray!), there's no homework (wow!), and you can stay up as late as you like (whee!). If summer isn't a kid's idea of heaven, I don't know what is! This menu is great for vacation birthdays, but you don't need a special occasion to invite the gang over to your house. The kid-pleasing recipes take very little time to prepare, so that Mom and Dad can enjoy the party, too.

Easy Refrigerator Shake Pickles (301) O
Sweet 'n' Sour Vegetable Salad (134) O
The Best Baked Beans (170) 2
Frankfurter and Sauerkraut Pizza (226) 6
*Chocolate Brownie Cake with Raspberry Glaze
and White Chocolate Topping (267)* |

SIZZLING SUMMER DAYS FAMILY REUNION POTLUCK

■ ■ ■

There's no summer tradition I enjoy more than inviting family members from far and near to share in a healthy potluck meal! Sitting under the trees, nibbling on foods beloved since childhood, everyone feels those special ties that bind us to those we love. Let's cherish the good times together!

Dilly Deviled Eggs (299) 5
Cabbage Mardi Gras Salad (130) O
Tuna Macaroni Salad (143) 6
Crunchy Grande Baked Chicken (190) 2
Pear and Raspberry Crumb Pie (252) 7

"SEE YOU IN SEPTEMBER"
BACK-TO-SCHOOL PICNIC

■ ■ ■

Of course you want to make the summer last—everyone does! But before you know it, the kids will be back in school, and it'll be time to buckle down again at the office. Here's a splendid end-of-summer menu to make the most of the sunny days and starlit nights you've got left. And perhaps some dancing under a golden moon . . . ?

Crispy Vegetable Slaw (133) 0
Ham-Broccoli-Pasta Salad (147) 5
Tuna-Potato Salad Casserole (181) 6
Barbecued Loose-Meat Sandwiches (208) 8
Perfect Apple Pie (255) 7

(handwritten: 26 FG)

HARVEST TIME/HALFTIME
"REAP WHAT YOU SOW" SUPPER

■ ■ ■

As the leaves turn glorious colors and drift down from the trees, as the bounty of our fields graces our tables, why not welcome the harvest with a heartwarming family meal? There's something about that little chill in the air that boosts everyone's appetites, but with these tasty dishes, you can feast without fear.

Midwest Ham and Corn Chowder (106) 2
Green Pot Luck (135) 0
Baked Hash Browns au Gratin (166) 2
Pot Roast Meatloaf (200) 7
German Chocolate Crazy Cake (268) 4

(handwritten: 15 FG)

"THANKS FOR EVERYTHING" POST–TURKEY DAY DINNER

■ ■ ■

I've never believed in saving my gratitude for life's gifts for just one day in late November. Expressing thanks for the joy in my life has been a daily practice—and a wonderful time to acknowledge a precious relationship with the Lord. If you haven't taken a few minutes lately to count your blessings, do it today—and invite your dearest friends to gather round your table.

The BEST Turkey Chowder (99) 2
Super Spinach Squares (160) 9
German Scalloped Potatoes (167) 3
Creamy Cajun Turkey Skillet (195) 4 8
Banana Peanut Butter Dream Pie (248) 8

26 FG

HEALTHY AND HEARTFELT HOLIDAY BUFFET

■ ■ ■

So many people fear the holidays as a time of overeating and depressing weight gains. Wouldn't it be wonderful this year to view those weeks from Thanksgiving to New Year's as a season to celebrate a year of living healthy? With a few well-chosen Healthy Exchanges recipes, you can dine deliciously—and party till you drop!

Italian Tomato Corn Chowder (93) 0
Calico Ham Dip (296) 3
Confetti Meatloaf (199) 8 7
Salisbury Pasta Skillet (206) 7
Cranberry-Walnut Glazed Cheesecake (257) 7

25 FG

THE
RECIPES

HOW TO READ
A HEALTHY
EXCHANGES RECIPE

■ ■ ■

THE HEALTHY EXCHANGES
NUTRITIONAL ANALYSIS

Before using these recipes, you may wish to consult your physician or health-care provider to be sure they are appropriate for you. The information in this book is not intended to take the place of any medical advice. It reflects my experiences, studies, research, and opinions regarding healthy eating.

Each recipe includes nutritional information calculated in three ways:

Healthy Exchanges Weight Loss Choices™ or Exchanges
Calories; Fat, Protein, Carbohydrates, and Fiber in grams; Sodium and
  Calcium in milligrams
Diabetic Exchanges

In every Healthy Exchanges recipe, the diabetic exchanges have been calculated by a registered dietitian. All the other calculations were done by computer, using the Food Processor II software. When the ingredient listing gives more than one choice, the first ingredient listed is the one used in the recipe analysis. Due to inevitable variations in the ingredients you choose to use, the nutritional values should be considered approximate.

The annotation "(limited)" following Protein counts in some recipes indicates that consumption of whole eggs should be limited to four per week.

Please note the following symbols:

☆　　　This star means read the recipe's directions carefully for special instructions about **division** of ingredients.

❋　　　This symbol indicates **FREEZES WELL.**

HEARTWARMING SOUPS

■ ■ ■

When I remember the soups I dearly loved as a child, I think mostly about my mother's potato soup. Whenever we weren't feeling well, that's what my mother would comfort us with. I can still see, in my mind's eye, me as a little girl snuggled up in bed, and Mom hand-feeding me. That wonderfully warm and cozy soup told me with every spoonful just how much I was loved.

Her Bohemian ancestors had passed down delicious recipes for hearty broths and rich stews thick with whatever fresh ingredients were easily found. When she served my favorite potato soup with cheese dumplings and noodles, I believed nothing would ever be as soothing as that dish.

Now whenever I stir potatoes into one of my soup recipes, all those old feelings wash over me as I recall my mother's tender loving care, delivered in a bowl of soup that smelled as good as it tasted.

My Healthy Exchanges blends aren't quite as starchy as some of the more old-fashioned versions, but I'm willing to bet you'll take comfort and courage from a filling bowl of such soul-satisfying recipes as *Chicken Cabbage Chowder, Salmon Supper Soup,* and *The BEST Turkey Chowder,* all of which feature the proud potato! They're hearty, tangy, and perfect for filling the hungriest tummy on a chilly night. Some can be prepared in just minutes, while others take a little more time for all the flavors to blend beautifully. Why not stir up a pot of soup today, and enjoy it all week long?

"As one whom his mother comforts, so will I comfort you . . ."
—ISAIAH 66:13

Maxi Minestrone	Oriental Chicken Noodle Soup
Garden Patch Vegetable Chili	The BEST Turkey Chowder
Mexican Onion Soup	Brunswick Bean Soup
Creole Tomato Rice Soup	Chili with Rice
Italian Tomato Corn Chowder	Grandma's Quick Comfort Soup
Cheesy Tuna Chowder	Creamy Stroganoff Soup
Salmon Supper Soup	Beefy Onion and Noodle Soup
Chicken Cabbage Chowder	Peasant's Bean Soup
Mexican Chicken-Broccoli Soup	Midwest Ham and Corn Chowder

Maxi Minestrone

■ ❋ ■

I always think of minestrone as the "kitchen sink" of soups, a soothing and satisfying meal-in-a-bowl. This one is a true celebration of abundance—and delivers, in one dish, a day's worth of healthy veggies! *Serves 4 (1½ cups)*

2 cups (one 16-ounce can)
  Healthy Request Chicken
  Broth
½ cup chopped onion
1 cup shredded carrots
1 cup (5 ounces) diced raw
  potatoes
2 cups shredded cabbage
½ cup diced celery

1 cup (one 8-ounce can) Hunt's
  Tomato Sauce
⅓ cup (¾ ounce) uncooked
  rotini pasta
10 ounces (one 16-ounce can)
  navy beans, rinsed and
  drained
1 cup diced unpeeled zucchini
1 teaspoon Italian seasoning

In a large saucepan, combine chicken broth, onion, carrots, potatoes, cabbage, and celery. Bring mixture to a boil. Stir in tomato sauce, uncooked rotini pasta, navy beans, zucchini, and Italian seasoning. Lower heat, cover, and simmer for 15 to 20 minutes or until vegetables are tender, stirring occasionally.

HINT: 1 cup diced cooked chicken breast may be added with tomato sauce.

Each serving equals:
HE: 3½ Vegetable, 1¼ Protein, ½ Bread, 8 Optional Calories
196 Calories, 0 gm Fat, 11 gm Protein, 38 gm Carbohydrate, 641 mg Sodium, 98 mg Calcium, 10 gm Fiber
DIABETIC: 3 Vegetable, 1½ Starch, 1 Meat

Garden Patch Vegetable Chili

■ ❄ ■

If one of your healthy lifestyle goals is to share more meatless meals with your family, this tasty chili should please all palates! You also get a wonderful boost of fiber in this easy-to-fix main dish soup. *Serves 4 (1¼ cups)*

1 cup chopped onion
¾ cup chopped green bell pepper
2 cups chopped unpeeled zuc-
    chini
1¾ cups (one 14½-ounce can)
    stewed tomatoes, undrained
2 teaspoons Italian seasoning

10 ounces (one 16-ounce can) red
    kidney beans, rinsed and
    drained
1 (10¾-ounce) can Healthy
    Request Tomato Soup
¼ cup (¾ ounce) grated Kraft
    fat-free Parmesan cheese

In a large saucepan sprayed with olive oil–flavored cooking spray, sauté onion, green pepper, and zucchini for 10 minutes or until tender. Add undrained stewed tomatoes, Italian seasoning, kidney beans, and tomato soup. Mix well to combine. Bring mixture to a boil. Lower heat, cover, and simmer 15 minutes, stirring occasionally. When serving, sprinkle 1 tablespoon Parmesan cheese over top of each bowl.

Each serving equals:

HE: 2¾ Vegetable, 1½ Protein, ½ Slider, 5 Optional Calories

181 Calories, 1 gm Fat, 7 gm Protein, 36 gm Carbohydrate, 629 mg Sodium, 100 mg Calcium, 8 gm Fiber

DIABETIC: 3 Vegetable, 1 Meat, 1 Starch

Mexican Onion Soup

Why should the French have all the fun when it comes to onion soup? I like to think that this south-of-the-border version deserves more than a few festive *Olés!*   *Serves 4 (1¼ cups)*

3 cups thinly sliced onion
1 cup Healthy Request tomato
juice or any reduced-sodium
tomato juice
1¾ cups (one 14½-ounce can)
Swanson Beef Broth
½ cup chunky salsa (mild,
medium, or hot)

1 teaspoon chili seasoning
½ teaspoon dried minced garlic
4 slices reduced-calorie white
bread, toasted and cubed
4 (¾-ounce) slices Kraft reduced-
fat Cheddar cheese

Preheat oven to 400 degrees. In a large saucepan sprayed with butter-flavored cooking spray, sauté onion for 10 minutes or until tender. Add tomato juice, beef broth, salsa, chili seasoning, and garlic. Bring mixture to a boil. Lower heat and simmer for 10 minutes, stirring occasionally. Evenly spoon soup mixture into 4 individual casserole bowls. Top each with 1 slice toast and 1 slice Cheddar cheese. Place bowls on a baking sheet and bake for 10 to 12 minutes.

Each serving equals:
HE: 2¼ Vegetable, 1 Protein, ½ Bread, 9 Optional Calories
172 Calories, 4 gm Fat, 10 gm Protein, 24 gm Carbohydrate, 801 mg Sodium, 226 mg Calcium, 5 gm Fiber
DIABETIC: 2½ Vegetable, 1 Meat, ½ Starch

Creole Tomato Rice Soup

■ ■ ■

Five ingredients, ten minutes, and *voilà!* You've stirred up a filling and flavorful soup that both warms the heart and tickles the tastebuds!   *Serves 4 (1 cup)*

1 (10¾-ounce) can Healthy
   Request Tomato Soup
1½ cups water
1 cup (one 8-ounce can) cut
   green beans, rinsed and
   drained

2 tablespoons Hormel Bacon
   Bits
⅔ cup (2 ounces) uncooked
   Minute Rice

In a medium saucepan sprayed with butter-flavored cooking spray, combine tomato soup, water, green beans, and bacon bits. Bring mixture to a boil. Stir in uncooked rice. Lower heat, cover, and simmer for 10 minutes or until rice is tender, stirring occasionally.

Each serving equals:
HE: ½ Bread, ½ Vegetable, ½ Slider, 18 Optional Calories

85 Calories, 1 gm Fat, 3 gm Protein, 16 gm Carbohydrate, 356 mg Sodium, 19 mg Calcium, 1 gm Fiber

DIABETIC: 1 Starch, ½ Vegetable

Italian Tomato Corn Chowder

■ ❄ ■

Take two tasty treasures—a fragrant tomato soup and a hearty chowder—and prove without a doubt that two together are better than one alone.

Serves 4 (1½ cups)

¾ cup chopped onion
1¾ cups (one 14½-ounce can)
  stewed tomatoes, undrained
1 cup Healthy Request tomato
  juice or any reduced-sodium
  tomato juice
1½ cups frozen whole-kernel
  corn, thawed

1 teaspoon dried parsley flakes
1 teaspoon Italian seasoning
3 tablespoons all-purpose flour
1½ cups (one 12-fluid-ounce can)
  Carnation Evaporated Skim
  Milk
¼ cup (¾ ounce) grated Kraft
  fat-free Parmesan cheese

In a large saucepan sprayed with olive oil–flavored cooking spray, sauté onion for 5 minutes or until tender. Add undrained stewed tomatoes, tomato juice, corn, parsley flakes, and Italian seasoning. Mix well to combine. In a covered jar, combine flour and evaporated skim milk. Shake well to blend. Pour milk mixture into tomato mixture. Continue cooking until mixture thickens and is heated through, stirring often. When serving, sprinkle 1 tablespoon Parmesan cheese over top of each bowl.

HINT: Thaw corn by placing in a colander and rinsing under hot water for one minute.

Each serving equals:
HE: 1¾ Vegetable, 1 Bread, ¾ Skim Milk, ¼ Protein
216 Calories, 0 gm Fat, 12 gm Protein, 42 gm Carbohydrate, 544 mg Sodium, 346 mg Calcium, 4 gm Fiber
DIABETIC: 1½ Vegetable, 1 Starch, 1 Skim Milk, ½ Meat

Cheesy Tuna Chowder

When the north wind blows cold outside and your kids are clamoring for "Lunch, now, please, Mommy," here's a speedy, satisfying answer that's ready in a jiffy!

Serves 4 (1 full cup)

¼ cup finely chopped onion
1 (10¾-ounce) can Healthy
    Request Cream of Mushroom
    Soup
¾ cup (3 ounces) shredded Kraft
    reduced-fat Cheddar cheese
½ cup skim milk

1 ¾ cups (one 14½-ounce can)
    stewed tomatoes, undrained
1 (6-ounce) can white tuna,
    packed in water, drained
    and flaked
1 teaspoon dried parsley flakes
⅛ teaspoon black pepper

In a medium saucepan sprayed with butter-flavored cooking spray, sauté onion for 5 minutes or until tender. Stir in mushroom soup, Cheddar cheese, and skim milk. Add undrained stewed tomatoes, tuna, parsley flakes, and black pepper. Mix well to combine. Lower heat, cover, and simmer for 5 minutes or until cheese melts, stirring occasionally.

Each serving equals:

HE: 1¾ Protein, 1 Vegetable, ¾ Slider, 12 Optional Calories

185 Calories, 5 gm Fat, 19 gm Protein, 16 gm Carbohydrate, 854 mg Sodium, 291 mg Calcium, 1 gm Fiber

DIABETIC: 2 Meat, 1 Vegetable, ½ Starch/Carbohydrate

Salmon Supper Soup

■ ■ ■

When a dish is as good to look at as it is to taste, you know you've got a winner you can serve with pride to friends and family. With this colorful dish you can also meet your goal of putting more fish meals on the menu. *Serves 6 (1⅓ cups)*

¾ cup finely chopped onion
1 cup thinly sliced carrots
1 cup finely chopped celery
1½ cups (7½ ounces) diced raw
   potatoes
2 cups water
1¾ cups (one 14½-ounce can)
   stewed tomatoes, chopped and
   undrained

1 tablespoon white vinegar
2 teaspoons pourable Sugar Twin
¼ teaspoon dried dill weed
1 (14¾-ounce) can pink salmon,
   drained, boned, and flaked
6 tablespoons Land O Lakes
   no-fat sour cream

In a large saucepan sprayed with butter-flavored cooking spray, sauté onion for 5 minutes or until tender. Stir in carrots, celery, and potatoes. Add water, undrained stewed tomatoes, vinegar, Sugar Twin, and dill weed. Mix well to combine. Bring mixture to a boil. Stir in salmon. Lower heat, cover, and simmer for 20 to 25 minutes, or until vegetables are tender, stirring occasionally. When serving, top each bowl with 1 tablespoon sour cream.

Each serving equals:
HE: 2⅓ Protein, 1½ Vegetable, ¼ Bread, 16 Optional Calories

143 Calories, 3 gm Fat, 14 gm Protein, 15 gm Carbohydrate, 604 mg Sodium, 172 mg Calcium, 2 gm Fiber

DIABETIC: 2½ Meat, 1 Vegetable, ½ Starch

Chicken Cabbage Chowder

■ ❋ ■

Terrifically tummy-filling, this would make a perfect Sunday supper during the fall or winter, when Jack Frost is nipping at everybody's noses! It's also a thrifty choice when your budget is feeling the pinch.   *Serves 4 (1½ cups)*

2 cups (one 16-ounce can)
    Healthy Request Chicken
    Broth
2 cups (10 ounces) diced raw
    potatoes
½ cup chopped celery
½ cup chopped onion

8 ounces skinned and boned
    uncooked chicken breast,
    cut into 12 pieces
2 cups chopped cabbage
1 (10¾-ounce) can Healthy
    Request Cream of Chicken
    Soup

In a large saucepan, combine chicken broth, potatoes, celery, onion, and chicken pieces. Bring mixture to a boil. Lower heat, cover, and simmer for 15 to 20 minutes or until chicken and potatoes are tender. Stir in cabbage and chicken soup. Continue simmering for 10 to 12 minutes or until cabbage is tender, stirring often.

Each serving equals:

HE: 1½ Protein, 1½ Vegetable, ½ Bread, ½ Slider, 13 Optional Calories

170 Calories, 2 gm Fat, 17 gm Protein, 21 gm Carbohydrate, 600 mg Sodium, 37 mg Calcium, 2 gm Fiber

DIABETIC: 1½ Meat, 1 Vegetable, 1 Starch

Mexican Chicken-Broccoli Soup

■ ❄ ■

Did you know that spicy food can be just the ticket when you're fighting off a cold? A bowl of this steamy concoction, and you'll soon be feeling like your old self!   *Serves 4 (1½ cups)*

2 cups (one 16-ounce can) Healthy Request Chicken Broth

3 cups frozen cut broccoli

½ cup chopped onion

1 cup chopped celery

1 cup (one 8-ounce can) Hunt's Tomato Sauce

1 full cup (6 ounces) diced cooked chicken breast

2 teaspoons chili seasoning

1 (10¾-ounce) can Healthy Request Cream of Chicken Soup

¾ cup (3 ounces) shredded Kraft reduced-fat Cheddar cheese

In a large saucepan, combine chicken broth, broccoli, onion, and celery. Bring mixture to a boil. Stir in tomato sauce, chicken, and chili seasoning. Lower heat and simmer for 9 to 10 minutes or until vegetables are tender. Add chicken soup and Cheddar cheese. Mix well to combine. Continue simmering for 5 minutes or until cheese melts, stirring often.

HINT: If you don't have leftovers, purchase a chunk of cooked chicken breast from your local deli.

Each serving equals:

HE: 3¼ Vegetable, 2½ Protein, ½ Slider, 13 Optional Calories

230 Calories, 6 gm Fat, 25 gm Protein, 19 gm Carbohydrate, 965 mg Sodium, 203 mg Calcium, 4 gm Fiber

DIABETIC: 3 Vegetable, 2 Meat

Oriental Chicken Noodle Soup

■ ❄ ■

It takes just a few ingredients to give a traditional chicken noodle soup the delightful flavors of the mysterious East! This dish is crunchy and colorful, which makes it appealing to all your senses. *Serves 4 (1½ cups)*

> 2 cups (one 16-ounce can) Healthy Request Chicken Broth
> ¾ cup water
> ¾ cup sliced celery
> ½ cup chopped carrots
> ¼ cup chopped onion
> 1½ cups (8 ounces) diced cooked chicken breast

> ¼ cup (one 2-ounce jar) diced pimiento, drained
> 1 cup (one 8-ounce can) sliced water chestnuts, drained
> Scant 1 cup (1½ ounces) uncooked noodles
> 1 teaspoon Oriental seasoning
> 1 cup fresh snow peas

In a large saucepan, combine chicken broth, water, celery, carrots, and onion. Bring mixture to a boil. Stir in chicken, pimiento, water chestnuts, uncooked noodles, and Oriental seasoning. Lower heat and simmer for 15 minutes. Add snow peas. Mix well to combine. Continue simmering for 10 minutes or until vegetables and noodles are tender, stirring occasionally.

HINT: If you don't have leftovers, purchase a chunk of cooked chicken breast from your local deli.

Each serving equals:
HE: 2 Protein, 1¼ Vegetable, 1 Bread, 8 Optional Calories

203 Calories, 3 gm Fat, 23 gm Protein, 21 gm Carbohydrate, 315 mg Sodium, 46 mg Calcium, 4 gm Fiber

DIABETIC: 2 Meat, 1 Vegetable, 1 Starch

The BEST Turkey Chowder

■ ❄ ■

If we held a contest at the Iowa State Fair for the best way to serve holiday leftovers, this would be my entry—and I bet it would win. (Especially if Cliff is doing the judging!) The ginger gives it a special zing all its own.

Serves 4 (1½ cups)

1 cup finely chopped celery
½ cup chopped onion
2 cups (one 16-ounce can)
   Healthy Request Chicken
   Broth
⅔ cup Carnation Nonfat Dry
   Milk Powder
1 cup (one 8-ounce can) cream-
   style corn

½ cup (one 2.5-ounce jar) sliced
   mushrooms, drained
1½ cups (8 ounces) diced cooked
   potatoes
1½ cups (8 ounces) diced cooked
   turkey breast
½ teaspoon ground ginger

In a large saucepan sprayed with butter-flavored cooking spray, sauté celery and onion for 10 minutes or until tender. In a medium bowl, combine chicken broth and dry milk powder. Stir broth mixture and corn into vegetable mixture. Add mushrooms, potatoes, turkey, and ginger. Mix well to combine. Lower heat and simmer for 15 minutes or until mixture is heated through, stirring occasionally.

HINT: If you don't have leftovers, purchase a chunk of cooked turkey breast
     from your local deli.

Each serving equals:
HE: 2 Protein, 1 Bread, 1 Vegetable, ½ Skim Milk
238 Calories, 2 gm Fat, 26 gm Protein, 29 gm Carbohydrate, 638 mg Sodium, 171 mg Calcium, 3 gm Fiber
DIABETIC: 2 Meat, 1 Starch, 1 Vegetable, ½ Skim Milk

Brunswick Bean Soup

■ ❄ ■

If ever there was a hale-and-hearty dish, it would be this gathering of beans, chicken, and ham in one happy pot! High in fiber, rich in protein, it's like a cozy hug from someone who loves you.

Serves 4 (1 full cup)

10 ounces (one 16-ounce can) great northern beans, rinsed and drained
2 cups (one 16-ounce can) Healthy Request Chicken Broth
1 cup (5 ounces) diced cooked chicken breast

Full ½ cup (3 ounces) diced Dubuque 97% fat-free ham or any extra-lean ham
1 cup shredded carrots
½ cup chopped onion
1 teaspoon dried parsley flakes
⅛ teaspoon black pepper

Place great northern beans in a medium saucepan. Mash gently with a fork. Add chicken broth, chicken, ham, carrots, onion, parsley flakes, and black pepper. Bring mixture to a boil. Lower heat, cover, and simmer for 20 minutes or until vegetables are tender, stirring occasionally.

HINT: If you don't have leftovers, purchase a chunk of cooked chicken breast from your local deli.

Each serving equals:
HE: 3 Protein, ¾ Vegetable, 8 Optional Calories
190 Calories, 2 gm Fat, 22 gm Protein, 21 gm Carbohydrate, 458 mg Sodium, 67 mg Calcium, 5 gm Fiber
DIABETIC: 3 Meat, 1 Starch, ½ Vegetable

Chili with Rice

When your belly is begging "Fill me up!" I suggest this truly substantial classic blend of meat and beans. And when you serve it with rice, you'll quickly discover that a bowlful will leave you practically "stuffed." *Serves 4 (1½ cups)*

8 ounces ground 90% lean turkey
  or beef
½ cup chopped onion
½ cup finely chopped celery
3 cups Healthy Request tomato
  juice or any reduced-sodium
  tomato juice
1 cup water

10 ounces (one 16-ounce can) red
  kidney beans, rinsed and
  drained
1 teaspoon Worcestershire sauce
2 teaspoons chili seasoning
⅛ teaspoon black pepper
⅔ cup (2 ounces) uncooked
  Minute Rice

In a large saucepan sprayed with olive oil–flavored cooking spray, brown meat, onion, and celery. Stir in tomato juice, water, kidney beans, Worcestershire sauce, chili seasoning, and black pepper. Bring mixture to a boil. Lower heat and simmer for 15 minutes. Add uncooked rice. Mix well to combine. Cover and continue simmering for 10 minutes or until rice is tender, stirring occasionally.

Each serving equals:

HE: 2¾ Protein, 2 Vegetable, ½ Bread

217 Calories, 5 gm Fat, 16 gm Protein, 27 gm Carbohydrate, 188 mg Sodium, 43 mg Calcium, 6 gm Fiber

DIABETIC: 2 Meat, 2 Vegetable, 1½ Starch

Grandma's Quick Comfort Soup

■ ❄ ■

If necessity is the *mother* of invention, this is one *grandmother's* idea of creative cooking when time is short and appetites are big. Try it on a night when everyone's in a hurry to head for soccer or a PTA meeting. Best of all, you'll likely find most of the ingredients in your pantry and freezer.

Serves 6 (1½ cups)

8 ounces ground 90% lean turkey
   or beef
1¾ cups (one 15-ounce can)
   Hunt's Tomato Sauce
1¾ cups (one 14½-ounce can)
   Swanson Beef Broth
1½ cups water
⅔ cup (2 ounces) uncooked
   instant rice

1½ cups frozen sliced carrots
1½ cups frozen cut green beans
½ cup chopped onion
½ cup (one 2.5-ounce jar) sliced
   mushrooms, undrained
1 teaspoon dried parsley flakes
⅛ teaspoon black pepper

In a large saucepan sprayed with butter-flavored cooking spray, brown meat. Stir in tomato sauce, beef broth, and water. Add uncooked rice, carrots, green beans, onion, mushrooms, parsley flakes, and black pepper. Mix well to combine. Bring mixture to a boil. Lower heat, cover, and simmer for 20 minutes, or until vegetables and rice are tender, stirring occasionally.

Each serving equals:

HE: 2½ Vegetable, 1 Protein, ⅓ Bread, 6 Optional Calories

111 Calories, 3 gm Fat, 9 gm Protein, 12 gm Carbohydrate, 779 mg Sodium, 34 mg Calcium, 3 gm Fiber

DIABETIC: 2½ Vegetable, 1 Meat

Creamy Stroganoff Soup

■ ❋ ■

Inspired by chilly Russian winter nights, stroganoff is one of the coziest dishes I know! This tastes as if there's a cup of cream in every bowl—but you know better!
Serves 4 (1½ cups)

8 ounces ground 90% lean turkey or beef

½ cup chopped onion

½ cup finely chopped celery

1 (10¾-ounce) can Healthy Request Cream of Mushroom Soup

2 cups skim milk

1 teaspoon dried parsley flakes

½ cup (one 2.5-ounce jar) sliced mushrooms, drained

⅛ teaspoon black pepper

1½ cups hot cooked noodles, rinsed and drained

½ cup frozen peas, thawed

½ cup Land O Lakes no-fat sour cream

In a large saucepan sprayed with butter-flavored cooking spray, brown meat, onion, and celery. Stir in mushroom soup, skim milk, mushrooms, parsley flakes, and black pepper. Add noodles and peas. Mix well to combine. Lower heat and simmer for 15 minutes, stirring occasionally. Fold in sour cream. Cover and continue to simmer for 2 minutes. Gently stir again just before serving.

HINTS: 1. 1¼ cups uncooked noodles usually cooks to about 1½ cups.
2. Thaw peas by placing in a colander and rinsing under hot water for one minute.

Each serving equals:
HE: 1½ Protein, 1 Bread, ¾ Vegetable, ½ Skim Milk, ¾ Slider, 11 Optional Calories

304 Calories, 8 gm Fat, 20 gm Protein, 38 gm Carbohydrate, 558 mg Sodium, 259 mg Calcium, 3 gm Fiber

DIABETIC: 2 Starch, 1½ Meat, ½ Vegetable, ½ Skim Milk

Beefy Onion and Noodle Soup

■ ❋ ■

Teaching your teens to cook for themselves just got easier! Hand them this
recipe, then just stand back and enjoy the festivities. This soup is filling, flavorful, and frankly fun to cook!

Serves 4 (1½ cups)

1¾ cups (one 14½-ounce can)
   Swanson Beef Broth
2¾ cups water
1 teaspoon Worcestershire sauce
2 cups sliced onion
Scant 1 cup (1½ ounces)
   uncooked noodles

1½ cups (8 ounces) diced cooked
   lean roast beef
¼ cup (¾ ounce) grated Kraft
   fat-free Parmesan cheese

In a large saucepan, combine beef broth, water, and Worcestershire sauce. Stir
in onion. Bring mixture to a boil. Lower heat, cover, and simmer for 15 minutes. Add noodles and roast beef. Mix well to combine. Continue simmering
for 15 minutes or until noodles are tender, stirring occasionally. When serving,
sprinkle 1 tablespoon Parmesan cheese over top of each bowl.

HINT: If you don't have leftovers, purchase a chunk of cooked lean roast beef
     from your local deli.

Each serving equals:
HE: 2¼ Protein, 1 Vegetable, ½ Bread, 9 Optional Calories

197 Calories, 5 gm Fat, 21 gm Protein, 17 gm Carbohydrate, 552 mg Sodium,
24 mg Calcium, 2 gm Fiber

DIABETIC: 2 Meat, 1 Vegetable, 1 Starch

Peasant's Bean Soup

■ ❄ ■

Does "stretching" six ounces of meat and a can of beans to feed four seem impossible? Well, it's not—it's just a smart and thrifty way to cook healthy! And it certainly doesn't scrimp on taste.

Serves 4 (1½ cups)

1 full cup (6 ounces) diced Dubuque 97% fat-free ham or any extra-lean ham

1 cup (5 ounces) diced raw potatoes

Scant 1 cup (1½ ounces) uncooked noodles

½ cup finely chopped onion

2 cups water

2 cups (one 16-ounce can) Healthy Request Chicken Broth

10 ounces (one 16-ounce can) great northern beans, rinsed and drained

¼ teaspoon dried minced garlic

1 teaspoon dried parsley flakes

⅛ teaspoon black pepper

In a large saucepan, combine ham, potatoes, uncooked noodles, onion, chicken broth, and water. Bring mixture to a boil. Cook over medium heat for 10 minutes or until potatoes and noodles are tender. Stir in great northern beans, garlic, parsley flakes, and black pepper. Lower heat, cover, and simmer for 10 minutes, stirring occasionally.

Each serving equals:

HE: 2¼ Protein, ¾ Bread, ¼ Vegetable, 8 Optional Calories

218 Calories, 2 gm Fat, 17 gm Protein, 33 gm Carbohydrate, 594 mg Sodium, 62 mg Calcium, 5 gm Fiber

DIABETIC: 2 Meat, 2 Starch

Midwest Ham and Corn Chowder

■ ❋ ■

Have you been using your microwave just to heat up frozen dinners and reheat old coffee? It's time you celebrated the miraculous powers of this kitchen whiz, and here's just the dish to do it!   *Serves 4 (1 full cup)*

1 full cup (6 ounces) diced
   Dubuque 97% fat-free ham or
   any extra-lean ham
½ cup finely chopped onion
1 cup finely chopped celery
½ cup frozen whole-kernel corn
2 tablespoons water
1 cup (one 8-ounce can) cream-
   style corn

1½ cups (one 12-fluid-ounce can)
   Carnation Evaporated Skim
   Milk
⅓ cup (1 ounce) instant potato
   flakes
1 teaspoon dried parsley flakes
⅛ teaspoon black pepper

In an 8-cup glass measuring bowl, combine ham, onion, celery, whole-kernel corn, and water. Cover and microwave on HIGH (100% power) for 4 to 5 minutes, stirring after 2 minutes. Stir in cream-style corn, evaporated skim milk, potato flakes, parsley flakes, and black pepper. Re-cover and continue to microwave on HIGH for 3 to 4 minutes, stirring after 2 minutes. Let set for 2 to 3 minutes. Gently stir again just before serving.

Each serving equals:
HE: 1 Bread, 1 Protein, ¾ Skim Milk, ¾ Vegetable

226 Calories, 2 gm Fat, 17 gm Protein, 35 gm Carbohydrate, 866 mg Sodium, 300 mg Calcium, 3 gm Fiber

DIABETIC: 1½ Starch, 1 Meat, 1 Vegetable

SWEET AND SATISFYING SALADS

■ ■ ■

I always think about my husband, Cliff, when I'm creating recipes for this section, because he just loves fluffy sweet salads. They're a wonderful Midwestern
tradition that we've enjoyed all our lives, and it's been one of my pleasures
sharing these festive side dishes, these fruity and colorful "go-alongs," with the rest
of the nation!

Cliff drops by my kitchen from time to time, checking out what's being stirred
up on any given day. If a new sweet salad is on the taste-testing menu, his eyes
begin to sparkle—and I can almost hear his tummy rumble impatiently, hungry for
a mouth-pleasing morsel as soon as possible!

We grow a lot of beautiful fruit in our own garden and orchards, and those
fruits find their way into many of my sweet salads. Cliff's a particular fan of
creamy-sweet dishes starring cherries. I've told him, "If you'll pick 'em, I'll fix

'em!" *Because they have a rather short season, he's also happy to see a luscious blend that features bananas or strawberries (check out my* Banana Split Gelatin Salad), *so I don't have to worry about the harvest when I'm creating a dish that will make Cliff smile!*

The splendidly sweet salads in this section don't fill you up or fill you OUT, but they will find a home in your heart. Served as part of a healthy meal, they provide a fresh and fruity palate-clearer alongside a meat dish or casserole. They also make a terrific afternoon snack or light family dessert. Whether the menu offers my *Lemon Fruit Surprise Salad* or *Pineapple-Coconut Cream Salad*, you're bound to receive a little extra thanks from the lucky folks gathered together around your table!

> *"He that is married careth for the things that are of the world, how he may please his wife. . . . She that is married careth for the things of the world, how she may please her husband."*
> —I Corinthians 7:33–34

Blueberry Orange Salad

Strawberry Glow Salad

Hawaiian Strawberry Salad

Banana Split Gelatin Salad

Lemon Fruit Surprise Salad

Southern Apricot Hash Salad

Dessert Salad

Sunshine Salad

Tropical Ambrosia Salad

Marshmallow Waldorf Salad

Old-Time Peanut Fruit Salad

Pineapple-Coconut Cream Salad

Special Fruit Salad

Cottage Pistachio Salad

Fruit and Cream Rice Salad

Lemon Fruit Pasta Salad

Pear Salad with Blue Cheese
  Dressing

Blueberry Orange Salad

■ ■ ■

This splendid summer salad just shimmers with color and flavor. When the berries at the farm stand (or in your berry patch, if you're lucky) look ready to BURST, quick—stir them gently into this delightful dish!   *Serves 6*

1 cup unsweetened orange juice
1 (4-serving) package JELL-O
*   sugar-free orange gelatin*

¾ cup Diet Mountain Dew
¾ cup Cool Whip Free
1½ cups fresh blueberries

In a medium saucepan, bring orange juice to a boil. Remove from heat. Stir in dry gelatin, mixing well to dissolve gelatin. Add Diet Mountain Dew. Mix well to combine. Refrigerate for 30 minutes. Gently fold in Cool Whip Free and blueberries. Pour mixture into an 8-by-8-inch dish. Refrigerate until firm, about 3 hours. Divide into 6 servings.

Each serving equals:
HE: ⅔ Fruit, ¼ Slider, 2 Optional Calories
56 Calories, 0 gm Fat, 1 gm Protein, 13 gm Carbohydrate, 47 mg Sodium, 6 mg Calcium, 1 gm Fiber
DIABETIC: 1 Fruit

Strawberry Glow Salad

■ ■ ■

I'd choose this pretty party-on-a-plate for a bridal shower or birthday lunch—it's that special! Make sure you don't add the Cool Whip to the mixture until it's really cool, or your watery result could be a party "pooper"!   *Serves 6*

1 (4-serving) package JELL-O sugar-free strawberry gelatin

1 (4-serving) package JELL-O sugar-free vanilla cook-and-serve pudding mix

1 cup water

1 cup (one 8-ounce can) crushed pineapple, packed in fruit juice, undrained

2 cups frozen unsweetened strawberries

¾ cup Cool Whip Free

In a large saucepan, combine dry gelatin, dry pudding mix, undrained pineapple, and water. Stir in frozen strawberries. Cook over medium heat until strawberries thaw and mixture starts to boil, stirring often. Remove from heat. Place saucepan on a wire rack and allow to cool completely. Fold in Cool Whip Free. Pour mixture into an 8-by-8-inch dish. Refrigerate until firm, about 3 hours. Divide into 6 servings.

Each serving equals:

HE: ⅔ Fruit, ¼ Slider, 15 Optional Calories

72 Calories, 0 gm Fat, 1 gm Protein, 17 gm Carbohydrate, 119 mg Sodium, 13 mg Calcium, 1 gm Fiber

DIABETIC: 1 Fruit

Hawaiian Strawberry Salad

■ ■ ■

This taste-of-the-tropics salad just brims with lip-smacking fruit flavors, transporting you directly to Maui after just one bite! Say a happy "Aloha" at your next card party, and invite your friends to try an impromptu hula. *Serves 6*

1 (4-serving) package JELL-O sugar-free strawberry gelatin
1 cup boiling water
1 cup (one 8-ounce can) crushed pineapple, packed in fruit juice, undrained
⅓ cup (1 ripe medium) mashed banana
2 cups sliced fresh strawberries

¾ cup Yoplait plain fat-free yogurt
⅓ cup Carnation Nonfat Dry Milk Powder
Sugar substitute to equal 2 tablespoons sugar
1 teaspoon coconut extract
¾ cup Cool Whip Free
2 tablespoons flaked coconut

In a large bowl, combine dry gelatin and boiling water. Mix well to dissolve gelatin. Stir in undrained pineapple and mashed banana. Fold in strawberries. Mix gently to combine. Pour mixture into an 8-by-8-inch dish. Refrigerate until set, about 3 hours. In a medium bowl, combine yogurt and dry milk powder. Add sugar substitute, coconut extract, and Cool Whip Free. Mix gently to combine. Spread mixture evenly over set gelatin. Evenly sprinkle coconut over top. Cover and refrigerate for at least 15 minutes. Divide into 6 servings.

Each serving equals:
HE: 1 Fruit, ⅓ Skim Milk, ¼ Slider, 9 Optional Calories

104 Calories, 0 gm Fat, 4 gm Protein, 22 gm Carbohydrate, 88 mg Sodium, 116 mg Calcium, 1 gm Fiber

DIABETIC: 1 Fruit, ½ Starch/Carbohydrate

Banana Split Gelatin Salad

■ ■ ■

Here's a great idea for a sweet salad sundae that my husband, Cliff, scored a perfect 10! I love imagining a time when soda fountains across America will serve all my Banana Split recipes in every yummy category! *Serves 6*

1 (4-serving) package JELL-O sugar-free strawberry gelatin
¾ cup boiling water
1 cup (one 8-ounce can) crushed pineapple, packed in fruit juice, undrained
1½ cups cold water ☆
1 cup (1 medium) sliced banana
2 cups sliced fresh strawberries

1 (4-serving) package JELL-O sugar-free instant banana cream pudding mix
⅔ cup Carnation Nonfat Dry Milk Powder
½ cup Cool Whip Free
2 tablespoons (½ ounce) mini chocolate chips
3 maraschino cherries, halved

In a large bowl, combine dry gelatin and boiling water. Mix well to dissolve gelatin. Stir in undrained pineapple and ½ cup cold water. Add banana and strawberries. Mix well to combine. Pour mixture into an 8-by-8-inch dish. Refrigerate until firm, about 3 hours. In a large bowl, combine dry pudding mix, dry milk powder, and remaining 1 cup water. Mix well using a wire whisk. Blend in Cool Whip Free. Spread mixture evenly over set gelatin. Evenly sprinkle chocolate chips over top. Garnish with maraschino cherry halves. Cover and refrigerate for at least 30 minutes. Divide into 6 servings.

HINT: To prevent banana from turning brown, mix with 1 teaspoon lemon juice or sprinkle with Fruit Fresh.

Each serving equals:
HE: 1 Fruit, ⅓ Skim Milk, ½ Slider, 11 Optional Calories
200 Calories, 4 gm Fat, 4 gm Protein, 37 gm Carbohydrate, 310 mg Sodium, 111 mg Calcium, 2 gm Fiber 4
DIABETIC: 1½ Starch/Carbohydrate, 1 Fruit

Lemon Fruit Surprise Salad

■ ■ ■

Don't you just love surprises—especially when you get more than one per spoonful? The fresh berries and tangy orange are sure to transform the slightest frown into a happy grin.

Serves 8

1 (4-serving) package JELL-O
   sugar-free lemon gelatin
1 cup boiling water
¾ cup cold water
1 cup Cool Whip Free

1 cup (one 11-ounce can) mandarin oranges, rinsed and
   drained
1½ cups fresh blueberries

In a large bowl, combine dry gelatin and boiling water. Mix well to dissolve gelatin. Stir in cold water. Refrigerate for 15 minutes. Fold in Cool Whip Free. Add mandarin oranges and blueberries. Mix gently to combine. Pour mixture into an 8-by-8-inch dish. Refrigerate until firm, about 3 hours. Divide into 8 servings.

Each serving equals:
HE: ½ Fruit, ¼ Slider

48 Calories, 0 gm Fat, 1 gm Protein, 11 gm Carbohydrate, 35 mg Sodium, 5 mg Calcium, 0 gm Fiber

DIABETIC: ½ Fruit

Southern Apricot Hash Salad

■ ■ ■

"Hash" is one of those wonderful words that promise a mélange of flavors, some unexpected, and all delectable. This spirited bonanza should please old and young alike!

Serves 6 (½ cup)

- 1 (4-serving) package JELL-O sugar-free vanilla cook-and-serve pudding mix
- 1 (4-serving) package JELL-O sugar-free lemon gelatin
- 2 cups (one 16-ounce can) sliced apricots, packed in fruit juice, drained, and ⅓ cup liquid reserved
- 1 cup water
- 2 tablespoons (½ ounce) chopped pecans
- ¾ cup Cool Whip Free
- 9 (2½-inch) graham cracker squares, broken into large pieces
- ½ cup (1 ounce) miniature marshmallows

In a large saucepan, combine dry pudding mix and dry gelatin. Add reserved fruit juice and water. Mix well to combine. Cook over medium heat until mixture thickens and starts to boil, stirring often. Remove from heat. Stir in apricots and pecans. Spoon mixture into a large bowl. Place bowl on a wire rack and allow to cool for 30 minutes, stirring occasionally. Fold in Cool Whip Free. Cover and refrigerate for at least 15 minutes. Just before serving, stir in graham cracker pieces and marshmallows.

Each serving equals:

HE: ⅔ Fruit, ½ Bread, ⅓ Fat, ½ Slider, 3 Optional Calories

126 Calories, 2 gm Fat, 2 gm Protein, 25 gm Carbohydrate, 157 mg Sodium, 11 mg Calcium, 1 gm Fiber

DIABETIC: 1 Fruit, ½ Starch/Carbohydrate, ½ Fat

Dessert Salad

Sweet salads served alongside a main dish are a classic Midwestern tradition, but this one is pretty enough, and special enough, to feature for dessert! Its lovely blend of colors and textures will dazzle the senses and tempt any tummy.

Serves 8

1 cup Cool Whip Free
½ cup Kraft fat-free mayonnaise
Sugar substitute to equal 2 tablespoons sugar
1 cup (one 8-ounce can) pineapple chunks, packed in fruit
juice, drained
1 cup (1 medium) diced banana

1 cup (6 ounces) white seedless
grapes, halved
¼ cup raisins
¼ cup (1 ounce) chopped pecans
6 (2½-inch) graham cracker
squares, broken into bite-size
pieces
4 maraschino cherries, halved

In a large bowl, combine Cool Whip Free, mayonnaise, and sugar substitute. Add pineapple, grapes, banana, raisins, pecans, and graham cracker pieces. Mix gently to combine. Evenly spoon into 8 dessert dishes. Top each with maraschino cherry half. Refrigerate for at least 15 minutes.

HINTS: 1. To prevent banana from turning brown, mix with 1 teaspoon lemon
juice or sprinkle with Fruit Fresh.
2. To plump up raisins without "cooking," place in a glass measuring
cup and microwave on HIGH for 20 seconds.

Each serving equals:
HE: 1 Fruit, ½ Fat, ¼ Bread, ¼ Slider, 12 Optional Calories

135 Calories, 3 gm Fat, 1 gm Protein, 26 gm Carbohydrate, 153 mg Sodium,
11 mg Calcium, 1 gm Fiber

DIABETIC: 1 Fruit, ½ Fat, ½ Starch/Carbohydrate

Sunshine Salad

■ ■ ■

Want to tell your favorite honey that he is your "sunshine"? This fresh 'n' fruity concoction says it all for you!

Serves 8 (½ cup)

1 (4-serving) package JELL-O sugar-free instant vanilla pudding mix

1 (4-serving) package JELL-O sugar-free orange gelatin

⅔ cup Carnation Nonfat Dry Milk Powder

1 cup (one 8-ounce can) pineapple tidbits, packed in fruit juice, drained, and ⅓ cup liquid reserved

¾ cup water

¾ cup Cool Whip Free

½ cup Yoplait plain fat-free yogurt

1 cup (1 medium) sliced banana

2 cups chopped fresh strawberries

1 cup (one 11-ounce can) mandarin oranges, rinsed and drained

In a large bowl, combine dry pudding mix, dry gelatin, dry milk powder, reserved pineapple liquid, and water. Mix well using a wire whisk. Blend in Cool Whip Free and yogurt. Add banana, strawberries, oranges, and pineapple. Mix gently to combine. Cover and refrigerate for at least 30 minutes. Gently stir again just before serving.

HINTS: 1. If you can't find pineapple tidbits, use chunk pineapple and coarsely chop.
2. To prevent banana from turning brown, mix with 1 teaspoon lemon juice or sprinkle with Fruit Fresh.

Each serving equals:
HE: 1 Fruit, ⅓ Skim Milk, ¼ Slider, 9 Optional Calories

120 Calories, 0 gm Fat, 5 gm Protein, 25 gm Carbohydrate, 245 mg Sodium, 103 mg Calcium, 1 gm Fiber

DIABETIC: 1 Fruit, ½ Starch/Carbohydrate

Tropical Ambrosia Salad

■ ■ ■

This festive dish recalls the much-adored and widely served taste treat every 1950s homemaker served with pride—and why not! This heavenly mixture is truly refreshing.

Serves 4 (¾ cup)

¾ cup Yoplait plain fat-free
  yogurt
⅓ cup Carnation Nonfat Dry
  Milk Powder
Sugar substitute to equal 2 tablespoons sugar
1 teaspoon coconut extract
1 cup (one 8-ounce can) pineapple chunks, packed in fruit
  juice, drained

1 cup (one 11-ounce can) mandarin oranges, rinsed and
  drained
1 tablespoon flaked coconut
¼ cup (½ ounce) miniature
  marshmallows

In a large bowl, combine yogurt and dry milk powder. Stir in sugar substitute and coconut extract. Add pineapple, mandarin oranges, coconut, and marsh-mallows. Mix gently to combine. Cover and refrigerate for at least 1 hour. Gently stir again just before serving.

Each serving equals:
HE.   1 Fruit, ½ Skim Milk, 13 Optional Calories
116 Calories, 0 gm Fat, 5 gm Protein, 24 gm Carbohydrate, 71 mg Sodium, 170 mg Calcium, 1 gm Fiber   2
DIABETIC: 1 Fruit, ½ Skim Milk

Marshmallow Waldorf Salad

■ ■ ■

Hmm, tastes familiar, but there's something different, something new, something unexpected in this salad classic. *Whee!* Must be those sweetly surprising marshmallows that are lighter than air but very satisfying! *Serves 6 (¾ cup)*

3 cups (6 small) cored, unpeeled, and diced Red Delicious apples
1 tablespoon lemon juice
1 cup (2 ounces) miniature marshmallows

1 cup chopped celery
¼ cup (1 ounce) chopped walnuts
⅓ cup Kraft fat-free mayonnaise
Sugar substitute to equal 1 teaspoon sugar

In a large bowl, combine apples and lemon juice. Stir in marshmallows, celery, and walnuts. Add mayonnaise and sugar substitute. Mix gently to combine. Cover and refrigerate for at least 15 minutes. Gently stir again just before serving.

Each serving equals:
HE: 1 Fruit, ⅓ Fat, ⅓ Vegetable, ¼ Slider, 16 Optional Calories
103 Calories, 3 gm Fat, 1 gm Protein, 18 gm Carbohydrate, 136 mg Sodium, 17 mg Calcium, 2 gm Fiber
DIABETIC: 1 Fruit, ½ Fat, ½ Starch/Carbohydrate

Old-Time Peanut Fruit Salad

■ ■ ■

There's something so lusciously old-fashioned about this blend of fruity-nutty flavors. It's perfect for a summer potluck where the guests range in age from 3 to 103! Keeping happy taste memories alive is one of my favorite assignments.

Serves 8 (½ cup)

2 cups (4 small) cored, unpeeled, and diced Red Delicious apples
1 cup (1 medium) diced banana
¼ cup raisins
¼ cup (1 ounce) chopped dry-roasted peanuts
2 tablespoons Peter Pan reduced-fat peanut butter

Sugar substitute to equal 2 tablespoons sugar
2 tablespoons Kraft fat-free mayonnaise
2 tablespoons skim milk
½ cup Cool Whip Free

In a large bowl, combine apples, banana, raisins, and peanuts. In a small bowl, combine peanut butter, sugar substitute, mayonnaise, and skim milk. Blend in Cool Whip Free. Add peanut butter mixture to fruit mixture. Mix gently to combine. Cover and refrigerate for at least 30 minutes. Gently stir again just before serving.

HINTS: 1. To prevent banana from turning brown, mix with 1 teaspoon lemon juice or sprinkle with Fruit Fresh.
2. To plump up raisins without "cooking," place in a glass measuring cup and microwave on HIGH for 20 seconds.
3. Peter Pan reduced-fat peanut butter blends best at room temperature.

Each serving equals:
HE: 1 Fruit, ½ Fat, ⅓ Protein, 13 Optional Calories
90 Calories, 2 gm Fat, 2 gm Protein, 16 gm Carbohydrate, 44 mg Sodium, 12 mg Calcium, 2 gm Fiber
DIABETIC: 1 Fruit, ½ Fat, ½ Starch/Carbohydrate

Pineapple-Coconut Cream Salad

■ ■ ■

I confess—I think I was dreaming of a piña colada under a palm tree when I created this creamy salad! You don't even need a drop of rum to feel as if you're lying on a beach in Paradise, just a nibble or two of this outrageously luscious combo. Enjoy!

Serves 8 (½ cup)

1 (4-serving) package JELL-O sugar-free vanilla cook-and-serve pudding mix
⅔ cup Carnation Nonfat Dry Milk Powder
½ cup water
1 cup (one 8-ounce can) crushed pineapple, packed in fruit juice, undrained

1 cup (one 8-ounce can) pineapple tidbits, packed in fruit juice, drained, and ¼ cup liquid reserved
1 teaspoon coconut extract
1 cup Cool Whip Free
1 cup (2 ounces) miniature marshmallows
3 tablespoons flaked coconut

In a medium saucepan, combine dry pudding mix, dry milk powder, water, undrained crushed pineapple, and reserved pineapple liquid. Cook over medium heat until mixture thickens and starts to boil, stirring constantly. Remove from heat. Stir in pineapple tidbits and coconut extract. Place saucepan on a wire rack and allow to cool completely, stirring occasionally. Spoon mixture into a large bowl. Blend in Cool Whip Free. Add marshmallows and coconut. Mix gently to combine. Cover and refrigerate for at least 1 hour. Gently stir again just before serving.

HINT: If you can't find tidbits, use chunk pineapple and coarsely chop.

Each serving equals:
HE: ½ Fruit, ¼ Skim Milk, ½ Slider, 3 Optional Calories

104 Calories, 0 gm Fiber, 2 gm Protein, 24 gm Carbohydrate, 101 mg Sodium, 78 mg Calcium, 1 gm Fiber

DIABETIC: 1 Starch/Carbohydrate, ½ Fruit

Special Fruit Salad

■ ■ ■

Sure, you could scoop some cottage cheese on a plate and add a pineapple slice or two, but that's too much like dieting, don't you agree? This combination takes a bit more time but the scrumptious result is definitely worth it!

Serves 6 (¾ cup)

2 cups fat-free cottage cheese
1 (4-serving) package JELL-O
   sugar-free raspberry gelatin
¾ cup Cool Whip Free
1 cup (one 8-ounce can) crushed
   pineapple, packed in fruit
   juice, drained

2 cups (one 16-ounce can) fruit
   cocktail, packed in fruit juice,
   drained

In a large bowl, combine cottage cheese and dry gelatin. Blend in Cool Whip Free. Add pineapple and fruit cocktail. Mix gently to combine. Cover and refrigerate for at least 30 minutes. Gently stir again just before serving.

Each serving equals:
HE: 1 Fruit, ⅔ Protein, ¼ Slider, 2 Optional Calories

136 Calories, 0 gm Fat, 11 gm Protein, 23 gm Carbohydrate, 326 mg Sodium, 45 mg Calcium, 1 gm Fiber

DIABETIC: 1 Fruit, 1 Meat, ½ Starch/Carbohydrate

Cottage Pistachio Salad

■ ■ ■

I love "building" beautiful salads that please the eye as completely as they do the appetite. Pistachio pudding is one of my favorite "building blocks" for its lovely color and tiny nutty bits every now and then. This salad is protein-rich and sweetly flavorful.

Serves 8 (¾ cup)

1 (4-serving) package JELL-O sugar-free instant pistachio pudding mix
⅓ cup Carnation Nonfat Dry Milk Powder
¾ cup Yoplait plain fat-free yogurt
1 cup (one 8-ounce can) crushed pineapple, packed in fruit juice, undrained

2 cups fat-free cottage cheese
1 cup Cool Whip Free
1 cup (one 11-ounce can) mandarin oranges, rinsed and drained
½ cup (1 ounce) miniature marshmallows
¼ cup (1 ounce) chopped pecans
4 maraschino cherries, quartered

In a large bowl, combine dry pudding mix and dry milk powder. Add yogurt and undrained pineapple. Mix gently to combine. Blend in cottage cheese and Cool Whip Free. Add oranges, marshmallows, pecans, and maraschino cherries. Mix gently to combine. Cover and refrigerate for at least 30 minutes. Gently stir again just before serving.

Each serving equals:
HE: ½ Protein, ½ Fruit, ½ Fat, ¼ Skim Milk, ¼ Slider, 19 Optional Calories
150 Calories, 2 gm Fat, 10 gm Protein, 23 gm Carbohydrate, 411 mg Sodium, 110 mg Calcium, 0 gm Fiber
DIABETIC: 1 Meat, 1 Starch/Carbohydrate, ½ Fruit, ½ Fat

Fruit and Cream Rice Salad

■ ■ ■

This kissing cousin of rice pudding is downright delectable, and delivers tons of flavor in every bite. It appeals equally to young children and the grown-ups who still love its cold, creamy comfort!   *Serves 6*

1 (4-serving) package JELL-O
   sugar-free instant vanilla
   pudding mix
⅔ cup Carnation Nonfat Dry
   Milk Powder
2 cups (one 16-ounce can) fruit
   cocktail, packed in fruit juice,
   drained, and ½ cup liquid
   reserved

1 cup (one 8-ounce can) crushed
   pineapple, packed in fruit
   juice, drained, and ⅓ cup
   liquid reserved
½ cup water
½ cup Cool Whip Free
1½ cups cold cooked rice
3 maraschino cherries, halved

In a large bowl, combine dry pudding mix and dry milk powder. Add reserved fruit liquids and water. Mix well using a wire whisk. Blend in Cool Whip Free. Add fruit cocktail and pineapple. Mix well to combine. Fold in rice. Evenly spoon mixture into 6 salad dishes. Top each with a maraschino cherry half. Refrigerate for at least 30 minutes.

HINT: 1 cup uncooked rice usually cooks to about 1½ cups.

Each serving equals:
HE: 1 Fruit, ½ Bread, ⅓ Skim Milk, ¼ Slider, 12 Optional Calories
160 Calories, 0 gm Fat, 4 gm Protein, 36 gm Carbohydrate, 269 mg Sodium, 108 mg Calcium, 1 gm Fiber
DIABETIC: 1 Fruit, 1 Starch/Carbohydrate

Lemon Fruit Pasta Salad

■ ■ ■

A sweet pasta salad? True, it's not what you might expect, but I bet you'll be delighted by its palate-pleasing potential! And each of the fruits retains its special identity—tart, sweet, and crunchy.

Serves 8 (¾ cup)

1 (4-serving) package JELL-O sugar-free instant vanilla pudding mix

1 (4-serving) package JELL-O sugar-free lemon gelatin

⅔ cup Carnation Nonfat Dry Milk Powder

1 cup (one 8-ounce can) crushed pineapple, packed in fruit juice, undrained

⅔ cup water

1 cup Cool Whip Free

2 cups cold cooked shell macaroni, rinsed and drained

1 cup (one 11-ounce can) mandarin oranges, rinsed and drained

1 cup (6 ounces) halved seedless green grapes

1 cup (2 small) cored, unpeeled, and chopped Red Delicious apples

In a large bowl, combine dry pudding mix, dry gelatin, and dry milk powder. Add undrained pineapple and water. Mix well using a wire whisk. Blend in Cool Whip Free. Stir in macaroni. Add mandarin oranges, grapes, and apples. Mix well to combine. Cover and refrigerate for at least 30 minutes. Gently stir again just before serving.

HINT: 1⅓ cups uncooked shell macaroni usually cooks to about 2 cups.

Each serving equals:
HE: 1 Fruit, ½ Bread, ¼ Skim Milk, ¼ Slider, 13 Optional Calories

152 Calories, 0 gm Fat, 5 gm Protein, 33 gm Carbohydrate, 231 mg Sodium, 82 mg Calcium, 1 gm Fiber

DIABETIC: 1 Fruit, 1 Starch/Carbohydrate

Pear Salad with Blue Cheese Dressing

■ ■ ■

This dish provides a refreshing contrast of flavors and textures. It takes seconds to prepare and yet looks attractive enough for a ladies' luncheon. Isn't it fun to impress your friends with so little effort?

Serves 4

4 cups shredded lettuce
4 ripe (medium-sized) pears,
    cored and diced

½ cup Kraft Fat Free Blue
    Cheese Dressing
Dash ground nutmeg

For each serving, place 1 cup of lettuce on a salad plate, evenly sprinkle 1 diced pear over lettuce, drizzle 2 tablespoons Blue Cheese dressing over pear, and lightly sprinkle nutmeg over top.

Each serving equals:

HE: 2 Vegetable, 1 Fruit, ½ Slider, 10 Optional Calories

80 Calories, 0 gm Fat, 1 gm Protein, 19 gm Carbohydrate, 250 mg Sodium, 68 mg Calcium, 4 gm Fiber

DIABETIC: 1 Fruit, ½ Starch/Carbohydrate, 1 Free Food

SAVORY SALADS TO
FEED THE SPIRIT

. . .

O ut here in Iowa, there's something special about the fall season, when the gardens are in all their glory. I remember when we lived on the farm, neighboring farmers would always help each other out, whether it meant pitching in at the harvest or sorting the hogs. Whenever there was a big job to be done, something that was just too much for one farmer, you'd call on your two or three closest neighbors for help instead of hiring outside hands.

These occasions were also a time for feasting with friends, at great groaning buffet tables laden with a huge spread of food to serve the crowd of workers. You'd always see cucumber salad and at least two kinds of coleslaw. My son James used to say he couldn't ever remember a family gathering that didn't feature coleslaw. In fact, when he brought Pam, his future wife, home for a visit, there was coleslaw on the table. He nudged her and said, "See? What did I tell you?" As a little boy he used to call it "cold slop," but whatever he called it, he gobbled it down!

Because no summer picnic is complete without a tasty potato salad, I've given you a few festive choices in this chapter, including one that uses sweet potatoes to make this American classic (*Honey Dijon Sweet Potato Salad*). There's a mélange of slaws that taste so fresh and crunchy, someone just might say "*Shhhh!*" especially if you're serving *Crispy Vegetable Slaw*. Some of my favorites here are all vegetarian (*Party Broccoli Salad*), while others blend in tasty bits of healthy protein (*West Coast Seafood Salad*). And because I'm known everywhere now as the Pie Lady, I've included—yes!—*Layered Summer Salad Pie*.

> "Your words were found, and I ate them,
> And Your word was to me the joy and rejoicing of my heart."
> —JEREMIAH 15:16

Jellied Gazpacho Salad

Lemon Perfection Salad

Cabbage Mardi Gras Salad

Crunchy Broccoli Salad

Party Broccoli Salad

Crispy Vegetable Slaw

Sweet 'n' Sour Vegetable Salad

Green Pot Luck

Chili Corn Salad

Layered Tomato and Mozzarella Salad

Zucchini Bean Salad

Stuffed Tomato–Potato Salad

Springtime Potato Salad

Honey Dijon Sweet Potato Salad

Layered Summer Salad Pie

Tuna Macaroni Salad

West Coast Seafood Salad

Italian Pasta Salmon Salad

Mexican Chicken Salad

Ham-Broccoli-Pasta Salad

Jellied Gazpacho Salad

■ ■ ■

Savory gelatin salads have been enjoying a kind of rebirth recently, and this crunchy-tangy blend will make a believer out of you! (Make sure you use only white vinegar in this recipe, as other types won't produce a properly tasty result.)

Serves 6

1 cup unpeeled and chopped
    fresh tomatoes
1 cup diced unpeeled cucumber
¼ cup chopped green bell pepper
¼ cup chopped onion
1½ cups Healthy Request tomato
    juice or any reduced-sodium
    tomato juice

1 (4-serving) package JELL-O
    sugar-free lemon gelatin
¼ cup cold water
2 tablespoons white vinegar

In a large bowl, combine tomatoes, cucumber, green pepper, and onion. In a medium saucepan, bring tomato juice to a boil. Remove from heat. Add dry gelatin. Mix well to dissolve gelatin. Stir in water and vinegar. Let set for 10 minutes. Add partially cooled gelatin mixture to vegetable mixture. Mix gently to combine. Pour mixture into an 8-by-8-inch dish. Refrigerate until firm, about 3 hours. Divide into 6 servings.

HINT: Good served with a dollop of fat-free sour cream.

Each serving equals:
HE: 1⅓ Vegetable, 7 Optional Calories

32 Calories, 0 gm Fat, 2 gm Protein, 6 gm Carbohydrate, 75 mg Sodium, 10 mg Calcium, 1 gm Fiber

DIABETIC: 1 Vegetable

Lemon Perfection Salad

■ ■ ■

Remember those recommendations to get "Five a Day," meaning five fruit and vegetable servings daily? Well, if it seems like too much trouble, try this recipe, which solves one-fifth of your day's requirements quickly and deliciously.

Serves 8

1 (4-serving) package JELL-O sugar-free lemon gelatin
1 cup boiling water
⅔ cup cold water
1 cup (one 8-ounce can) crushed pineapple, packed in fruit juice, undrained
1 teaspoon white vinegar

Sugar substitute to equal 2 teaspoons sugar
1 cup shredded cabbage
½ cup shredded carrots
½ cup chopped celery
1 cup (2 small) cored, unpeeled, and diced Red Delicious apples

In a large bowl, combine dry gelatin and boiling water. Mix well to dissolve gelatin. Stir in cold water, undrained pineapple, vinegar, and sugar substitute. Add cabbage, carrots, celery, and apples. Mix well to combine. Pour mixture into an 8-by-8-inch dish. Refrigerate until firm, about 3 hours. Divide into 8 servings.

Each serving equals:
HE: ½ Fruit, ½ Vegetable, 5 Optional Calories

36 Calories, 0 gm Fat, 1 gm Protein, 8 gm Carbohydrate, 39 mg Sodium, 15 mg Calcium, 1 gm Fiber

DIABETIC: ½ Fruit

Cabbage Mardi Gras Salad

■ ■ ■

There's no more exciting party than Mardi Gras in New Orleans or Rio, where the atmosphere is festive, costumes come in every color of the rainbow, and the music goes on all night. This salad might just turn your ordinary weekday dinner into a party that never ends! *Serves 6*

1 (4-serving) package JELL-O sugar-free lime gelatin
1 cup boiling water
1 cup (one 8-ounce can) crushed pineapple, packed in fruit juice, undrained

½ cup (1 ounce) miniature marshmallows
¾ cup fat-free cottage cheese
1 cup shredded cabbage
½ cup Kraft fat-free mayonnaise
½ cup Cool Whip Free

In a large bowl, combine dry gelatin and boiling water. Mix well to dissolve gelatin. Add undrained pineapple and marshmallows. Mix well to combine. Stir in cottage cheese. Refrigerate for at least 15 minutes. Add cabbage, mayonnaise, and Cool Whip Free. Mix gently to combine. Pour mixture into an 8-by-8-inch dish. Cover and refrigerate until firm, about 3 hours. Divide into 6 servings.

Each serving equals:
HE: ⅓ Fruit, ⅓ Vegetable, ¼ Protein, ¼ Slider, 18 Optional Calories
88 Calories, 0 gm Fat, 5 gm Protein, 17 gm Carbohydrate, 323 mg Sodium, 24 gm Calcium, 1 gm Fiber
DIABETIC: 1 Starch/Carbohydrate

Crunchy Broccoli Salad

■ ■ ■

If there's one food that every nutritionist encourages us to eat more of, it's broccoli. And raw is better than cooked for making sure you get the most from all those great nutrients (especially fiber) that broccoli contains. This salad takes something wonderful and makes it even better, with tasty bits of this and that to tickle your tastebuds.

Serves 6 (⅔ cup)

3¾ cups chopped fresh broccoli
¼ cup chopped red onion
½ cup raisins
⅓ cup (1½ ounces) chopped
   walnuts
2 tablespoons Hormel Bacon
   Bits

⅔ cup Kraft fat-free mayonnaise
2 tablespoons skim milk
Sugar substitute to equal 2 tablespoons sugar
1 tablespoon white vinegar

In a large bowl, combine broccoli, onion, raisins, walnuts, and bacon bits. In a small bowl, combine mayonnaise, skim milk, sugar substitute, and vinegar. Add mayonnaise mixture to broccoli mixture. Mix gently to combine. Cover and refrigerate for at least 30 minutes. Gently stir again just before serving.

HINT: To plump up raisins without "cooking," place in a glass measuring cup and microwave on HIGH for 20 seconds.

Each serving equals:
HE: 1⅓ Vegetable, ⅔ Fruit, ½ Fat, ¼ Protein, ¼ Slider, 5 Optional Calories
124 Calories, 4 gm Fat, 4 gm Protein, 18 gm Carbohydrate, 332 mg Sodium,
47 mg Calcium, 3 gm Fiber
DIABETIC: 1 Vegetable, 1 Fruit, ½ Fat

Party Broccoli Salad

■ ■ ■

You don't even need to decorate the table when you make this super-salad the centerpiece of your next dinner party—it's just that colorfully vibrant and full of mouth-pleasing textures! Not only that, but it's low in calories, contains NO fat, and delivers a wallop of fiber that would make your doctor cheer!

Serves 6 (1 cup)

2 cups chopped fresh broccoli
2 cups chopped fresh cauliflower
1 cup frozen peas, thawed
1 cup (one 8-ounce can) sliced
  water chestnuts, drained
½ cup chopped red radishes

½ cup Kraft Fat Free Ranch
  Dressing
¼ cup Kraft fat-free mayonnaise
1 teaspoon dried onion flakes
2 teaspoons dried parsley flakes

In a large bowl, combine broccoli, cauliflower, peas, water chestnuts, and radishes. In a small bowl, combine Ranch dressing, mayonnaise, onion flakes, and parsley flakes. Add dressing mixture to vegetable mixture. Mix well to combine. Cover and refrigerate for at least 30 minutes. Gently stir again just before serving.

HINT: Thaw peas by placing in a colander and rinsing under hot water for one
    minute.

Each serving equals:
HE: 1½ Vegetable, ⅔ Bread, ½ Slider
88 Calories, 0 gm Fat, 3 gm Protein, 19 gm Carbohydrate, 324 mg Sodium, 33 mg Calcium, 4 gm Fiber
DIABETIC: 1½ Vegetable, ½ Starch/Carbohydrate

Crispy Vegetable Slaw

■ ■ ■

Don't you just love biting down and crunch-crunch-crunching on a mouthful of fresh and tangy veggies? There's so much mouth satisfaction in it, especially when you add a little cheese and dressing to the mix.   *Serves 4 (1 cup)*

2¾ cups purchased coleslaw mix
1 cup chopped fresh cauliflower
¼ cup sliced green onion
½ cup chopped celery
1 tablespoon Hormel Bacon Bits
⅓ cup Kraft fat free mayonnaise

2 tablespoons Kraft Fat Free
   Italian Dressing
Sugar substitute to equal 1 tablespoon sugar
¼ cup (¾ ounce) grated Kraft
   fat-free Parmesan cheese

In a medium bowl, combine coleslaw mix, cauliflower, green onion, celery, and bacon bits. In a small bowl, combine mayonnaise, Italian dressing, sugar substitute, and Parmesan cheese. Add dressing mixture to vegetable mixture. Mix gently to combine. Cover and refrigerate for at least 1 hour. Gently stir again just before serving.

HINT: 2 cups shredded cabbage and ¼ cup shredded carrots may be used in
      place of purchased coleslaw mix.

Each serving equals:
HE: 2¼ Vegetable, ¼ Protein, ¼ Slider, 12 Optional Calories
72 Calories, 0 gm Fat, 2 gm Protein, 16 gm Carbohydrate, 514 mg Sodium,
36 mg Calcium, 3 gm Fiber
DIABETIC: 1 Vegetable, ½ Meat, ½ Starch/Carbohydrate

Sweet 'n' Sour Vegetable Salad

■ ■ ■

If you've never made a cooked dressing like the one in this recipe, I bet you'll be pleasantly surprised by how well the different flavors combine. This dish blends fresh and frozen veggies for a magnificent mélange that satisfies in every way.

Serves 8 (1 cup)

1½ cups finely diced celery
½ cup finely chopped onion
1½ cups shredded carrots
1½ cups frozen cut green beans, thawed
1 cup frozen whole-kernel corn, thawed

1 cup frozen peas, thawed
¾ cup Kraft Fat Free French Dressing
2 tablespoons white vinegar
1 tablespoon Brown Sugar Twin
1 teaspoon prepared mustard
1 teaspoon dried parsley flakes

In a large bowl, combine celery, onion, carrots, green beans, corn, and peas. In a small saucepan, combine French dressing, vinegar, Brown Sugar Twin, mustard, and parsley flakes. Bring mixture to a boil, stirring constantly. Pour hot mixture over vegetables. Mix gently to combine. Cover and refrigerate for at least 1 hour. Gently stir again just before serving.

HINT: Thaw frozen vegetables by placing in a colander and rinsing under hot water for one minute.

Each serving equals:
HE: 1¼ Vegetable, ½ Bread, ¼ Slider, 18 Optional Calories
92 Calories, 0 gm Fat, 2 gm Protein, 21 gm Carbohydrate, 263 mg Sodium, 30 mg Calcium, 3 gm Fiber
DIABETIC: 1 Vegetable, 1 Starch

Green Pot Luck

■ ■ ■

Imagine that you opened your fridge and spotted a couple of lonely cucumbers and a few green onions. Then you opened your cabinet and noticed a can of your favorite tiny peas. What could you do, you wonder, with these "green" ingredients? Here's my suggestion! *Serves 4 (¾ cup)*

2 cups (one 16-ounce can) tiny
   green peas, rinsed and drained
1¼ cups diced unpeeled
   cucumber
¼ cup sliced green onion
1 teaspoon dried parsley flakes

¼ cup Kraft fat-free mayonnaise
⅛ teaspoon black pepper
1 teaspoon lemon juice
Sugar substitute to equal 2 teaspoons sugar

In a medium bowl, combine peas, cucumber, and green onion. Add parsley flakes, mayonnaise, black pepper, lemon juice, and sugar substitute. Mix gently to combine. Cover and refrigerate for at least 1 hour. Gently stir again just before serving.

Each serving equals:
HE: 1 Bread, ¾ Vegetable, 11 Optional Calories
76 Calories, 0 gm Fat, 4 gm Protein, 15 gm Carbohydrate, 133 mg Sodium, 26 mg Calcium, 4 gm Fiber
DIABETIC: 1 Starch

Chili Corn Salad

■ ■ ■

Cliff loves the combination of chili and corn, so I came up with this new way to deliver those favorite flavors—but in a crunchy, healthy salad! The creamy dressing is a wonderful contrast with the fresh veggie chunks, and you can make it as spicy as you like it.

Serves 4 (¾ cup)

⅓ cup Kraft fat-free mayonnaise
2 tablespoons Land O Lakes no-
    fat sour cream
1 teaspoon lemon juice
1½ teaspoons chili seasoning
1½ cups frozen whole-kernel
    corn, thawed

10 ounces (one 16-ounce can) red
    kidney beans, rinsed and
    drained
½ cup thinly sliced celery
¼ cup chopped red bell pepper
¼ cup chopped red onion

In a large bowl, combine mayonnaise, sour cream, lemon juice, and chili seasoning. Add kidney beans, corn, celery, red pepper, and onion. Mix well to combine. Cover and refrigerate for at least 30 minutes. Gently stir again just before serving.

HINT: Thaw corn by placing in a colander and rinsing under hot water for one
    minute.

Each serving equals:
HE: 1¼ Protein, ¾ Bread, ½ Vegetable, ¼ Slider, 1 Optional Calorie
144 Calories, 0 gm Fat, 6 gm Protein, 30 gm Carbohydrate, 200 mg Sodium,
35 mg Calcium, 7 gm Fiber
DIABETIC: 2 Starch, 1 Meat

Layered Tomato and Mozzarella Salad

■ ■ ■

Tomatoes and mozzarella make a splendid pair no matter how they're served, but I thought layering them together would be festive and fun. Choose the most luscious bright-red tomatoes you can find for this dish—you'll make what's already good even better!   *Serves 4*

4 (medium-sized) fresh ripe
   tomatoes
8 (¾-ounce) slices Kraft reduced-
   fat mozzarella cheese
½ cup Kraft Fat Free Italian
   Dressing

¼ cup (1 ounce) chopped ripe
   olives
¼ cup chopped fresh basil or 2
   teaspoons dried basil leaves

Slice top off of each tomato and discard; then cut each tomato into 3 slices. For each salad, place bottom slice on a salad plate, arrange 1 slice of mozzarella cheese over bottom, place center slice of tomato over cheese, arrange another slice of cheese over tomato slice, place top of tomato over cheese, drizzle 2 tablespoons Italian dressing over top, and garnish with 1 tablespoon olives and 1 tablespoon basil or ½ teaspoon dried basil leaves. Refrigerate for at least 30 minutes.

Each serving equals:
HE: 2 Protein, 1½ Vegetable, ¼ Fat, 16 Optional Calories
167 Calories, 7 gm Fat, 13 gm Protein, 13 gm Carbohydrate, 625 mg Sodium, 384 mg Calcium, 2 gm Fiber
DIABETIC: 2 Meat, 1½ Vegetable, ½ Fat

Zucchini Bean Salad

■ ■ ■

Here's my nominee for a salad that helps you use up all those extra zucchini the end of summer invariably brings! It's especially appealing to anyone trying to boost fiber and lower sodium—high in the first and low in the second. Try to give it the full two hours in the fridge so that all those good flavors can join hands.

Serves 6 (¾ cup)

2¼ cups chopped unpeeled zucchini
½ cup chopped green bell pepper
¼ cup chopped onion
10 ounces (one 16-ounce can)
   red kidney beans, rinsed and
   drained
¼ cup (¾ ounce) grated Kraft
   fat-free Parmesan cheese

1 tablespoon chopped fresh parsley or 1 teaspoon dried parsley
   flakes
⅛ teaspoon black pepper
⅓ cup Kraft Fat Free Italian
   Dressing

In a large bowl, combine zucchini, green pepper, and onion. Add kidney beans, Parmesan cheese, parsley, and black pepper. Mix well to combine. Stir in Italian dressing. Cover and refrigerate for at least 2 hours. Gently stir again just before serving.

Each serving equals:

HE: 1 Protein, 1 Vegetable, 7 Optional Calories

64 Calories, 0 gm Fat, 3 gm Protein, 13 gm Carbohydrate, 193 mg Sodium, 22 mg Calcium, 4 gm Fiber

DIABETIC: 1 Meat, 1 Vegetable, ½ Starch

Stuffed Tomato–Potato Salad

■ ■ ■

Won't your guests be intrigued next time you serve a light lunch, and they discover that their tomatoes aren't filled with a scoop of tuna or chicken salad, but potatoes instead! This recipe is a great example of not letting yourself get into a rut when it comes to healthy eating. When you try something new or even outrageous, you'll feel energized by the change!

Serves 4

4 (medium-sized) fresh ripe
   tomatoes
1½ cups (8 ounces) diced cooked
   potatoes
½ cup frozen peas, thawed
½ cup fat-free cottage cheese

1 teaspoon dried parsley flakes
⅛ teaspoon black pepper
3 tablespoons (¾ ounce) shredded Kraft reduced-fat Cheddar cheese

Cut tops off tomatoes. Cut tomatoes into quarters, being careful not to cut all the way through the bottom. Spread wedges slightly apart. In a medium bowl, combine potatoes, peas, cottage cheese, parsley flakes, and black pepper. Evenly spoon about ½ cup potato mixture into center of each tomato. Sprinkle 2 full teaspoons Cheddar cheese over top of each. Cover and refrigerate for at least 30 minutes.

HINT: Thaw peas by placing in a colander and rinsing under hot water for one minute.

Each serving equals:

HE: 1 Vegetable, ¾ Bread, ½ Protein

109 Calories, 1 gm Fat, 8 gm Protein, 17 gm Carbohydrate, 165 mg Sodium, 63 mg Calcium, 3 gm Fiber

DIABETIC: 1 Vegetable, 1 Starch, ½ Meat

Springtime Potato Salad

■ ■ ■

This pretty potato salad looks extra-festive on the table with the green peas and red onion peeking through the creamy dressing. If you've never used dill weed in your recipes, treat yourself to a small container of this "talented" spice—it can do wonderful things!

Serves 4 (¾ cup)

¼ cup *Kraft fat-free mayonnaise*
2 tablespoons *Land O Lakes*
   no-fat sour cream
2 tablespoons *skim milk*
½ teaspoon *dried dill weed*
⅛ teaspoon *black pepper*

¾ cup *frozen peas, partially*
   thawed
2 cups (10 ounces) *diced*
   unpeeled cooked new potatoes
½ cup *finely chopped red onion*

In a large bowl, combine mayonnaise, sour cream, skim milk, dill weed, and black pepper. Add peas, potatoes, and onion. Mix gently to combine. Cover and refrigerate for at least 30 minutes. Gently stir again just before serving.

Each serving equals:

HE: 1 Bread, ¼ Vegetable, ¼ Slider, 1 Optional Calorie

88 Calories, 0 gm Fat, 3 gm Protein, 19 gm Carbohydrate, 149 mg Sodium, 34 mg Calcium, 2 gm Fiber

DIABETIC: 1 Starch

Honey Dijon Sweet Potato Salad

■ ■ ■

Everyone at Healthy Exchanges who taste-tested this dish really seemed to enjoy the "surprise" of finding sweet potatoes in potato salad! This is a wonderful recipe to try during holiday season—maybe you'll start a new family tradition for Thanksgiving.

Serves 6 (⅔ cup)

3½ cups (18 ounces) diced
   cooked sweet potatoes
½ cup raisins
¼ cup (1 ounce) chopped pecans
⅔ cup Kraft Fat Free Honey
   Dijon Dressing

2 tablespoons Kraft fat-free mayonnaise
1 teaspoon dried parsley flakes

In a large bowl, combine sweet potatoes, raisins, and pecans. Add Honey Dijon dressing, mayonnaise, and parsley flakes. Mix well to combine. Cover and refrigerate for at least 1 hour. Gently stir again just before serving.

HINT: To plump up raisins without "cooking," place in a glass measuring cup and microwave on HIGH for 20 seconds.

Each serving equals:
HE: 1 Bread, ⅔ Fruit, ⅔ Fat, ½ Slider, 8 Optional Calories

191 Calories, 3 gm Fat, 2 gm Protein, 39 gm Carbohydrate, 387 mg Sodium, 27 mg Calcium, 4 gm Fiber   3

DIABETIC: 1½ Starch, 1 Fruit, ½ Fat

Layered Summer Salad Pie

■ ■ ■

It's a revolutionary concept, I suspect, to serve a salad in a freshly baked piecrust, but doesn't it sound like fun? Instead of a baked filling (as in a quiche), this one is truly a colorful toss of veggies made almost magical by adding little bits of goodies like bacon, eggs, and cheese. Yum! *Serves 8*

1 Pillsbury refrigerated unbaked
  9-inch piecrust
1¼ cups shredded lettuce
½ cup chopped celery
1 cup (one 8-ounce can) sliced
  water chestnuts, drained
¼ cup sliced green onion
1 cup Kraft fat-free mayonnaise
2 teaspoons prepared mustard

1 teaspoon dried parsley flakes
1 cup frozen peas, thawed
¾ cup (3 ounces) shredded Kraft
  reduced-fat Cheddar cheese
2 hard-boiled eggs, chopped
1 cup chopped fresh tomato
2 tablespoons Hormel Bacon
  Bits

Preheat oven to 450 degrees. Place piecrust in a 9-inch pie plate. Flute edges and prick bottom and sides with tines of a fork. Bake for 9 to 11 minutes or until lightly browned. Place pie plate on a wire rack and allow to cool completely. Layer lettuce in cooled piecrust. Sprinkle celery, water chestnuts, and green onion evenly over lettuce. In a medium bowl, combine mayonnaise, mustard, and parsley flakes. Spread half of dressing mixture evenly over top. Sprinkle peas and Cheddar cheese over dressing mixture. Spread remaining dressing mixture over Cheddar cheese. Evenly sprinkle eggs, tomato, and bacon bits over the top. Cover and refrigerate for at least 1 hour. Cut into 8 servings.

HINTS: 1. Thaw peas by placing in a colander and rinsing under hot water for
      one minute.
    2. If you want the look and feel of egg without the cholesterol, toss out
      the yolk and dice the whites.

Each serving equals:
HE: 1 Bread, ¾ Protein (¼ limited), ¾ Vegetable, ¾ Slider, 16 Optional Calories
209 Calories, 9 gm Fat, 7 gm Protein, 25 gm Carbohydrate, 556 mg Sodium,
90 mg Calcium, 2 gm Fiber
DIABETIC: 1 Starch, 1 Meat, 1 Vegetable, 1 Fat

Tuna Macaroni Salad

■　■　■

If your family LOVES macaroni and cheese, I'm sure they'll cheer this tasty salad. The recipe easily adds extra pizzazz to that beloved classic by stirring in tuna and egg, then makes it sparkle with one of my favorite additions: pickle relish! This is a great picnic dish too!

Serves 4 (1¼ cups)

1⅓ cups (3 ounces) uncooked
   elbow macaroni
1 cup water
¾ cup (3 ounces) shredded Kraft
   reduced-fat Cheddar cheese
¼ cup skim milk
1 teaspoon dried parsley flakes

⅛ teaspoon black pepper
1 (6-ounce) can white tuna,
   packed in water, drained and
   flaked
¼ cup Kraft fat-free mayonnaise
2 tablespoons sweet pickle relish
1 hard-boiled egg, chopped

In a medium saucepan, cook macaroni in water until tender. Drain and return warm macaroni to saucepan. Add Cheddar cheese, skim milk, parsley flakes, and black pepper. Mix well to combine. Continue cooking over medium heat until cheese melts, stirring often. Remove from heat. Pour mixture into a medium bowl. Stir in tuna, mayonnaise, and pickle relish. Fold in egg. Cover and refrigerate for at least 30 minutes. Gently stir again just before serving.

HINT: If you want the look and feel of egg without the cholesterol, toss out the yolk and dice the white.

Each serving equals:
HE: 2 Protein (¼ limited), 1 Bread, ¼ Slider, 3 Optional Calories

294 Calories, 6 gm Fat, 24 gm Protein, 36 gm Carbohydrate, 533 mg Sodium, 180 mg Calcium, 1 gm Fiber

DIABETIC: 2½ Meat, 2 Starch

West Coast Seafood Salad

■　■　■

Here's one of those recipes that make even the most inexperienced cook feel like a whiz! The secret, of course, is in the list of ingredients, but the process couldn't be simpler. This is the kind of cold salad Cliff and I often saw on menus out West as we traveled to promote my Healthy Exchanges cookbooks.

Serves 4

½ cup Kraft fat-free mayonnaise
2 tablespoons Land O Lakes no-
　fat sour cream
¼ cup chili sauce
½ teaspoon seafood seasoning
1 (4.5-ounce drained weight) can
　imitation crabmeat, chopped

1 hard-boiled egg, chopped
2 tablespoons chopped onion
¼ cup (1 ounce) chopped green
　olives
¼ cup (one 2-ounce jar) chopped
　pimiento, drained
2 cups finely shredded lettuce

In a medium bowl, combine mayonnaise, sour cream, chili sauce, and seafood seasoning. Stir in crabmeat, egg, onion, green olives, and pimiento. Cover and refrigerate for at least 30 minutes. For each serving, place ½ cup lettuce on a plate and spoon about ½ cup salad mixture on top.

HINT: Imitation crabmeat is lower in cholesterol and less expensive than "the real thing."

Each serving equals:
HE: 1¼ Protein (¼ limited), 1 Vegetable, ¼ Fat, ½ Slider, 3 Optional Calories
115 Calories, 3 gm Fat, 10 gm Protein, 12 gm Carbohydrate, 577 mg Sodium, 68 mg Calcium, 1 gm Fiber
DIABETIC: 2 Meat, ½ Starch/Carbohydrate

Italian Pasta Salmon Salad

■ ■ ■

Cold salads are perfect for the steamy hot summers we get here in Iowa, when the last thing any cook wants to do is turn on the oven—or even the microwave! This is a perfect last-minute meal that requires very little effort and not much time in the kitchen either. Maybe you've got time for a refreshing shower before dinner. . . .   *Serves 4 (1½ cups)*

2 cups cold cooked shell maca-
  roni, rinsed and drained
½ cup chopped green bell pepper
¼ cup sliced green onion
¼ cup sliced radishes
½ cup shredded carrots
1 cup cherry tomatoes, halved

1 (6½-ounce) can pink salmon,
  drained, boned, and flaked
¼ cup (¾ ounce) grated Kraft
  fat-free Parmesan cheese
½ cup Kraft Fat Free Italian
  Dressing

In a large bowl, combine macaroni, green pepper, onion, radishes, carrots, and tomatoes. Add salmon and Parmesan cheese. Mix well to combine. Stir in Italian dressing. Cover and refrigerate for at least 30 minutes. Gently stir again just before serving.

HINT: 1⅓ cups uncooked shell macaroni usually cooks to about 2 cups.

Each serving equals:
HE: 1¾ Protein, 1¼ Vegetable, 1 Bread, 16 Optional Calories
190 Calories, 2 gm Fat, 12 gm Protein, 31 gm Carbohydrate, 629 mg Sodium, 81 mg Calcium, 3 gm Fiber
DIABETIC: 2 Meat, 1½ Starch, 1 Vegetable

Mexican Chicken Salad

■ ■ ■

Here's another tasty and satisfying cold supper that delivers plenty of fireworks in the flavor department! Be adventurous—experiment with different kinds of lettuce if your market offers a variety. This looks beautiful when presented on dark green romaine or the dark red of radicchio.   *Serves 4*

1½ cups (8 ounces) diced cooked chicken breast
½ cup chopped celery
1 cup frozen whole-kernel corn, thawed
¼ cup (1 ounce) sliced ripe olives

½ cup chunky salsa (mild, medium, or hot)
¼ cup Land O Lakes no-fat sour cream
1 teaspoon dried parsley flakes
1 cup finely shredded lettuce

In a medium bowl, combine chicken, celery, corn, and olives. In a small bowl, combine salsa, sour cream, and parsley flakes. Add salsa mixture to chicken mixture. Mix gently to combine. Cover and refrigerate for at least 1 hour. For each serving, arrange ¼ cup lettuce on a plate and spoon about ¾ cup chicken mixture over top.

HINTS: 1. If you don't have leftovers, purchase a chunk of cooked chicken breast from your local deli.
2. Thaw corn by placing in a colander and rinsing under hot water for one minute.

Each serving equals:
HE: 2 Protein, 1 Vegetable, ½ Bread, ¼ Fat, 15 Optional Calories
167 Calories, 3 gm Fat, 19 gm Protein, 16 gm Carbohydrate, 261 mg Sodium, 80 mg Calcium, 2 gm Fiber
DIABETIC: 2 Meat, ½ Vegetable, ½ Starch, ½ Fat

Ham-Broccoli-Pasta Salad

■ ■ ■

It's always seemed to me that the challenge of a pasta salad is keeping all the flavors and textures from running together. This one features lots of crunch, along with the tangy pleasures of ham and cheese with mustard, and provides extra fun if you choose the rotini pasta that comes in different colors.

Serves 4 (1¼ cups)

1½ cups cold cooked rotini
    pasta, rinsed and drained
1 full cup (6 ounces) diced
    Dubuque 97% fat-free ham or
    any extra-lean ham
¾ cup (3 ounces) shredded Kraft
    reduced-fat Cheddar cheese

2 cups chopped fresh broccoli
½ cup Kraft fat-free mayonnaise
2 tablespoons skim milk
Sugar substitute to equal 1
    teaspoon sugar
1 teaspoon dried onion flakes
1 teaspoon prepared mustard

In a large bowl, combine rotini pasta, ham, Cheddar cheese, and broccoli. In a small bowl, combine mayonnaise, skim milk, sugar substitute, onion flakes, and mustard. Add dressing mixture to pasta mixture. Mix well to combine. Cover and refrigerate for at least 1 hour. Gently stir again just before serving.

HINT: 1 cup uncooked rotini pasta usually cooks to about 1½ cups.

Each serving equals:
HE: 2 Protein, 1 Vegetable, ¾ Bread, ¼ Slider, 3 Optional Calories
205 Calories, 5 gm Fat, 16 gm Protein, 24 gm Carbohydrate, 831 mg Sodium, 176 mg Calcium, 2 gm Fiber
DIABETIC: 2 Meat, 1 Vegetable, 1 Starch

VEGETABLES TO NOURISH AND SOOTHE

∎ ∎ ∎

Each group of immigrants that settled the nation brought its unique style of cooking along for the ride, and that's nowhere more true than in the delightful variety of vegetable dishes that play an important part at nearly every heartland meal!

The dish that I remember best from growing up was my mother's carrots and cabbage boiled together with a bit of onion. A classic Irish dish that was as economical as it was filling, it was a favorite that Mom used to fix for my father. Not only that, it was exceedingly high in fiber and beta-carotene, though I don't think any of us gave its health benefits much thought at the time. What mattered then, as it still does now, is that this vegetable combination tasted good and warmed us through and through on a cold evening. What more can we ask from a recipe than that it nourish our bodies and satisfy our souls?

Even if you weren't brought up on cabbage, as I was, I hope you'll give one of my cabbage recipes a try—and I bet you'll be pleasantly surprised at how good this good-for-you veggie actually is! (Try *Creamy Cabbage with Peas*—it's fast and flavorful.) As usual, I'm offering a varied menu of green bean dishes, since that's Cliff's first-choice vegetable. (His pick of this group: he's torn between *Nutty Green Beans* and *Tex-Mex Green Beans*, so try them both!) Whether your passion is peas or potatoes, broccoli or zucchini, you'll find some fresh and inventive variations on traditional side dishes that will surely please your friends and family.

"I sought the Lord and He heard me,
And delivered me from all my fears."
—PSALM 34:4

Nutty Green Beans	Glazed Carrots and Zucchini
Tex-Mex Green Beans	Baked Carrot Croquettes with Creamed Pea Sauce
Zucchini Mexicali	Creole Cabbage
Sautéed Mushrooms and Peppers	Creamy Cabbage with Peas
Italian Asparagus-Tomato Stir Fry	Peas Lorraine
Country Tomatoes	Baked Hash Browns au Gratin
Harvard Beets	German Scalloped Potatoes
Baked Onions au Gratin	Celery Alfredo Pasta
Broccoli Party Casserole	Broccoli-Noodle Side Dish
Cauliflower with Tomato-Cheese Sauce	The Best Baked Beans
Super Spinach Squares	Vegetable Stuffing Side Dish

Nutty Green Beans

■ ■ ■

It doesn't take much to make an everyday dish a truly soul-satisfying one. In this speedy treat, some fat-free dressing and a few chopped nuts provide the "Abracadabra"—you just bring the hearty appetite!   *Serves 4 (1 cup)*

4 cups frozen cut green beans
1 cup water
¼ cup Kraft Fat Free French
  Dressing

¼ cup (1 ounce) chopped dry-
  roasted peanuts

In a medium saucepan, cook green beans in water for 5 minutes or until tender. Drain and return beans to saucepan. Stir in French dressing and peanuts. Continue to cook for 5 minutes or until mixture is heated through, stirring often.

Each serving equals:
HE: 2 Vegetable, ½ Fat, ¼ Protein, ¼ Slider, 5 Optional Calories

91 Calories, 3 gm Fat, 3 gm Protein, 13 gm Carbohydrate, 153 mg Sodium, 39 mg Calcium, 3 gm Fiber

DIABETIC: 2 Vegetable, 1 Fat

Tex-Mex Green Beans

■ ■ ■

Who really has time to stand over a hot stove for hours these days? I certainly don't, and I'm sure you can't either. Now you don't have to, when you can deliver a dish with that slow-cooked, spicy-tangy flavor in just a few minutes of preparation.

Serves 6 (½ cup)

½ cup chopped onion
1 (10¾-ounce) can Healthy
   Request Tomato Soup
2 tablespoons Brown Sugar Twin
2 teaspoons chili seasoning

4 cups (two 16-ounce cans) cut
   green beans, rinsed and
   drained
¼ cup Hormel Bacon Bits

In a large skillet sprayed with butter-flavored cooking spray, sauté onion for 5 minutes or until tender. Stir in tomato soup, Brown Sugar Twin, and chili seasoning. Add green beans and bacon bits. Mix well to combine. Lower heat and simmer for 10 minutes, stirring occasionally.

Each serving equals:
HE: 1½ Vegetable, ½ Slider, 8 Optional Calories
73 Calories, 1 gm Fat, 4 gm Protein, 12 gm Carbohydrate, 322 mg Sodium, 31 mg Calcium, 2 gm Fiber
DIABETIC: 1½ Vegetable, ½ Starch/Carbohydrate

Zucchini Mexicali

■ ❋ ■

Can't you just hear the music of the mariachi band playing as you set a bowl of this colorful summer veggie blend on your picnic table? There's no more spirited way to celebrate the pleasures of a summer harvest than with this fiesta of flavors.

Serves 4 (1 cup)

1 cup shredded carrots
¾ cup chopped onion
2½ cups thinly sliced unpeeled
    zucchini
¼ cup chopped green bell pepper
½ cup chunky salsa (mild,
    medium, or hot)

1 tablespoon Brown Sugar Twin
1 teaspoon taco seasoning
1½ cups peeled and coarsely
    chopped fresh tomatoes
⅓ cup (1½ ounces) shredded
    Kraft reduced-fat Cheddar
    cheese

In a large skillet sprayed with olive oil–flavored cooking spray, sauté carrots, onion, zucchini, and green pepper for 5 minutes or until vegetables are tender. Stir in salsa, Brown Sugar Twin, and taco seasoning. Add tomatoes. Mix well to combine. Lower heat and simmer for 6 to 8 minutes or until mixture is heated through, stirring occasionally. Evenly sprinkle Cheddar cheese over top. Remove from heat. Cover and let set for 2 to 3 minutes or until cheese melts.

Each serving equals:
HE: 3¼ Vegetable, ½ Protein, 1 Optional Calorie
102 Calories, 2 gm Fat, 5 gm Protein, 16 gm Carbohydrate, 714 mg Sodium, 140 mg Calcium, 4 gm Fiber
DIABETIC: 3 Vegetable, ½ Meat

Sautéed Mushrooms and Peppers

■ ■ ■

This dish is so easy and good for you, I hope it'll soon appear regularly on your table. If you're feeling adventurous, you may want to try this with some red and yellow peppers for added color (and vitamin A).   *Serves 4 (½ cup)*

2 teaspoons reduced-calorie margarine
½ cup chopped onion
1 cup chopped green bell pepper

2 cups chopped fresh mushrooms
2 tablespoons Kraft Fat Free Italian Dressing
¼ teaspoon lemon pepper

In a large skillet, melt margarine. Add onion and sauté for 5 minutes. Stir in green pepper, mushrooms, Italian dressing, and lemon pepper. Continue to sauté for 3 to 5 minutes or until vegetables are just tender.

Each serving equals:
HE: 1¾ Vegetable, ¼ Fat, 4 Optional Calories
33 Calories, 1 gm Fat, 1 gm Protein, 5 gm Carbohydrate, 89 mg Sodium, 8 mg Calcium, 1 gm Fiber
DIABETIC: 1½ Vegetable

Italian Asparagus-Tomato Stir Fry

■ ■ ■

This recipe lets you in on a wonderful culinary secret—you can actually stir-fry veggies using fat-free dressing! The trick, of course, is to keep those veggies moving. Asparagus season isn't that long, so put this on the menu as soon as you spot those lovely green stalks in your market. *Serves 4*

2 tablespoons Kraft Fat Free Italian Dressing
2 cups chopped fresh asparagus
½ cup sliced green onion
1½ cups sliced fresh mushrooms

1½ cups coarsely chopped fresh tomatoes
¼ cup (¾ ounce) grated Kraft fat-free Parmesan cheese

In a large skillet, heat Italian dressing. Add asparagus, onion, and mushrooms. Mix well to combine. Sauté for 4 to 5 minutes. Stir in tomatoes. Continue to sauté for 2 to 3 minutes or until tomatoes are heated through. For each serving, spoon about ¾ cup vegetable mixture on a plate and sprinkle 1 tablespoon Parmesan cheese on top.

Each serving equals:
HE: 2¾ Vegetable, ¼ Protein, 4 Optional Calories

72 Calories, 0 gm Fat, 4 gm Protein, 14 gm Carbohydrate, 414 mg Sodium, 28 mg Calcium, 5 gm Fiber

DIABETIC: 2½ Vegetable

Country Tomatoes

■ ■ ■

Tomatoes used to be known as "love apples"—and yes, they're actually considered a fruit. Here's a great way to show your love and get lots of healthy vitamins in every bite! This will take you back to those good old days, when every cook stewed and canned the tomatoes from her garden. *Serves 4 (½ cup)*

1 cup chopped celery
½ cup chopped onion
2 cups (one 16-ounce can) tomatoes, coarsely chopped and undrained

1 tablespoon pourable Sugar Twin
⅛ teaspoon black pepper
2 tablespoons Hormel Bacon Bits

In a large skillet sprayed with butter-flavored cooking spray, sauté celery and onion for 10 minutes or until tender. Add undrained tomatoes, Sugar Twin, and black pepper. Mix well to combine. Stir in bacon bits. Lower heat and simmer for 5 minutes, stirring occasionally.

Each serving equals:
HE: 1¾ Vegetable, 14 Optional Calories
45 Calories, 1 gm Fat, 2 gm Protein, 7 gm Carbohydrate, 160 mg Sodium, 21 mg Calcium, 2 gm Fiber
DIABETIC: 2 Vegetable

Harvard Beets

■ ■ ■

One of the country's oldest and most prestigious universities, Harvard is also well known for its school color: crimson. I decided to dedicate this classic beet dish to the folks in Cambridge, Massachusetts, who root fiercely for their men and women in red!

Serves 4 (½ cup)

2 cups (one 16-ounce can) diced beets, drained, and ⅓ cup liquid reserved
¼ cup vinegar
1 tablespoon cornstarch

1 tablespoon pourable Sugar Twin
1 tablespoon + 1 teaspoon reduced-calorie margarine

In a covered jar, combine reserved beet liquid, vinegar, Sugar Twin, and cornstarch. Shake well to blend. Pour mixture into a medium saucepan. Add margarine. Mix well to combine. Cook over medium heat until mixture thickens, stirring often. Stir in beets. Lower heat and simmer for 5 minutes or until beets are heated through, stirring occasionally.

Each serving equals:
HE: 1 Vegetable, ½ Fat, 11 Optional Calories

89 Calories, 5 gm Fat, 1 gm Protein, 10 gm Carbohydrate, 306 mg Sodium, 13 mg Calcium, 2 gm Fiber

DIABETIC: 1 Vegetable, ½ Fat

Baked Onions au Gratin

■ ■ ■

You can make this dish with any onions you happen to have on hand, though I bet it would be especially good if prepared with sweet onions (like Vidalia). If you've never contemplated eating onions on their own, I hope this recipe will win you over.

Serves 6

6 cups sliced onion
1 (10¾-ounce) can Healthy
   Request Tomato Soup
3 tablespoons Hormel Bacon
   Bits

¾ cup (3 ounces) shredded Kraft
   reduced-fat Cheddar cheese
1 teaspoon dried parsley flakes

Preheat oven to 350 degrees. Spray an 8-by-8-inch baking dish with butter-flavored cooking spray. Evenly arrange onion in prepared baking dish. In a large bowl, combine tomato soup, bacon bits, Cheddar cheese, and parsley flakes. Spoon soup mixture evenly over onion. Cover and bake for 45 minutes. Uncover and continue baking for 15 minutes or until onions are tender. Place baking dish on a wire rack and let set for 5 minutes. Divide into 6 servings.

Each serving equals:
HE: 2 Vegetable, ⅔ Protein, ½ Slider, 3 Optional Calories
144 Calories, 4 gm Fat, 7 gm Protein, 20 gm Carbohydrate, 402 mg Sodium, 132 mg Calcium, 3 gm Fiber
DIABETIC: 2 Vegetable, ½ Meat, ½ Starch/Carbohydrate

Broccoli Party Casserole

■ ❄ ■

This festive dish is almost a vegetable quiche, but even better, I think, because it's got lots and lots of broccoli in it! You might want to serve this as part of a holiday buffet, or just some evening when you want to treat your family like company.

Serves 6

1 (16-ounce) package frozen cut broccoli, cooked and drained

14 small fat-free saltine crackers, made into fine crumbs

Scant 1 cup (3¾ ounces) shredded Kraft reduced-fat Cheddar cheese

1 (10¾-ounce) can Healthy Request Cream of Mushroom Soup

1 egg or equivalent in egg substitute

½ cup Kraft fat-free mayonnaise

Preheat oven to 400 degrees. Spray an 8-by-8-inch baking dish with butter-flavored cooking spray. In a large bowl, combine broccoli, cracker crumbs, and Cheddar cheese. In a small bowl, combine mushroom soup, egg, and mayonnaise. Add soup mixture to broccoli mixture. Mix well to combine. Spread mixture into prepared baking dish. Bake for 30 to 35 minutes. Place baking dish on a wire rack and let set for 5 minutes. Divide into 6 servings.

HINT: A self-seal sandwich bag works great for crushing saltine crackers.

Each serving equals:
HE: 1 Protein, 1 Vegetable, ⅓ Bread, ½ Slider, 8 Optional Calories

149 Calories, 5 gm Fat, 9 gm Protein, 17 gm Carbohydrate, 637 mg Sodium, 190 mg Calcium, 2 gm Fiber   3

DIABETIC: 1 Meat, 1 Vegetable, 1 Starch/Carbohydrate

Cauliflower with Tomato-Cheese Sauce

■ ■ ■

You can really boost your daily veggie intake by serving this scrumptious side dish, which would be a terrific pasta accompaniment. It takes so little cheese to deliver a luscious amount of flavor.

Serves 4 (¾ cup)

1 cup (one 8-ounce can) Hunt's Tomato Sauce
¾ cup water
⅓ cup Carnation Nonfat Dry Milk Powder
1 teaspoon pourable Sugar Twin
1 teaspoon Worcestershire sauce

½ teaspoon dried minced garlic
1 teaspoon dried parsley flakes
3 cups frozen chopped cauliflower, cooked and drained
½ cup + 1 tablespoon (2¼ ounces) shredded Kraft reduced-fat Cheddar cheese

In a large saucepan sprayed with butter-flavored cooking spray, combine tomato sauce, water, dry milk powder, Sugar Twin, Worcestershire sauce, garlic, and parsley flakes. Cook over medium heat for 5 minutes or until mixture is heated through, stirring often. Add cauliflower. Mix well to combine. Stir in Cheddar cheese. Continue cooking until cheese melts, stirring often.

Each serving equals:
HE: 2½ Vegetable, ¾ Protein, ¼ Skim Milk
94 Calories, 2 gm Fat, 9 gm Protein, 10 gm Carbohydrate, 650 mg Sodium, 209 mg Calcium, 3 gm Fiber
DIABETIC: 2½ Vegetable, ½ Meat

Super Spinach Squares

∎ ∎ ∎

These inventive hors d'oeuvres are sure to lend sparkle to your next festive occasion and will definitely put those good old reliable frozen tidbits to shame! When I served these up for testing, I couldn't get the baking dish out of the oven fast enough—and everyone wanted us to mix up several more batches ASAP.

Serves 12 (2 each)

1 (8-ounce) can Pillsbury
   Reduced Fat Crescent Rolls
1 (10¾-ounce) can Healthy
   Request Cream of Mushroom
   Soup
¼ cup (1 ounce) chopped pecans
1 tablespoon dried onion flakes
3 eggs, beaten, or equivalent in
   egg substitute

¼ cup (¾ ounce) grated Kraft
   fat-free Parmesan cheese
2 (10-ounce) packages frozen
   chopped spinach, thawed, and
   thoroughly drained
5 (¾-ounce) slices Kraft reduced-
   fat Swiss cheese, shredded

Preheat oven to 350 degrees. Spray a 10-by-15-inch rimmed baking sheet with butter-flavored cooking spray. Unroll crescent rolls and pat into prepared baking sheet, being sure to seal perforations. In a large bowl, combine mushroom soup, pecans, onion flakes, eggs, and Parmesan cheese. Add spinach and Swiss cheese. Mix well to combine. Spread spinach mixture evenly over rolls. Bake for 40 to 45 minutes or until filling is firm and a toothpick inserted in center comes out clean. Place baking sheet on a wire rack and let set for at least 10 minutes. Cut into 24 squares.

HINT: Do NOT use inexpensive rolls as they don't cover the pan properly.

Each serving equals:
HE: ¾ Protein (¼ limited), ⅔ Bread, ⅓ Fat, ⅓ Vegetable, 14 Optional Calories
161 Calories, 9 gm Fat, 6 gm Protein, 14 gm Carbohydrate, 470 mg Sodium,
77 mg Calcium, 2 gm Fiber
DIABETIC: 1 Meat, 1 Starch, ½ Fat, ½ Vegetable

Glazed Carrots and Zucchini

■ ■ ■

Sweet and tangy says it all: the carrots made more irresistibly sweet with a bit of brown sugar flavor, the zucchini turned even more tangy than it tastes served fresh from the garden (or the farm stand!). If you haven't discovered the magic of lemon pepper on your vegetables yet, choose today to celebrate this culinary marvel!

Serves 4 (½ cup)

2 cups shredded carrots

2 cups shredded unpeeled zucchini

2 tablespoons Brown Sugar Twin

¼ teaspoon lemon pepper

1 teaspoon dried parsley flakes

⅓ cup water

In a large skillet sprayed with butter-flavored cooking spray, sauté carrots and zucchini for 5 to 8 minutes or until just tender. Add Brown Sugar Twin, lemon pepper, parsley flakes, and water. Mix gently to combine. Lower heat, cover, and simmer for 5 minutes or until most of liquid is absorbed, stirring occasionally.

Each serving equals:

HE: 2 Vegetable, 2 Optional Calories

32 Calories, 0 gm Fat, 1 gm Protein, 7 gm Carbohydrate, 21 mg Sodium, 26 mg Calcium, 2 gm Fiber

DIABETIC: 2 Vegetable

Baked Carrot Croquettes
with Creamed Pea Sauce

■ ■ ■

If you'd like to do something elegant and different the next time you have company for dinner, I think this festive recipe will provide the dazzle you're looking for! It takes a little bit more work than some of my recipes, but it's easy work, and even the kids can help form the croquettes.   *Serves 4*

*2 cups (one 16-ounce can) cut
    carrots, rinsed and drained
1 egg, beaten, or equivalent in
    egg substitute
½ teaspoon ground nutmeg
6 tablespoons (1½ ounces) dried
    fine bread crumbs*

*1½ cups (one 12-fluid-ounce can)
    Carnation Evaporated Skim
    Milk
3 tablespoons all-purpose flour
½ cup frozen peas, thawed
¼ teaspoon lemon pepper
1 teaspoon dried parsley flakes*

Preheat oven to 350 degrees. Spray a baking sheet with butter-flavored cooking spray. In a medium bowl, mash carrots using a potato masher or fork. Add egg, nutmeg, and bread crumbs. Mix well to combine. Form into 24 (1-inch) balls. Place carrot balls on prepared baking sheet. Bake for 25 to 30 minutes. Meanwhile, in a covered jar, combine evaporated skim milk and flour. Shake well to blend. Pour milk mixture into a medium saucepan sprayed with butter-flavored cooking spray. Cook over medium heat until mixture starts to thicken, stirring often. Add peas, lemon pepper, and parsley flakes. Mix well to combine. Lower heat and simmer, stirring often, until croquettes are browned. For each serving, place 6 croquettes on a plate and spoon a full ⅓ cup pea sauce over top.

HINT: Thaw peas by placing in a colander and rinsing under hot water for one
        minute.

Each serving equals:
HE: 1 Bread, 1 Vegetable, ¾ Skim Milk, ¼ Protein (limited)

194 Calories, 2 gm Fat, 12 gm Protein, 32 gm Carbohydrate, 237 mg Sodium,
335 mg Calcium, 4 gm Fiber   3

DIABETIC: 1 Starch, 1 Vegetable, 1 Skim Milk

Creole Cabbage

The varied cultures who created the cuisine known as Creole cooking drew from many different food traditions, but dishes in this style are always rich in flavor and tangy-sweet. This baked cabbage casserole will make you take a fresh look at this familiar vegetable.   *Serves 6*

1¾ cups (one 15-ounce can)
   Hunt's Tomato Sauce
¾ cup chopped onion
¾ cup chopped green bell pepper
1 tablespoon Brown Sugar Twin

⅛ teaspoon black pepper
6 cups coarsely chopped cabbage
1 cup water
¾ cup (3 ounces) shredded Kraft
   reduced-fat Cheddar cheese

Preheat oven to 350 degrees. Spray an 8-by-8-inch baking dish with butter-flavored cooking spray. In a large skillet, combine tomato sauce, onion, green pepper, Brown Sugar Twin, and black pepper. Cook over medium heat for 10 minutes, stirring occasionally. Meanwhile, in another large skillet, combine cabbage and water. Cover and cook over medium heat for 6 to 8 minutes or until cabbage is just tender. Drain well, then spread cabbage into prepared baking dish. Evenly spoon sauce mixture over cabbage. Bake for 20 minutes. Sprinkle Cheddar cheese evenly over top. Continue baking for 10 minutes. Place baking dish on a wire rack and let set for 5 minutes. Divide into 6 servings.

Each serving equals:
HE: 3⅔ Vegetable, ⅔ Protein, 1 Optional Calorie
90 Calories, 2 gm Fat, 6 gm Protein, 12 gm Carbohydrate, 565 mg Sodium, 142 mg Calcium, 3 gm Fiber
DIABETIC: 2½ Vegetable, ½ Meat

Creamy Cabbage with Peas

■ ■ ■

Here's an intriguing way to serve this wonderfully high-fiber vegetable. It's amazingly creamy, yet still so low in calories you can enjoy it often. You could, if you wish, try this dish with Healthy Request Cream of Broccoli or Cream of Celery soup.

Serves 4 (1 full cup)

½ cup chopped onion
1½ cups frozen peas, thawed
3 cups shredded cabbage
1 (10¾-ounce) can Healthy Request Cream of Mushroom Soup

½ cup skim milk
1 tablespoon Land O Lakes no-fat sour cream
1 teaspoon dried parsley flakes

In a large skillet sprayed with butter-flavored cooking spray, sauté onion for 5 minutes. Stir in peas and cabbage. Add mushroom soup, skim milk, sour cream, and parsley flakes. Mix well to combine. Lower heat, cover, and simmer for 10 minutes, stirring occasionally.

HINT: Thaw peas by placing in a colander and rinsing under hot water for one minute.

Each serving equals:
HE: 1¾ Vegetable, ¾ Bread, ¾ Slider, 13 Optional Calories

122 Calories, 2 gm Fat, 5 gm Protein, 21 gm Carbohydrate, 359 mg Sodium, 141 mg Calcium, 4 gm Fiber

DIABETIC: 2½ Vegetable, ½ Meat

Peas Lorraine

■ ■ ■

Here's a rich and intriguing side dish that turns any meal into a special occasion! It's crunchy, creamy, tangy, and oh-so-tummy-pleasing—truly luxurious eating that tastes sinful but isn't.

Serves 4 (½ cup)

⅓ cup Land O Lakes no-fat sour cream

2 tablespoons Hormel Bacon Bits

½ cup (one 2.5-ounce jar) sliced mushrooms, drained

2 teaspoons dried onion flakes

1 (8-ounce) can water chestnuts, drained and chopped

2 cups (one 16-ounce can) small peas, rinsed and drained

In a large skillet sprayed with butter-flavored cooking spray, combine sour cream, bacon bits, onion flakes, and mushrooms. Add water chestnuts and peas. Mix gently to combine. Cook over medium-low heat for 5 minutes or until mixture is heated through, stirring occasionally.

Each serving equals:

HE: 1½ Bread, ¼ Vegetable, ¼ Slider, 12 Optional Calories

129 Calories, 1 gm Fat, 7 gm Protein, 23 gm Carbohydrate, 241 mg Sodium, 44 mg Calcium, 6 gm Fiber

DIABETIC: 1 Starch, 1 Vegetable

Baked Hash Browns au Gratin

■ ❋ ■

When I pulled this dish from the oven, melted cheese bubbling, everyone in the kitchen grabbed a fork and pleaded for a taste! And when a dish looks and smells that scrumptious, you know it's going to taste sooo good—and it does. Of course, you may have trouble convincing people it's low in fat and good for them. . . .

Serves 4

4½ cups (15 ounces) shredded
　loose-packed frozen potatoes
⅔ cup Carnation Nonfat Dry
　Milk Powder
1 cup water

¼ teaspoon lemon pepper
1 teaspoon dried parsley flakes
⅓ cup (1½ ounces) shredded
　Kraft reduced-fat Cheddar
　cheese

Preheat oven to 375 degrees. Spray an 8-by-8-inch baking dish with butter-flavored cooking spray. Arrange potatoes in prepared baking dish. In a small bowl, combine dry milk powder, water, lemon pepper, and parsley flakes. Evenly pour milk mixture over potatoes. Bake for 45 minutes. Evenly sprinkle Cheddar cheese over top. Continue baking for 5 to 7 minutes or until cheese melts. Place baking dish on a wire rack and let set for 5 minutes. Divide into 4 servings.

Each serving equals:
HE: ¾ Bread, ½ Skim Milk, ½ Protein
166 Calories, 2 gm Fat, 10 gm Protein, 27 gm Carbohydrate, 151 mg Sodium, 221 mg Calcium, 3 gm Fiber
DIABETIC: 1 Starch, ½ Skim Milk, ½ Meat

German Scalloped Potatoes

■ ❋ ■

I love finding up to date ways of serving great traditional dishes from the world's cuisines. Here's a dish I transformed with my magical whisk—and made nearly all the fat vanish, while keeping that irresistible flavor! Why not start a new tradition at your house tonight?

Serves 6

5 cups (24 ounces) diced cooked unpeeled potatoes	*1 (10¾-ounce) can Healthy Request Cream of Celery Soup*
¾ cup chopped onion	*¼ cup white vinegar*
¾ cup finely diced celery	*¼ cup pourable Sugar Twin*
¼ cup Hormel Bacon Bits	*1 teaspoon prepared mustard*

Preheat oven to 350 degrees. Spray an 8-by-8-inch baking dish with butter-flavored cooking spray. In a large bowl, combine potatoes, onion, celery, and bacon bits. In a small bowl, combine celery soup, vinegar, Sugar Twin, and mustard. Add soup mixture to potato mixture. Mix well to combine. Spread mixture into prepared baking dish. Cover and bake for 45 minutes. Uncover and continue baking for 10 to 15 minutes. Place baking dish on a wire rack and let set for 5 minutes. Divide into 6 servings.

Each serving equals:

HE: 1 Bread, ½ Vegetable, ½ Slider, 8 Optional Calories

135 Calories, 3 gm Fat, 5 gm Protein, 22 gm Carbohydrate, 581 mg Sodium, 35 mg Calcium, 2 gm Fiber

DIABETIC: 1½ Starch, ½ Vegetable

Celery Alfredo Pasta

This creamy, cheesy dish used to be off-limits to anyone trying to live a healthy lifestyle, but now it's back—and better than ever, with the tasty addition of celery and luscious fat-free Parmesan cheese! What a cozy way to warm the soul on a crisp fall evening . . .

Serves 4 (1 scant cup)

1½ cups finely diced celery
1 (10¾-ounce) can Healthy
 Request Cream of Celery or
 Mushroom Soup
1⅓ cups skim milk

1 teaspoon dried onion flakes
½ cup (1½ ounces) grated Kraft
 fat-free Parmesan cheese
2 cups hot cooked rotini pasta,
 rinsed and drained

In a large skillet sprayed with butter-flavored cooking spray, sauté celery for 6 to 8 minutes or until just tender. Stir in celery soup, skim milk, onion flakes, and Parmesan cheese. Add rotini pasta. Mix well to combine. Lower heat and simmer for 5 minutes, stirring often.

HINT: 1½ cups uncooked rotini pasta usually cooks to about 2 cups.

Each serving equals:
HE: 1 Bread, ¾ Vegetable, ½ Protein, ⅓ Skim Milk, ½ Slider, 1 Optional Calorie

202 Calories, 2 gm Fat, 8 gm Protein, 38 gm Carbohydrate, 528 mg Sodium, 168 mg Calcium, 2 gm Fiber

DIABETIC: 1½ Starch/Carbohydrate, ½ Vegetable, ½ Meat

Broccoli-Noodle Side Dish

■ ❋ ■

Here's another quick and healthy quick-fix accompaniment that's great for non-cooks—none of the ingredients needs advance preparation, and you only use one pan! Broccoli is usually a no-no with Cliff, but it's so full of healthy nutrients, I recommend putting it on the menu as often as you can.

Serves 4 (scant 1 cup)

1½ cups frozen cut broccoli, thawed
1¾ cups (3 ounces) uncooked noodles
1½ cups water
½ cup (one 2.5-ounce jar) sliced mushrooms, undrained

1 (10¾-ounce) can Healthy Request Cream of Mushroom Soup
1 teaspoon dried onion flakes
⅛ teaspoon black pepper

In a large saucepan, combine broccoli, uncooked noodles, and water. Bring mixture to a boil. Lower heat and simmer for 10 minutes or until broccoli and noodles are tender. Drain well. Return mixture to saucepan. Stir in undrained mushrooms, mushroom soup, onion flakes, and black pepper. Continue simmering for 5 minutes or until mixture is heated through, stirring occasionally.

HINT: Thaw broccoli by placing in a colander and rinsing under hot water for one minute.

Each serving equals:
HE: 1 Bread, 1 Vegetable, ½ Slider, 1 Optional Calorie
151 Calories, 3 gm Fat, 5 gm Protein, 26 gm Carbohydrate, 397 mg Sodium, 77 mg Calcium, 3 gm Fiber
DIABETIC: 1½ Starch, 1 Vegetable

The Best Baked Beans

■ ■ ■

I don't use the word "best" lightly, so I hope you'll trust me when I do. I've experimented with so many different combinations of ingredients that go into this classic cookout treat, you might think I couldn't eat another bean! But the journey was more than worth it—and here's the blue-ribbon winner!   *Serves 6*

¾ *cup finely chopped onion*
1 *(10¾-ounce) can Healthy*
   Request Tomato Soup
¼ *cup Hormel Bacon Bits*

⅛ *teaspoon black pepper*
48 *ounces (three 16-ounce cans)*
   great northern beans, rinsed
   and drained

Preheat oven to 350 degrees. Spray an 8-by-8-inch baking dish with butter-flavored cooking spray. In a large skillet sprayed with butter-flavored cooking spray, sauté onion for 5 minutes or until tender. Stir in tomato soup, bacon bits, and black pepper. Add great northern beans. Mix well to combine. Spread mixture into prepared baking dish. Bake for 45 minutes. Place baking dish on a wire rack and let set for 5 minutes. Divide into 6 servings.

Each serving equals:
HE: 2½ Protein, ¼ Vegetable, ½ Slider, 7 Optional Calories

226 Calories, 2 gm Fat, 14 gm Protein, 38 gm Carbohydrate, 323 mg Sodium, 106 mg Calcium, 9 gm Fiber

DIABETIC: 2 Meat, 2 Starch

Vegetable Stuffing Side Dish

■ ❄ ■

Would your family be pleased to find stuffing instead of rice or potatoes on their dinner plates tonight? I bet they'll applaud when you serve this delectable surprise, which delivers more than a full serving of vegetables along with the fragrant stuffing!

Serves 6

2 cups shredded unpeeled zucchini

2 cups shredded carrots

½ cup chopped onion

1 (10¾-ounce) can Healthy Request Cream of Mushroom Soup

¼ cup Land O Lakes no-fat sour cream

1 teaspoon dried parsley flakes

1 teaspoon lemon pepper

3 cups (4½ ounces) unseasoned dry bread cubes

Preheat oven to 350 degrees. Spray an 8-by-12-inch baking dish with butter-flavored cooking spray. In a large skillet sprayed with butter-flavored cooking spray, sauté zucchini, carrots, and onion for 6 to 8 minutes. In a large bowl, combine mushroom soup, sour cream, parsley flakes, and lemon pepper. Add bread cubes. Mix well to combine. Stir in sautéed vegetables. Spread mixture into prepared baking dish. Cover and bake for 30 minutes. Uncover and continue baking for 15 minutes. Place baking dish on a wire rack and let set for 5 minutes. Divide into 6 servings.

HINT: Pepperidge Farm bread cubes work great.

Each serving equals:
HE: 1½ Vegetable, 1 Bread, ¼ Slider, 18 Optional Calories
166 Calories, 2 gm Fat, 5 gm Protein, 32 gm Carbohydrate, 493 mg Sodium, 73 mg Calcium, 3 gm Fiber
DIABETIC: 1½ Starch/Carbohydrate, 1 Vegetable

MAIN DISHES TO DELIGHT THE SOUL

■ ■ ■

In so many families, a particular main dish is traditionally associated with the annual celebration of an important holiday or occasion. The Lund household is no different: with us, it's always ham on Easter, turkey for Thanksgiving, and nothing else for Christmas but my son James's pot roast!

When I join James in the kitchen as he's preparing the family meal, I am reminded of when he was a young boy learning to cook from my mother. He loved to hang around and watch, no matter what was on the menu, and everything he learned from her lives on in his creative cooking.

Back when James was in fifth grade, he began making dinner for the family regularly, and he used my mother's recipes, especially her pot roast, when he wanted to show off for us. Okay, I know I'm his mother, and so maybe I'm not *completely objective, but I'll put his pot roast up against any other pot roast in America—and I bet he'll come out on top!*

Dinner is often just dinner, but I rarely meet anyone who doesn't treasure family food memories that frequently are associated with a special food or particular occasion. In some families, happy times are recalled with simple and inexpensive dishes like meatloaf or shepherd's pie. In others, the images that keep us warm inside involve special dishes or company food that we cherished because we only had it occasionally. I hope that this collection of main dish recipes will inspire some new sweet recollections, whether you choose *Confetti Meatloaf, Cowboy Pot Pie, Creamy Cajun Turkey Skillet, or Scandinavian Fish Bake.* Just remember that when any dish is prepared and served with love and care, it's what the generations that follow us will always hold dear.

> *"I will lift up my eyes to the hills—*
> *From whence comes my help.*
> *My help comes from the Lord . . ."*
> —PSALM 121:1

Three-Cheese Scalloped Tomatoes

Tomato Fettuccine

Green Beans Frittata

Frontier Fireside Skillet

Pizza Rice Skillet

Scandinavian Fish Bake

Tuna–Potato Salad Casserole

Crunchy Tuna Burgers

Tuna Pizza Treats

Tuna-Corn Sauce over Muffins

Seafood Macaroni Bake

Island Shrimp and Rice

Salmon Cheese Loaf with Pea Sauce

Corn and Salmon Loaf

Baked Chicken in Mushroom Sauce

Crunchy Grande Baked Chicken

South-of-the-Border Chicken Breasts

Chicken Cordon Bleu Casserole

Creamed Chicken over Muffins

Chicken Pot Pie Sauce with Noodles

Creamy Cajun Turkey Skillet

Turkey Trot

Green Bean and Turkey Shepherd's Pie

Sauerbraten Meatloaf

Confetti Meatloaf

Pot Roast Meatloaf

Mexican Stroganoff

Cowboy Pot Pie

Tomato "Sausage" Polenta

Goulash Stew

Salisbury Pasta Skillet

Popeye's Burritos

Barbecued Loose-Meat Sandwiches

Meat and Cabbage Pie

"Sausage"-Stuffed Acorn Squash

"Cabbage Rolls" Skillet

Tommy's Hamburger Milk Gravy Skillet

Skillet Steak Dinner

Stuffed Beef Rounds

Swiss Steak Stew Skillet

Pork Via Veneto Skillet

Rio Bravo Pork Tenders

Pork Loin Potato Dish

Oktoberfest Pork Tenders

German Pork Stroganoff

Creamy Ham and Vegetables over Toast

Layered Green Bean and Ham Casserole

Ham and Potato Hot Dish

Ham and Maple Syrup–Stuffed Sweet Potatoes

Baked Ham and Pineapple Loaf

Frankfurter and Sauerkraut Pizza

Corned Beef Toasties

Potato Reuben Casserole

Three-Cheese Scalloped Tomatoes

■ ■ ■

This tummy-pleasing veggie casserole is truly delectable with its combination of—count 'em—THREE tasty cheeses! When your backyard tomato patch is hanging heavy with these gorgeous red globes, celebrate your personal harvest with this earthy dish.

Serves 6

4½ cups peeled and thinly sliced fresh tomatoes
¾ cup (3 ounces) shredded Kraft reduced-fat Cheddar cheese
¾ cup (3 ounces) shredded Kraft reduced-fat mozzarella cheese
3 slices reduced-calorie Italian bread, made into soft crumbs

⅔ cup Carnation Nonfat Dry Milk Powder
⅓ cup water
¼ cup (¾ ounce) grated Kraft fat-free Parmesan cheese
1 teaspoon dried basil
⅛ teaspoon black pepper

Preheat oven to 350 degrees. Spray an 8-by-8-inch baking dish with butter-flavored cooking spray. Evenly arrange tomatoes in prepared baking dish. Sprinkle Cheddar and mozzarella cheeses over top. Layer bread crumbs over cheeses. In a small bowl, combine dry milk powder, water, Parmesan cheese, basil, and black pepper. Pour mixture evenly over top. Bake for 55 to 60 minutes. Place baking dish on a wire rack and let set for 5 minutes. Divide into 6 servings.

Each serving equals:
HE: 1½ Protein, 1½ Vegetable, ⅓ Skim Milk, ¼ Bread
177 Calories, 5 gm Fat, 14 gm Protein, 19 gm Carbohydrate, 403 mg Sodium, 312 mg Calcium, 3 gm Fiber
DIABETIC: 2 Vegetable, 1 Meat, ½ Skim Milk

Tomato Fettuccine

■ ❄ ■

Here's a great "anytime, anyplace" meal that will warm you and fill you all at once! Even when the fridge is empty and the cupboard nearly bare, you've probably got the ingredients for this dish, which cooks up in just no time at all.

Serves 4 (1 cup)

1¾ cups (one 15-ounce can) Hunt's Tomato Sauce
1 teaspoon Italian seasoning
1 tablespoon chopped fresh parsley or 1 teaspoon dried parsley flakes
2 teaspoons reduced-calorie margarine

⅓ cup Carnation Nonfat Dry Milk Powder
⅔ cup warm water
¼ cup (¾ ounce) grated Kraft fat-free Parmesan cheese
2 cups hot cooked fettuccine, rinsed and drained

In a large skillet sprayed with butter-flavored cooking spray, combine tomato sauce, Italian seasoning, parsley, and margarine. Cook over medium heat for 5 minutes, or until mixture is heated through, stirring often. In a small bowl, combine dry milk powder, water, and Parmesan cheese. Stir milk mixture into tomato mixture. Add fettuccine. Mix well to combine. Serve at once.

HINT: 1½ cups broken uncooked fettuccine usually cooks to about 2 cups.

Each serving equals:
HE: 1¾ Vegetable, 1 Bread, ¼ Skim Milk, ¼ Protein, ¼ Fat
169 Calories, 1 gm Fat, 7 gm Protein, 33 gm Carbohydrate, 769 mg Sodium, 91 mg Calcium, 3 gm Fiber
DIABETIC: 2 Vegetable, 1½ Starch

Green Beans Frittata

■ ■ ■

It sounds fancy, but a "frittata" is just an unfolded omelet with some goodies mixed in. It's a great idea for hurried weekend lunches or a late supper after work when you don't feel much like cooking but everyone's still hungry. Isn't it good to know you can fix an appetizing meal for yourself without spending time or trouble?

Serves 4

4 cups (two 16-ounce cans) cut
green beans, rinsed and
drained
2 tablespoons Hormel Bacon
Bits
4 eggs, slightly beaten, or equivalent in egg substitute

¼ cup (¾ ounce) grated Kraft
fat-free Parmesan cheese
2 teaspoons dried parsley flakes
½ teaspoon lemon pepper

In a large skillet sprayed with butter-flavored cooking spray, combine green beans and bacon bits. Cook over medium heat for 2 to 3 minutes or until heated through. Meanwhile, in a medium bowl, combine eggs, Parmesan cheese, parsley flakes, and lemon pepper. Pour egg mixture over green beans. Lower heat, cover, and cook until eggs are just set. Cut into 4 wedges.

HINT: Also good with ½ cup sliced mushrooms added.

Each serving equals:
HE: 2 Vegetable, 1½ Protein (1 limited), 13 Optional Calories
134 Calories, 6 gm Fat, 10 gm Protein, 10 gm Carbohydrate, 271 mg Sodium,
63 mg Calcium, 2 gm Fiber
DIABETIC: 2 Vegetable, 1½ Meat

Frontier Fireside Skillet

■ ❋ ■

Cliff and I don't go camping often (who has time these days?), but when I asked him what he thought of this skillet supper, he said it was the kind of hearty dish he could imagine enjoying while seated around a campfire! The simple and inexpensive ingredients make it a thrifty family meal, but it's the taste that will win them over.

Serves 4 (1 cup)

½ cup chopped onion
½ cup chopped green bell pepper
1 (10¾-ounce) can Healthy
   Request Tomato Soup
1½ teaspoons chili seasoning

10 ounces (one 16-ounce can) red
   kidney beans, rinsed and
   drained
2 cups hot cooked elbow macaroni, rinsed and drained

In a large skillet sprayed with butter-flavored cooking spray, sauté onion and green pepper for 5 minutes or until tender. Stir in tomato soup, kidney beans, and chili seasoning. Add macaroni. Mix well to combine. Lower heat and simmer for 6 to 8 minutes, or until mixture is heated through, stirring occasionally.

HINT: 1⅓ cups uncooked elbow macaroni usually cooks to about 2 cups.

Each serving equals:
HE: 1¼ Protein, 1 Bread, ½ Vegetable, ½ Slider, 5 Optional Calories
218 Calories, 2 gm Fat, 8 gm Protein, 42 gm Carbohydrate, 233 mg Sodium, 35 mg Calcium, 7 gm Fiber
DIABETIC: 2 Starch, 1 Meat

Pizza Rice Skillet

■ ❋ ■

Love the flavor of pizza, but you're trying to cut down on the calls to the pizza place? I think you'll be delighted by this "pizza-in-a-pan" dish that delivers the flavors you adore! Close your eyes, trust your tastebuds, and enjoy!

Serves 4 (1 cup)

½ cup chopped onion
½ cup diced green bell pepper
1 cup (one 8-ounce can) Hunt's
   Tomato Sauce
1½ cups water
2 teaspoons pourable Sugar Twin
1½ teaspoons Italian seasoning
1⅓ cups (4 ounces) uncooked
   Minute Rice

¼ cup (1 ounce) sliced ripe olives
½ cup (one 2.5-ounce jar) sliced
   mushrooms, drained
¾ cup (3 ounces) shredded Kraft
   reduced-fat mozzarella cheese
¼ cup (¾ ounce) grated Kraft
   fat-free Parmesan cheese

In a large skillet sprayed with olive oil–flavored cooking spray, sauté onion and green pepper for 5 minutes or until just tender. Add tomato sauce, water, Sugar Twin, and Italian seasoning. Mix well to combine. Bring mixture to a boil. Stir in uncooked rice, olives, mushrooms, and mozzarella cheese. Lower heat, cover, and simmer for 6 to 8 minutes or until rice is tender. Add Parmesan cheese. Mix gently to combine. Serve at once.

Each serving equals:
HE: 2½ Vegetable, 1¼ Protein, 1 Bread, ¼ Fat
160 Calories, 4 gm Fat, 9 gm Protein, 22 gm Carbohydrate, 817 mg Sodium, 172 mg Calcium, 4 gm Fiber
DIABETIC: 2 Vegetable, 1 Starch, 1 Meat

Scandinavian Fish Bake

■ ■ ■

Do you sometimes stand in the store and think, "What am I going to do with this piece of plain fish?" Well, here's a delicate and delectable suggestion inspired by a cuisine that celebrates the glories of fish—and it tastes so luscious, no one will believe it's this low in calories and fat! *Serves 4*

3 tablespoons all-purpose flour
½ teaspoon dried dill weed
⅛ teaspoon black pepper
16 ounces white fish, cut into 4
    pieces

1 cup skim milk
½ cup Land O Lakes no-fat sour
    cream
6 tablespoons (1½ ounces) dried
    fine bread crumbs

Preheat oven to 350 degrees. Spray an 8-by-8-inch baking dish with butter-flavored cooking spray. In a shallow saucer, combine flour, dill weed, and black pepper. Coat fish pieces in flour mixture. Place fish into prepared baking dish. Sprinkle any remaining flour mixture over fish pieces. Evenly pour skim milk over top. Bake for 35 minutes. Spoon sour cream evenly over fish pieces. Sprinkle bread crumbs over top. Lightly spray tops with butter-flavored cooking spray. Continue baking for 15 to 20 minutes or until fish flakes easily. Evenly divide into 4 servings.

Each serving equals:

HE: 1½ Protein, ¾ Bread, ¼ Skim Milk, ¼ Slider, 10 Optional Calories

190 Calories, 2 gm Fat, 27 gm Protein, 16 gm Carbohydrate, 226 mg Sodium, 200 mg Calcium, 1 gm Fiber

DIABETIC: 3 Meat, 1 Starch/Carbohydrate

Tuna–Potato Salad Casserole

■ ❋ ■

Ever spot a couple and think, "Hmm, what did she see in him, or he in her?" That's the way it is sometimes with food combinations, and yet often it's the unlikely or unusual blends that provide unexpected pleasures. I love potato salad in all its forms, and I thought, why not create a tuna casserole that makes it a star? Why ask why? I did it, and it's a winner!   *Serves 4*

1 (10¾-ounce) can Healthy
   Request Cream of Celery or
   Mushroom Soup
¼ cup Kraft fat-free mayonnaise
1½ teaspoons dried onion flakes
1½ teaspoons dried parsley flakes
3 full cups (16 ounces) diced
   cooked potatoes

1 (6-ounce) can white tuna,
   packed in water, drained and
   flaked
4 (¾-ounce) slices Kraft reduced-
   fat Cheddar cheese

Preheat oven to 350 degrees. Spray an 8-by-8-inch baking dish with butter-flavored cooking spray. In a large bowl, combine celery soup, mayonnaise, onion flakes, and parsley flakes. Add potatoes and tuna. Mix well to combine. Spread mixture into prepared baking dish. Bake for 30 minutes. Evenly arrange Cheddar cheese slices over top. Continue baking for 10 minutes or until cheese melts. Place baking dish on a wire rack and let set for 5 minutes. Divide into 4 servings.

Each serving equals:
HE: 1¾ Protein, 1 Bread, ½ Slider, 11 Optional Calories
226 Calories, 6 gm Fat, 20 gm Protein, 23 gm Carbohydrate, 768 mg Sodium, 213 mg Calcium, 2 gm Fiber
DIABETIC: 2 Meat, 1½ Starch/Carbohydrate

Crunchy Tuna Burgers

■ ■ ■

This is fun food, perfect for serving to kids and teens, but it's also a yummy surprise for all those big kids who never really grew up when it comes to lunch! Instead of those unhealthy fried-fish fast-food sandwiches, why not give this home-grown version a try?

Serves 4

1 (6-ounce) can white tuna, packed in water, drained and flaked

2 tablespoons Kraft fat-free mayonnaise

½ cup (¾ ounce) crushed cornflakes

1 teaspoon dried onion flakes

1 teaspoon dried parsley flakes

4 reduced-calorie hamburger buns

In a large bowl, combine tuna, mayonnaise, cornflakes, onion flakes, and parsley flakes. Mix well to combine. Using a ⅓-cup measure as a guide, form into 4 patties. Place patties in a large skillet sprayed with butter-flavored cooking spray. Cook over medium heat for about 4 minutes on each side or until golden brown. For each sandwich, arrange a browned patty in a hamburger bun. Serve at once.

HINT: A self-seal sandwich bag works great for crushing cornflakes.

Each serving equals:

HE: 1¼ Bread, ¾ Protein, 5 Optional Calories

133 Calories, 1 gm Fat, 13 gm Protein, 18 gm Carbohydrate, 401 mg Sodium, 9 mg Calcium, 1 gm Fiber

DIABETIC: 1½ Meat, 1 Starch

Tuna Pizza Treats

■ ■ ■

I'm not sure why it's just more fun eating open-faced sandwiches, but it is! Maybe it's because it feels like you're nibbling on party food—and this recipe would be great as part of a summer gathering. Sure, you *could* just have a tuna fish sandwich for lunch, but isn't living well the best revenge?

Serves 8 (2 each)

1 (8-ounce) can Pillsbury
　　Reduced Fat Crescent Rolls
2 (6-ounce) cans white tuna,
　　packed in water, drained and
　　flaked
⅓ cup Kraft fat-free mayonnaise

2 tablespoons sweet pickle relish
1 teaspoon dried onion flakes
1½ cups (6 ounces) shredded
　　Kraft reduced-fat Cheddar
　　cheese ☆

Preheat oven to 375 degrees. Spray a rimmed 10-by-15-inch baking sheet with butter-flavored cooking spray. Pat rolls into prepared baking sheet, being sure to seal perforations. Bake for 8 minutes. Meanwhile, in a large bowl, combine tuna, mayonnaise, pickle relish, and onion flakes. Add 1 cup Cheddar cheese. Mix well to combine. Spread tuna mixture over partially baked crust. Evenly sprinkle remaining ½ cup Cheddar cheese over top. Continue baking for 5 minutes or until cheese melts. Place baking sheet on a wire rack and let set for 5 minutes. Cut into 16 pieces.

HINT: Do not use inexpensive rolls as they don't cover the pan properly.

Each serving equals:
HE: 1¾ Protein, 1 Bread, 10 Optional Calories

208 Calories, 8 gm Fat, 19 gm Protein, 16 gm Carbohydrate, 681 mg Sodium, 146 mg Calcium, 0 gm Fiber

DIABETIC: 2 Meat, 1 Starch, ½ Fat

Tuna-Corn Sauce over Muffins

■ ■ ■

There's such an old-fashioned feeling to this cozy supper dish, bringing back memories of a time when every family's favorite was tuna à la king! The cheesy, creamy taste and texture of this "saucy" recipe will create new happy memories at your house.

Serves 6

¼ cup Kraft fat-free mayonnaise
1 (10¾-ounce) can Healthy
  Request Cream of Mushroom
  Soup
½ cup skim milk
2 teaspoons dried onion flakes
1 (6-ounce) can white tuna,
  packed in water, drained and
  flaked

1 cup (one 8-ounce can) whole-
  kernel corn, rinsed and
  drained
½ cup + 1 tablespoon (2¼
  ounces) shredded Kraft
  reduced-fat Cheddar cheese
1 teaspoon dried parsley flakes
3 English muffins, split and
  toasted

In a medium saucepan, combine mayonnaise, mushroom soup, skim milk, and onion flakes. Stir in tuna, corn, Cheddar cheese, and parsley flakes. Cook over medium heat for 6 to 8 minutes or until mixture is heated through, stirring often. For each serving, place 1 muffin half on a plate and spoon about ½ cup tuna mixture over top.

Each serving equals:
HE: 1⅓ Bread, 1 Protein, ½ Slider, 2 Optional Calories
187 Calories, 3 gm Fat, 14 gm Protein, 26 gm Carbohydrate, 616 mg Sodium, 184 mg Calcium, 2 gm Fiber
DIABETIC: 2 Starch, 2 Meat

Seafood Macaroni Bake

■ ❄ ■

Imagine the fun of biting into what you think is a forkful of tuna casserole and finding shrimp, or crunching a slice of water chestnut when all you expect is a chunk of celery! Isn't it fun to defy expectations, surprise your family, and keep life interesting? This recipe can help you do it! *Serves 6*

1 (10¾-ounce) can Healthy Request Cream of Mushroom Soup

⅓ cup Kraft fat-free mayonnaise

⅓ cup skim milk

1 teaspoon dried onion flakes

2 teaspoons dried parsley flakes

1 (4.5-ounce drained weight) can small shrimp, rinsed and drained

1 (6-ounce) can white tuna, packed in water, drained and flaked

1 cup (one 8-ounce can) sliced water chestnuts, drained

1 cup finely chopped celery

2 cups hot cooked elbow macaroni, rinsed and drained

¼ teaspoon paprika

Preheat oven to 350 degrees. Spray an 8-by-8-inch baking dish with butter-flavored cooking spray. In a large bowl, combine mushroom soup, mayonnaise, and skim milk. Stir in onion flakes and parsley flakes. Add shrimp, tuna, water chestnuts, and celery. Mix well to combine. Stir in macaroni. Spread mixture into prepared baking dish. Evenly sprinkle paprika over top. Bake for 40 to 45 minutes. Place baking dish on a wire rack and let set for 5 minutes. Evenly divide into 6 servings.

HINT: 1⅓ cups uncooked elbow macaroni usually cooks to about 2 cups.

Each serving equals:
HE: 1¼ Protein, 1 Bread, ⅓ Vegetable, ½ Slider, 1 Optional Calorie
178 Calories, 2 gm Fat, 16 gm Protein, 24 gm Carbohydrate, 473 mg Sodium, 81 mg Calcium, 2 gm Fiber
DIABETIC: 1½ Meat, 1½ Starch/Carbohydrate

Island Shrimp and Rice

■ ■ ■

Yes, you could ask your travel agent to book you on the next plane to San Juan, but if your schedule and budget don't permit a Caribbean getaway *this* week, how about the next-best thing: a mouth-watering seafood special you stir up in minutes? And you won't need a bit of sunblock to enjoy this tropical delight!

Serves 6

1 cup (one 8-ounce can) pineapple chunks, packed in fruit
juice, drained, and 3 tablespoons liquid reserved
¾ cup chopped green bell pepper
¾ cup Kraft Fat Free French
Dressing

1 (10-ounce) package frozen
cooked cocktail shrimp,
thawed
1 tablespoon chopped fresh parsley or 1 teaspoon dried parsley
flakes
3 cups hot cooked rice

In a large skillet sprayed with butter-flavored cooking spray, combine reserved pineapple liquid and green pepper. Cook over medium heat for 5 minutes or until green pepper is just tender, stirring occasionally. Add French dressing, pineapple, shrimp, and parsley. Mix well to combine. Lower heat and simmer for 5 minutes, or until mixture is heated through, stirring occasionally. For each serving, place ½ cup rice on a plate and spoon about ½ cup shrimp mixture over top.

HINTS: 1. Thaw shrimp by placing in a colander and rinsing under hot water
for one minute.
2. 2 cups uncooked rice usually cooks to about 3 cups.

Each serving equals:
HE: 1⅔ Protein, 1 Bread, ⅓ Fruit, ¼ Vegetable, ⅛ Slider, 10 Optional Calories
205 Calories, 1 gm Fat, 12 gm Protein, 37 gm Carbohydrate, 410 mg Sodium,
35 mg Calcium, 2 gm Fiber
DIABETIC: 2 Starch/Carbohydrate, 1 ½ Meat, ½ Fruit

Salmon Cheese Loaf with Pea Sauce

■ ■ ■

Don't you just love a dish that makes leftovers worth hurrying home for? This recipe packs a nutritious calcium wallop in addition to a bundle of scrumptious flavor, and if there's any left after dinner is served, it reheats beautifully for a second meal.

Serves 6

1½ cups (one 12-fluid-ounce can) Carnation Evaporated Skim Milk ☆

1 egg or equivalent in egg substitute

1 (14¾-ounce) can pink salmon, drained, boned, and flaked

¼ cup finely chopped celery

28 small fat-free saltine crackers, made into fine crumbs

¼ cup finely chopped onion

¾ cup (3 ounces) shredded Kraft reduced-fat Cheddar cheese

1 teaspoon dried parsley flakes

⅛ teaspoon black pepper

1 (10¾-ounce) can Healthy Request Cream of Mushroom Soup

1 cup frozen peas, thawed

Preheat oven to 350 degrees. Spray a 9-by-5-inch loaf pan with butter-flavored cooking spray. In a large bowl, combine 1 cup evaporated skim milk and egg. Mix gently using a wire whisk. Add salmon, celery, onion, cracker crumbs, Cheddar cheese, parsley flakes, and black pepper. Mix well to combine. Let set for 2 to 3 minutes or until moisture is absorbed. Pat mixture into prepared loaf pan. Bake for 50 to 60 minutes. Place loaf pan on a wire rack and let set while preparing sauce. In a medium saucepan, combine mushroom soup, remaining ½ cup evaporated skim milk, and peas. Cook over medium heat for 5 minutes or until mixture is heated through, stirring often. Cut salmon loaf into 6 pieces. For each serving, place 1 piece of salmon loaf on a plate and spoon about ⅓ cup pea sauce over top.

HINT: A self-seal sandwich bag works great for crushing saltine crackers.

Each serving equals:

HE: 3 Protein, 1 Bread, ½ Skim Milk, ¼ Vegetable, ¼ Slider, 8 Optional Calories

279 Calories, 7 gm Fat, 26 gm Protein, 28 gm Carbohydrate, 875 mg Sodium, 427 mg Calcium, 2 gm Fiber

DIABETIC: 3 Meat, 1 Starch, ½ Skim Milk

Corn and Salmon Loaf

■ ■ ■

Any meatloaf lovers at your house? Mine, too. But since we're all trying to eat more fish these days, and since salmon is the "meatiest" of fish, why not try this delicious entree tonight? I think you'll find that the corn gives this dish a wonderful taste and texture. *Serves 6*

⅔ cup **Carnation Nonfat Dry Milk Powder**
½ cup water
1 teaspoon lemon juice
1 egg or equivalent in egg substitute
1 cup (one 8-ounce can) cream-style corn

1 (14¾-ounce) can pink salmon, drained, boned, and flaked
21 small fat-free saltine crackers, made into fine crumbs
½ cup frozen whole-kernel corn, thawed
2 teaspoons dried onion flakes
1 teaspoon dried parsley flakes

Preheat oven to 350 degrees. Spray a 9-by-5-inch loaf pan with butter-flavored cooking spray. In a large bowl, combine dry milk powder and water. Stir in lemon juice, egg, and cream-style corn. Add salmon, cracker crumbs, whole-kernel corn, onion flakes, and parsley flakes. Mix well to combine. Pat mixture into prepared loaf pan. Bake for 50 to 60 minutes. Place loaf pan on a wire rack and let set for 5 minutes. Cut into 6 servings.

HINTS: 1. A self-seal sandwich bag works great for crushing saltine crackers.
2. Thaw corn by placing in a colander and rinsing under hot water for one minute.

Each serving equals:
HE: 2⅔ Protein, 1 Bread, ⅓ Skim Milk

195 Calories, 3 gm Fat, 19 gm Protein, 23 gm Carbohydrate, 645 mg Sodium, 198 mg Calcium, 1 gm Fiber

DIABETIC: 2½ Meat, 1½ Starch

Baked Chicken in Mushroom Sauce

■ ❄ ■

If you're not a fan of skinless chicken breasts because they always turn out dry, I'm going to change your mind with this recipe! Isn't it nice to know that eating healthy doesn't mean eating your poultry grilled dry? This dish takes just minutes to prepare, and while it bakes, you can relax and de-stress. *Serves 4*

16 ounces skinned and boned uncooked chicken breast, cut into 4 pieces

1 (10¾-ounce) can Healthy Request Cream of Mushroom Soup

½ cup Land O Lakes no-fat sour cream

½ cup (one 2.5-ounce jar) sliced mushrooms, undrained

1 teaspoon dried onion flakes

1 teaspoon dried parsley flakes

Preheat oven to 350 degrees. Evenly arrange chicken pieces in an 8-by-8-inch baking dish. In a medium bowl, combine mushroom soup, sour cream, and undrained mushrooms. Add onion flakes and parsley flakes. Mix gently to combine. Evenly spoon mushroom mixture over chicken pieces. Bake for 40 to 50 minutes or until chicken is tender. Divide into 4 servings.

Each serving equals:

HE: 3 Protein, ¼ Vegetable, ¾ Slider, 11 Optional Calories

191 Calories, 3 gm Fat, 28 gm Protein, 13 gm Carbohydrate, 497 mg Sodium, 99 mg Calcium, 0 gm Fiber 4

DIABETIC: 3 Meat, 1 Starch/Carbohydrate

Crunchy Grande Baked Chicken

■ ■ ■

You know baked chicken is better for you than fried, but what can you do—you LOVE the crust! Well, now you can enjoy a crunchy meal that's good for you and tastes great. All it takes is a bit of spice, some salad dressing, and a cereal coating that bakes up downright yummy! *Serves 4*

½ cup Kraft Fat Free Catalina Dressing
1 teaspoon chili seasoning
1 teaspoon dried onion flakes
1½ cups (1½ ounces) corn-flakes, made into crumbs

16 ounces skinned and boned uncooked chicken breast, cut into 4 pieces

Preheat oven to 350 degrees. Spray an 8-by-8-inch baking dish with olive oil–flavored cooking spray. In a shallow saucer, combine Catalina dressing, chili seasoning, and onion flakes. Place cornflake crumbs on a plate. Dip chicken pieces first in dressing mixture, then in cornflake crumbs to coat evenly. Arrange chicken pieces in prepared baking dish. Evenly sprinkle any remaining cornflake crumbs over chicken pieces, then drizzle any remaining dressing mix-ture evenly over tops. Bake for 40 to 45 minutes or until chicken is tender.

HINT: A self-seal sandwich bag works great for making cornflake crumbs.

Each serving equals:
HE: 3 Protein, ½ Bread, ½ Slider, 10 Optional Calories
194 Calories, 2 gm Fat, 27 gm Protein, 17 gm Carbohydrate, 523 mg Sodium, 14 mg Calcium, 1 gm Fiber
DIABETIC: 3 Meat, 1 Starch/Carbohydrate

South-of-the-Border Chicken Breasts

You'll be delighted to discover how dipping skinned chicken breasts in a little flour can really seal in the juices! This tangy skillet dish is so easy to fix, I wouldn't be surprised to hear that you've put it on the menu just about every week or so. With dinner this simple to prepare, you've got time for a little siesta after work—or better yet, an energizing walk about the neighborhood.

Serves 4

3 tablespoons all-purpose flour
1 teaspoon chili seasoning
1 teaspoon dried parsley flakes
16 ounces skinned and boned
*   uncooked chicken breast, cut*
*   into 4 pieces*

1¾ cups (one 15-ounce can)
*   Hunt's Tomato Sauce*
½ cup chunky salsa (mild,
*   medium, or hot)*
1 tablespoon Brown Sugar Twin

In a shallow saucer, combine flour, chili seasoning, and parsley flakes. Coat chicken pieces in flour mixture. Place chicken in a large skillet sprayed with olive oil–flavored cooking spray. Brown chicken for 3 to 4 minutes on each side. In a large bowl, combine tomato sauce, salsa, Brown Sugar Twin, and any remaining flour mixture. Evenly spoon sauce over chicken. Lower heat, cover, and simmer for 15 to 20 minutes or until chicken is tender. When serving, evenly spoon sauce mixture over chicken pieces.

Each serving equals:
HE: 3 Protein, 2 Vegetable, ¼ Bread, 1 Optional Calorie
182 Calories, 2 gm Fat, 28 gm Protein, 13 gm Carbohydrate, 833 mg Sodium, 70 mg Calcium, 2 gm Fiber
DIABETIC: 3 Meat, 2 Vegetable

Chicken Cordon Bleu Casserole

■ ❈ ■

Prepared in a style that deserves a blue ribbon (the *cordon bleu*), this classic dish lets you treat your family like company any day of the week! It tastes sinful, with all that ham and the cheese bubbling away, but you can enjoy this with a clear conscience.

Serves 4

1 (10¾-ounce) can Healthy
   Request Cream of Chicken
   Soup
¼ cup Kraft fat-free mayonnaise
1 teaspoon dried parsley flakes
1 cup (5 ounces) diced cooked
   chicken breast

½ full cup (3 ounces) diced
   Dubuque 97% fat-free ham or
   any extra-lean ham
2 cups hot cooked noodles,
   rinsed and drained
4 (¾-ounce) slices Kraft
   reduced-fat Swiss cheese

Preheat oven to 350 degrees. Spray an 8-by-8-inch baking dish with butter-flavored cooking spray. In a large bowl, combine chicken soup, mayonnaise, and parsley flakes. Add chicken, ham, and noodles. Mix well to combine. Spread mixture into prepared baking dish. Bake for 20 minutes. Evenly arrange Swiss cheese slices over top. Continue baking for 10 minutes. Place baking dish on a wire rack and let set for 5 minutes. Divide into 4 servings.

HINTS: 1. If you don't have leftovers, purchase a chunk of cooked chicken breast from your local deli.
2. 1¾ cups uncooked noodles usually cooks to about 2 cups.

Each serving equals:

HE: 2¾ Protein, 1 Bread, ½ Slider, 15 Optional Calories

289 Calories, 9 gm Fat, 21 gm Protein, 31 gm Carbohydrate, 968 mg Sodium, 15 mg Calcium, 1 gm Fiber

DIABETIC: 2½ Meat, 1½ Starch/Carbohydrate

Creamed Chicken over Muffins

■ ■ ■

If you're having some friends over for lunch or a card party, this American classic will encourage reminiscing about old times. It's simple, it's luscious, and it's soothing in a way that makes us feel comforted. Use your prettiest dishes, make a pitcher of iced tea, and bring out the scrapbooks! *Serves 4*

½ cup finely chopped celery
1 (10¾-ounce) can Healthy
   Request Cream of Mushroom
   Soup
1½ cups (8 ounces) diced
   cooked chicken breast

2 teaspoons dried onion flakes
¼ cup (one 2-ounce jar)
   chopped pimiento, drained
⅛ teaspoon black pepper
2 English muffins, split and
   toasted

In a medium saucepan sprayed with butter-flavored cooking spray, sauté celery for 6 to 8 minutes or until tender. Add mushroom soup, chicken, onion flakes, pimiento, and black pepper. Mix well to combine. Lower heat and simmer for 6 to 8 minutes, or until mixture is heated through, stirring occasionally. For each serving, place 1 muffin half on a plate and spoon about ½ cup chicken mixture over top.

HINT: If you don't have leftovers, purchase a chunk of cooked chicken breast from your local deli.

Each serving equals:
HE: 2 Protein, 1 Bread, ¼ Vegetable, ½ Slider, 1 Optional Calorie
204 Calories, 4 gm Fat, 21 gm Protein, 21 gm Carbohydrate, 489 mg Sodium, 117 mg Calcium, 1 gm Fiber
DIABETIC: 2 Meat, 1½ Starch/Carbohydrate

Chicken Pot Pie Sauce with Noodles

■ ■ ■

Were you the kind of kid who ignored the crust and slurped up the creamy filling of every chicken pot pie your mom served? I must have had you in mind when I created this truly irresistible noodle-topping sauce! It's cozy and hearty all at once.

Serves 4

1 (10¾-ounce) can Healthy
  Request Cream of Chicken
  Soup
¾ cup (3 ounces) shredded
  Kraft reduced-fat Cheddar
  cheese
1 teaspoon dried onion flakes
1 teaspoon dried parsley flakes
1 full cup (6 ounces) diced
  cooked chicken breast

1 cup (one 8-ounce can) sliced
  carrots, rinsed and drained
1 cup (one 8-ounce can) cut
  green beans, rinsed and
  drained
2 cups hot cooked noodles,
  rinsed and drained

In a large skillet sprayed with butter-flavored cooking spray, combine chicken soup, Cheddar cheese, onion flakes, and parsley flakes. Cook over medium heat until cheese melts, stirring occasionally. Stir in chicken, carrots, and green beans. Lower heat and simmer for 6 to 8 minutes or until mixture is heated through, stirring occasionally. For each serving, place ½ cup noodles on a plate and spoon about ⅔ cup chicken sauce over top.

HINTS: 1. If you don't have leftovers, purchase a chunk of cooked chicken breast from your local deli.
2. 1¾ cups uncooked noodles usually cooks to about 2 cups.

Each serving equals:
HE: 2½ Protein, 1 Bread, 1 Vegetable, ½ Slider, 5 Optional Calories
287 Calories, 7 gm Fat, 24 gm Protein, 32 gm Carbohydrate, 532 mg Sodium, 176 mg Calcium, 2 gm Fiber
DIABETIC: 2 Meat, 1½ Starch/Carbohydrate, 1 Vegetable

Creamy Cajun Turkey Skillet

■ ❄ ■

Just as New Orleans is known as "The Big Easy," this recipe provides a simple yet scrumptious way to make something special out of turkey in a skillet! Cajuns are famous for spicy food and an appetite for all kinds of pleasures from eating to dancing. So don't be surprised if your dinner guests gobble this down, then roll up the rugs and run wild! *Serves 4 (1 full cup)*

¼ cup chopped green bell pepper
½ cup chopped onion
1 cup finely chopped celery
1 (10¾-ounce) can Healthy Request Cream of Chicken Soup
¼ cup Land O Lakes no-fat sour cream
1 teaspoon Cajun seasoning
1 teaspoon dried parsley flakes

1¾ cups (one 14½-ounce can) stewed tomatoes, chopped and undrained
½ cup (one 2.5-ounce jar) sliced mushrooms, drained
2 cups hot cooked noodles, rinsed and drained
1½ cups (8 ounces) diced cooked turkey breast

In a large skillet sprayed with butter-flavored cooking spray, sauté green pepper, onion, and celery for 8 to 10 minutes or until vegetables are tender. Stir in chicken soup, sour cream, Cajun seasoning, parsley flakes, and undrained stewed tomatoes. Add mushrooms, noodles, and turkey. Mix well to combine. Lower heat and simmer for 5 minutes, or until mixture is heated through, stirring occasionally.

HINTS: 1. 1¾ cups uncooked noodles usually cooks to about 2 cups.
         2. If you don't have leftovers, purchase a chunk of cooked turkey breast from your local deli.

Each serving equals:
HE: 2 Protein, 2 Vegetable, 1 Bread, ¾ Slider

288 Calories, 4 gm Fat, 25 gm Protein, 38 gm Carbohydrate, 793 mg Sodium, 110 mg Calcium, 3 gm Fiber

DIABETIC: 2 Meat, 2 Vegetable, 2 Starch/Carbohydrate

Turkey Trot

■ ■ ■

Richly satisfying and amazingly creamy, this recipe invites an abundance of healthy veggies to join hands with chunks of turkey in a lovable partnership of tummy-pleasing pleasure! If you're into running and health-walking, why not serve this for a lively weekend brunch after a workout with friends?   *Serves 6*

2 cups shredded unpeeled zuc-
    chini
1½ cups shredded carrots
¾ cup sliced celery
¼ cup chopped onion
1½ cups (8 ounces) diced
    cooked turkey breast
1 (10¾-ounce) can Healthy
    Request Cream of Chicken
    Soup

⅓ cup skim milk
½ teaspoon poultry seasoning
1 teaspoon dried parsley flakes
3 cups hot cooked noodles,
    rinsed and drained
6 tablespoons Land O Lakes no-
    fat sour cream

In a large skillet sprayed with butter-flavored cooking spray, sauté zucchini, carrots, celery, and onion for 6 to 8 minutes or until vegetables are tender. Add turkey, chicken soup, skim milk, poultry seasoning, and parsley flakes. Mix well to combine. Lower heat and simmer for 5 minutes or until mixture is heated through, stirring often. For each serving, place ½ cup noodles on a plate, spoon a full ½ cup turkey mixture over noodles, and top with 1 tablespoon sour cream.

HINTS: 1. If you don't have leftovers, purchase a chunk of cooked turkey breast from your local deli.
       2. 2⅔ cups uncooked noodles usually cooks to about 3 cups.

Each serving equals:
HE: 1½ Vegetable, 1⅓ Protein, 1 Bread, ½ Slider, 10 Optional Calories
231 Calories, 3 gm Fat, 18 gm Protein, 33 gm Carbohydrate, 279 mg Sodium, 68 mg Calcium, 3 gm Fiber
DIABETIC: 1½ Starch/Carbohydrate, 1 Meat, 1 Vegetable

Green Bean and Turkey Shepherd's Pie

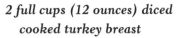

Calling all mashed-potato fans to join in the party! This old-fashioned dish was originally made with ground lamb (hence the name!) but is outrageously good when served with almost any meat or poultry. The reason couldn't be simpler: it's those rich mashed potatoes piled on top! *Mmm-mmm . . .*   *Serves 6*

2 full cups (12 ounces) diced cooked turkey breast

2 cups (one 16-ounce can) cut green beans, rinsed and drained

1 (10¾-ounce) can Healthy Request Cream of Chicken Soup

¼ cup Land O Lakes no-fat sour cream ☆

½ cup + 1 tablespoon (2¼ ounces) shredded Kraft reduced-fat Cheddar cheese

2½ cups boiling water

2 cups (4½ ounces) instant potato flakes

⅔ cup Carnation Nonfat Dry Milk Powder

1 teaspoon dried onion flakes

½ teaspoon paprika

Preheat oven to 350 degrees. Spray an 8-by-8-inch baking dish with butter-flavored cooking spray. In a large skillet sprayed with butter-flavored cooking spray, combine turkey, green beans, and chicken soup. Stir in 2 tablespoons sour cream and Cheddar cheese. Cook over medium heat until mixture is heated through and cheese melts, stirring often. Spoon hot mixture into prepared baking dish. In a large bowl, combine boiling water, potato flakes, dry milk powder, and onion flakes. Fold in remaining 2 tablespoons sour cream. Fluff gently with a fork. Spread potato mixture evenly over chicken mixture. Lightly sprinkle paprika over top. Bake for 20 to 25 minutes. Place baking dish on a wire rack and let set for 5 minutes. Divide into 6 servings.

HINT: If you don't have leftovers, purchase a chunk of cooked turkey breast from your local deli.

Each serving equals:

HE: 2½ Protein, 1 Bread, ⅔ Vegetable, ⅓ Skim Milk, ½ Slider

245 Calories, 5 gm Fat, 25 gm Protein, 25 gm Carbohydrate, 392 mg Sodium, 190 mg Calcium, 2 gm Fiber

DIABETIC: 2½ Meat, 1½ Starch/Carbohydrate, 1 Vegetable

Sauerbraten Meatloaf

■ ❄ ■

It's all in the spices, you'll soon discover, when you go a little bit out on a limb with me and this recipe! Whoever thought of stirring pumpkin pie spice into a hearty meatloaf? you may wonder. Well, you'll be pleased to taste the intriguing result—and I hope your family will, too!

Serves 6

16 ounces ground 90% lean
    turkey or beef
6 tablespoons purchased graham
    cracker crumbs or 6 (2½-inch)
    graham cracker squares, made
    into crumbs
1 tablespoon Brown Sugar Twin

1 teaspoon pumpkin pie spice
1 teaspoon dried parsley flakes
¾ cup chopped onion
¼ cup water
¾ cup Heinz Light Harvest
    Ketchup or any reduced-
    sodium ketchup ☆

Preheat oven to 350 degrees. Spray a 9-by-5-inch loaf pan with butter-flavored cooking spray. In a large bowl, combine meat, graham cracker crumbs, Brown Sugar Twin, pumpkin pie spice, parsley flakes, onion, water, and ¼ cup ketchup. Mix well to combine. Pat mixture into prepared loaf pan. Bake for 30 minutes. Spread remaining ½ cup ketchup over partially baked meatloaf. Continue baking for 15 to 20 minutes. Place loaf pan on a wire rack and let set for 5 minutes. Cut into 6 servings.

HINT: A self-seal sandwich bag works great for crushing graham crackers.

Each serving equals:
HE: 2 Protein, ⅓ Bread, ¼ Vegetable, ¼ Slider, 11 Optional Calories
183 Calories, 7 gm Fat, 14 gm Protein, 16 gm Carbohydrate, 124 mg Sodium, 15 mg Calcium, 1 gm Fiber
DIABETIC: 2 Meat, 1 Starch/Carbohydrate

Confetti Meatloaf

■ ❊ ■

Now, I'm not promising that your family will organize a parade in your honor down the main street of your town if you serve them this colorful dish, but it's definitely possible. If you've always made my meatloaf recipes with lean beef, why not round up the freshest ground turkey you can find and try it with this blend of ingredients?

Serves 6

16 ounces ground 90% lean
   turkey or beef
6 tablespoons (1½ ounces) dried
   fine bread crumbs
⅓ cup (1½ ounces) chopped
   green olives
¼ cup (one 2-ounce jar)
   chopped pimiento, drained

2 teaspoons dried onion flakes
1 cup (one 8-ounce can) Hunt's
   Tomato Sauce ☆
2 tablespoons pourable Sugar
   Twin
1 teaspoon dried parsley flakes

Preheat oven to 350 degrees. Spray a 9-by-5-inch loaf pan with olive oil–flavored cooking spray. In a large bowl, combine meat, bread crumbs, olives, pimiento, onion flakes, and ⅓ cup tomato sauce. Mix well to combine. Pat mixture into prepared loaf pan. Stir Sugar Twin and parsley flakes into remaining tomato sauce. Spoon sauce mixture evenly over top. Bake for 50 to 60 minutes. Place loaf pan on a wire rack and let set for 5 minutes. Divide into 6 servings.

Each serving equals:
HE: 2 Protein, ⅔ Vegetable, ⅓ Bread, ¼ Fat, 2 Optional Calories
160 Calories, 8 gm Fat, 14 gm Protein, 8 gm Carbohydrate, 543 mg Sodium, 26 mg Calcium, 1 gm Fiber
DIABETIC: 2 Meat, ½ Starch/Carbohydrate

Pot Roast Meatloaf

■ ❋ ■

It's a pot roast . . . It's a meatloaf . . . or, as the old commercial goes, maybe it's two-in-one! Actually, it's definitely a meatloaf, but I wanted it to taste like your favorite pot roast recipe, and so I've asked you to bake it in a dish with room for veggies on the side. After they cook in that pot roast–type gravy, they'll be so full of flavor, everyone will cheer!

Serves 6

⅔ cup *Carnation Nonfat Dry Milk Powder*
⅔ cup *water*
¼ cup *Heinz Light Harvest Ketchup or any reduced-sodium ketchup*
⅛ teaspoon *black pepper*
2 teaspoons *Worcestershire sauce*

½ cup (1½ ounces) *quick oats*
16 ounces *ground 90% lean turkey or beef*
1 cup *sliced onion*
2 cups *sliced carrots*
1½ cups *sliced celery*
2 cups (10 ounces) *sliced raw potatoes*
2 teaspoons *dried parsley flakes*

Preheat oven to 375 degrees. Spray an 8-by-12-inch baking dish with butter-flavored cooking spray. In a large bowl, combine dry milk powder, water, ketchup, black pepper, Worcestershire sauce, and oats. Add meat. Mix well to combine. Pat mixture into center of prepared baking dish. In a large bowl, combine onion, carrots, celery, potatoes, and parsley flakes. Evenly arrange vegetables around meatloaf. Cover and bake for 1 hour. Uncover and continue baking for 10 minutes or until vegetables are tender. Place baking dish on a wire rack and let set for 5 minutes. Cut meatloaf into 6 pieces. For each serving, place 1 piece of meatloaf on a plate and spoon 1 cup vegetables next to it.

Each serving equals:
HE: 2 Protein, 1½ Vegetable, ⅔ Bread, ⅓ Skim Milk, 10 Optional Calories
227 Calories, 7 gm Fat, 18 gm Protein, 23 gm Carbohydrate, 258 mg Sodium, 132 mg Calcium, 3 gm Fiber
DIABETIC: 2 Meat, 1 Vegetable, 1 Starch/Carbohydrate

Mexican Stroganoff

■ ❄ ■

America is often called a melting pot because of all the cultures that have come here from other countries to live together in harmony. This recipe is a perfect example of how we can take great ideas from two different worlds and mingle them for a delectable dish.

Serves 4

8 ounces ground 90% lean turkey or beef

½ cup chunky salsa (mild, medium, or hot)

1 cup (one 4-ounce jar) sliced mushrooms, undrained

¼ teaspoon dried minced garlic

1 teaspoon dried parsley flakes

½ cup Land O Lakes no-fat sour cream

2 cups hot cooked noodles, rinsed and drained

In a large skillet sprayed with butter-flavored cooking spray, brown meat. Stir in salsa, undrained mushrooms, garlic, and parsley flakes. Add sour cream. Mix well to combine. Lower heat and simmer for 6 to 8 minutes, or until mixture is heated through, stirring often. For each serving, place ½ cup noodles on a plate and spoon about ½ cup meat sauce over top.

HINT: 1¾ cups uncooked noodles usually cooks to about 2 cups.

Each serving equals:

HE: 1½ Protein, 1 Bread, ¾ Vegetable, ¼ Slider, 10 Optional Calories

230 Calories, 6 gm Fat, 16 gm Protein, 28 gm Carbohydrate, 375 mg Sodium, 88 mg Calcium, 2 gm Fiber

DIABETIC: 1½ Meat, 1½ Starch/Carbohydrate, ½ Vegetable

Cowboy Pot Pie

■ ❊ ■

When you're riding the range all day from dawn until the stars come out, you get a hankering for something so flavorful and filling, you'll find the strength to do it again tomorrow. Well, maybe your job isn't as physically demanding as herding steer, but a satisfying dinner will nourish you, too.

Serves 6

16 ounces ground 90% lean turkey or beef
½ cup chopped onion
½ cup chopped green bell pepper
10 ounces (one 16-ounce can) pinto beans, rinsed and drained
1 cup (one 8-ounce can) Hunt's Tomato Sauce

2 teaspoons chili seasoning
1 tablespoon Brown Sugar Twin
1 (7.5-ounce) can Pillsbury refrigerated buttermilk biscuits
1 teaspoon dried parsley flakes
3 tablespoons (¾ ounce) shredded Kraft reduced-fat Cheddar cheese

Preheat oven to 375 degrees. Spray an 8-by-8-inch baking dish with olive oil–flavored cooking spray. In a large skillet sprayed with olive oil–flavored cooking spray, brown meat, onion, and green pepper. Stir in pinto beans, tomato sauce, chili seasoning, and Brown Sugar Twin. Mix well to combine. Bring mixture to a boil. Spread hot mixture into prepared baking dish. Separate biscuits and cut each into 4 pieces. Evenly place biscuit pieces over meat mixture. Sprinkle parsley flakes over biscuits. Top with Cheddar cheese. Bake for 15 to 20 minutes or until biscuits are golden brown. Place baking dish on a wire rack and let set for 5 minutes. Divide into 6 servings.

Each serving equals:
HE: 3 Protein, 1¼ Bread, 1 Vegetable, 1 Optional Calorie
292 Calories, 8 gm Fat, 21 gm Protein, 34 gm Carbohydrate, 653 mg Sodium, 56 mg Calcium, 7 gm Fiber
DIABETIC: 2½ Meat, 1½ Starch, 1 Vegetable

Tomato "Sausage" Polenta

■ ❋ ■

If you've never eaten it before, polenta is a kind of cornmeal "mush" that can be served soft or baked into a firm cake. It takes on the flavors of whatever you cook it with and is a real tummy-pleaser in my book. This meaty dish is richly satisfying and a wonderful change of pace, so give it a try. As with most of my Healthy Exchanges recipes, here I've done my best to deliver lots of "main-dish" satisfaction in a meal that uses protein simply as an element of the overall entree. Many Americans are used to sitting down to an eight-ounce (or larger!) serving of beef, but living a healthier lifestyle is easier when you cut back somewhat on the protein

Serves 6

8 ounces ground 90% lean turkey or beef
½ cup chopped onion
½ teaspoon poultry seasoning
¼ teaspoon ground sage
¼ teaspoon garlic powder
½ cup frozen whole-kernel corn, thawed
1¾ cups (one 15-ounce can) Hunt's Tomato Sauce
6 tablespoons all-purpose flour
6 tablespoons (2¼ ounces) yellow cornmeal

1 tablespoon pourable Sugar Twin
1½ teaspoons baking powder
¼ cup (¾ ounce) grated Kraft fat-free Parmesan cheese
⅔ cup Carnation Nonfat Dry Milk Powder
½ cup water
1 egg or equivalent in egg substitute
2 teaspoons vegetable oil
¾ cup (3 ounces) shredded Kraft reduced-fat Cheddar cheese

Preheat oven to 375 degrees. Spray a 9-inch deep-dish pie plate with olive oil–flavored cooking spray. In a large skillet sprayed with olive oil–flavored cooking spray, brown meat and onion. Stir in poultry seasoning, sage, garlic powder, corn, and tomato sauce. Lower heat and simmer for 5 minutes. Meanwhile, in a large bowl, combine flour, cornmeal, Sugar Twin, baking powder, and Parmesan cheese. In a small bowl, combine dry milk powder, water, egg, and vegetable oil. Add milk mixture to flour mixture. Mix well to combine. Spread mixture into prepared pie plate. Evenly spoon meat mixture over top. Bake for 20 minutes. Sprinkle Cheddar cheese evenly over top. Continue baking for 5 minutes or until cheese melts. Divide into 6 servings.

HINT: My choice of seasoning may seem strange, especially if you prepare this with beef. But I'm trying to give this dish an old-time sausage flavor with spices you have on hand.

Each serving equals:

HE: 2 Protein, 1⅓ Vegetable, 1 Bread, ⅓ Skim Milk, ⅓ Fat, 1 Optional Calorie

248 Calories, 8 gm Fat, 17 gm Protein, 27 gm Carbohydrate, 814 mg Sodium, 273 mg Calcium, 2 gm Fiber

DIABETIC: 2 Meat, 1 Vegetable, 1 Starch

Goulash Stew

■ ❋ ■

Traditional goulash is ladled over noodles and is one of those old-fashioned dishes that emigrated to the United States with all the people who came here from eastern Europe. I decided to mix the noodles into the dish itself and create an earthy, hearty stew I think you'll love.   *Serves 4 (1¼ cups)*

8 ounces ground 90% lean turkey or beef	1½ cups thinly sliced carrots
	1 cup thinly sliced celery
1¾ cups (one 14½-ounce can) Swanson Beef Broth	1¾ cups (3 ounces) uncooked noodles
½ cup chopped onion	1 teaspoon dried parsley flakes

In a large skillet sprayed with butter-flavored cooking spray, brown meat. Stir in beef broth. Add onion, carrots, and celery. Mix well to combine. Bring mixture to a boil. Stir in uncooked noodles and parsley flakes. Lower heat, cover, and simmer for 15 minutes. Uncover and continue simmering for 5 minutes or until vegetables and noodles are tender and most of liquid is absorbed, stirring occasionally.

Each serving equals:

HE: 1½ Protein, 1¼ Vegetable, 1 Bread, 8 Optional Calories

213 Calories, 5 gm Fat, 15 gm Protein, 27 gm Carbohydrate, 455 mg Sodium, 38 mg Calcium, 2 gm Fiber

DIABETIC: 1½ Meat, 1½ Vegetable, 1 Starch

Salisbury Pasta Skillet

■ ❄ ■

If the men in your house could eat Salisbury steak three times a week, this might just win their votes for favorite new recipe! It's an easy-to-fix, homey-tasting, man-pleasing meal in a pan—but it doesn't skimp on flavor.   *Serves 4 (1 cup)*

8 ounces ground 90% lean turkey or beef
½ cup chopped onion
1 (10¾-ounce) can Healthy Request Cream of Mushroom Soup
2 teaspoons Worcestershire sauce

¼ cup Heinz Light Harvest Ketchup or any reduced-sodium ketchup
1 teaspoon dried parsley flakes
2 cups hot cooked rotini pasta, rinsed and drained

In a large skillet sprayed with butter-flavored cooking spray, brown meat and onion. Stir in mushroom soup, ketchup, Worcestershire sauce, and parsley flakes. Add rotini pasta. Mix well to combine. Lower heat and simmer for 6 to 8 minutes or until mixture is heated through, stirring occasionally.

HINT: 1½ cups uncooked rotini pasta usually cooks to about 2 cups.

Each serving equals:
HE: 1½ Protein, 1 Bread, ¼ Vegetable, ½ Slider, 16 Optional Calories
247 Calories, 7 gm Fat, 14 gm Protein, 32 gm Carbohydrate, 386 mg Sodium, 66 mg Calcium, 2 gm Fiber
DIABETIC: 2 Starch/Carbohydrate, 1½ Meat

Popeye's Burritos

■ ❊ ■

I have no idea if Olive Oyl was much of a cook, or if Popeye ate at home very often, but this recipe would probably please them both for its ease of preparation and its spicy blend of meat, cheese, and spinach! If you don't often serve burritos, your first tries at folding them neatly may be a bit off the mark, but don't worry, you'll soon get the hang of it.   *Serves 6*

    8 ounces ground 90% lean turkey
      or beef
    1 (10-ounce) package frozen
      chopped spinach, thawed, and
      well drained
    1 cup chunky salsa (mild,
      medium, or hot)

    1 tablespoon chili seasoning
    ¾ cup (3 ounces) shredded Kraft
      reduced-fat Cheddar cheese
    6 (6-inch) flour tortillas,
      warmed

In a large skillet sprayed with olive oil–flavored cooking spray, brown meat. Stir in spinach. Continue cooking for 3 to 4 minutes or until any excess moisture in spinach is absorbed. Add salsa, chili seasoning, and Cheddar cheese. Mix well to combine. Lower heat and simmer for 5 minutes, stirring occasionally. For each serving, spoon a scant ½ cup meat mixture in center of a tortilla, fold bottom edge up over filling, and fold sides to center, overlapping edges. Serve at once.

HINTS: 1. Thaw spinach by placing in a colander and rinsing under hot water for one minute.
       2. Warm tortillas in microwave for about 30 seconds.

Each serving equals:
HE: 1⅓ Protein, 1 Bread, 1 Vegetable
191 Calories, 7 gm Fat, 14 gm Protein, 18 gm Carbohydrate, 491 mg Sodium, 209 mg Calcium, 1 gm Fiber
DIABETIC: 1½ Meat, 1 Starch, 1 Vegetable

Barbecued Loose-Meat Sandwiches

■ ■ ■

Iowa is famous for corn and cornfields, but another great idea launched from our fields of dreams is the much-loved loose-meat sandwich! I've heard it described as a sort of Sloppy Joe, but the seasonings are a little different. This version is tangy-sweet like your favorite barbecue sauce, but made easy and healthy all at once.

Serves 6

*16 ounces ground 90% lean
   turkey or beef*
½ cup chopped onion
½ cup chopped green bell pepper
*1 (10¾-ounce) can Healthy
   Request Tomato Soup*

1 teaspoon prepared mustard
1 tablespoon Brown Sugar Twin
1 teaspoon dried parsley flakes
*6 reduced-calorie hamburger
   buns*

In a large skillet sprayed with butter-flavored cooking spray, brown meat, onion, and green pepper. Stir in tomato soup, water, mustard, Brown Sugar Twin, and parsley flakes. Lower heat and simmer for 6 to 8 minutes, stirring occasionally. For each sandwich, spoon about ½ cup meat mixture between halves of a hamburger bun.

Each serving equals:
HE: 2 Protein, 1 Bread, ⅓ Vegetable, ¼ Slider, 11 Optional Calories
224 Calories, 8 gm Fat, 16 gm Protein, 22 gm Carbohydrate, 396 mg Sodium, 13 mg Calcium, 2 gm Fiber
DIABETIC: 2 Meat, 1½ Starch/Carbohydrate

Meat and Cabbage Pie

■ ✳ ■

This homemade double-crust dinner pie won Cliff's heart as it baked up brown and oh-so-fragrant, but the real proof was in the eating, as usual—and he made quick work of his piece the night we tested this one. Refrigerated piecrusts are one of those convenience foods that are truly worth having on hand.   *Serves 8*

1 Pillsbury refrigerated unbaked
   9-inch piecrust
8 ounces ground 90% lean turkey
   or beef
1 cup chopped onion
3 cups shredded cabbage

1 cup (one 8-ounce can) Hunt's
   Tomato Sauce
1 tablespoon Brown Sugar Twin
1 teaspoon dried parsley flakes
⅛ teaspoon black pepper

Preheat oven to 350 degrees. Let piecrust set at room temperature for 15 minutes. Meanwhile, in a large skillet sprayed with butter-flavored cooking spray, brown meat and onion. Stir in cabbage. Add tomato sauce, Brown Sugar Twin, parsley flakes, and black pepper. Lower heat and simmer for 10 minutes, stirring occasionally. Cut the room temperature piecrust in half on the folded line. Gently roll each half into a ball. Wipe counter with a wet cloth and place a sheet of waxed paper over damp spot. Place one of the balls on the waxed paper, cover with another sheet of waxed paper, and roll out with a rolling pin. Carefully remove waxed paper on one side and place into an 8-inch pie plate. Remove other piece of waxed paper. Evenly spoon meat mixture into piecrust. Repeat process of rolling out remaining piecrust half. Place on top of meat mixture. Flute edges. Make about 8 slashes with a knife to allow steam to escape. Bake for 30 to 40 minutes or until crust is golden brown. Place pie plate on a wire rack and let set for 5 minutes. Cut into 8 servings.

Each serving equals:
HE: 1½ Vegetable, ¾ Protein, ½ Bread, ½ Slider, 11 Optional Calories

181 Calories, 9 gm Fat, 7 gm Protein, 18 gm Carbohydrate, 317 mg Sodium, 22 mg Calcium, 1 gm Fiber

DIABETIC: 1 Vegetable, 1 Meat, 1 Starch, ½ Fat

"Sausage"-Stuffed Acorn Squash

■ ■ ■

I haven't offered very many recipes using squash, but this one just seemed like such a good idea, I had to share it! Lots of people who weren't raised eating squash tend to pass it by in the supermarket, either because it looks like too much work to prepare properly or they fear they might not like it. I hope you'll give this nourishing dish a chance! *Serves 4*

2 (medium-sized) acorn squash
¾ cup water ☆
8 ounces ground 90% lean turkey
or beef
½ cup finely chopped onion

½ teaspoon poultry seasoning
¼ teaspoon ground sage
¼ teaspoon garlic powder
½ cup (¾ ounce) unseasoned dry
bread cubes

Preheat oven to 400 degrees. Cut squash into halves and remove seeds. Place squash cut side down in an 8-by-12-inch baking pan. Pour ½ cup water into pan. Cover and bake for 15 minutes. Meanwhile, in a large skillet sprayed with butter-flavored cooking spray, brown meat and onion. Stir in poultry seasoning, sage, garlic powder, remaining ¼ cup water, and bread cubes. Mix well to combine. Reduce heat to 350 degrees. Remove squash halves from baking pan and rearrange cut side up on a baking sheet. Evenly spoon stuffing mixture into squash cavities. Continue baking for 15 minutes or until squash is tender.

HINT: Pepperidge Farm bread cubes work great.

Each serving equals:
HE: 1½ Protein, 1¼ Bread, ¼ Vegetable

241 Calories, 5 gm Fat, 13 gm Protein, 36 gm Carbohydrate, 126 mg Sodium, 97 mg Calcium, 10 gm Fiber

DIABETIC: 2 Starch, 1½ Meat

"Cabbage Rolls" Skillet

■ ❋ ■

Do you love stuffed cabbage but think that it's just too much trouble? Well, sometimes it certainly feels like it is! But why should you miss out on one of your favorite meals because time is short? This skillet supper delivers all the flavor you're fond of but all stirred up together instead of rolled.

Serves 4 (1 cup)

8 ounces ground 90% lean turkey
   or beef
½ cup chopped onion
2½ cups shredded cabbage
1¾ cups (one 15-ounce can)
   Hunt's Tomato Sauce

½ cup water
2 teaspoons prepared mustard
2 tablespoons Brown Sugar Twin
1 teaspoon dried parsley flakes
⅔ cup (2 ounces) uncooked
   Minute Rice

In a large skillet sprayed with butter-flavored cooking spray, brown meat and onion. Stir in cabbage. Continue cooking for 6 to 8 minutes, stirring occasionally. In a medium bowl, combine tomato sauce, water, mustard, Brown Sugar Twin, and parsley flakes. Stir sauce mixture into meat mixture. Mix well to combine. Bring mixture to a boil. Stir in rice. Lower heat, cover, and simmer for 5 minutes or until rice is tender, stirring occasionally.

Each serving equals:
HE: 3¼ Vegetable, 1½ Protein, ½ Bread, 2 Optional Calories
165 Calories, 5 gm Fat, 13 gm Protein, 17 gm Carbohydrate, 744 mg Sodium, 46 mg Calcium, 3 gm Fiber
DIABETIC: 2 Vegetable, 1½ Meat, 1 Starch

Tommy's Hamburger Milk Gravy Skillet

I'm planning (don't tell her, please!) to give my daughter-in-law Angie her own personal cookbooklet filled with all the hamburger milk gravy recipes I've come up with over the years. I want Tom and Angie to have a long and happy marriage, and if the way to a man's you-know-what is . . . Here's the latest in a long line of tasty stovetop meals that won his heart.   *Serves 4 (1 cup)*

*8 ounces ground 90% lean turkey
    or beef
3 cups (15 ounces) shredded
    loose-packed frozen potatoes
½ cup (one 2.5-ounce jar) sliced
    mushrooms, drained*

*3 tablespoons all-purpose flour
2 cups skim milk
1 teaspoon dried parsley flakes
⅛ teaspoon black pepper*

In a large skillet sprayed with butter-flavored cooking spray, brown meat and potatoes. Stir in mushrooms. In a covered jar, combine flour and skim milk. Shake well to blend. Pour milk mixture over meat mixture. Add parsley flakes and black pepper. Mix gently to combine. Continue cooking for 6 to 8 minutes or until mixture thickens, stirring occasionally.

Each serving equals:
HE: 1½ Protein, 1 Bread, ½ Skim Milk, ¼ Vegetable

234 Calories, 6 gm Fat, 16 gm Protein, 29 gm Carbohydrate, 200 mg Sodium, 156 mg Calcium, 3 gm Fiber

DIABETIC: 1½ Meat, 1½ Starch, ½ Skim Milk

Skillet Steak Dinner

■ ❄ ■

Do you live with anyone who says, "Just steak and potatoes, that's all I like"? Or are you a fan of steak who figured you had to give it up to eat healthier? This easy meal tastes like you worked hard to prepare it, but you and I know it couldn't be simpler to make. (Let's keep it our secret, okay?) *Serves 4*

4 (4 ounce) lean minute or cube
   beef steaks
1 cup chopped onion
3 cups frozen French-cut green
   beans
½ cup (one 2.5-ounce jar) whole
   mushrooms, undrained

1 (10¾-ounce) can Healthy
   Request Cream of Mushroom
   Soup
¼ cup skim milk
⅛ teaspoon black pepper

In a large skillet sprayed with butter-flavored cooking spray, brown meat. Stir in onion, frozen green beans, and undrained mushrooms. In a medium bowl, combine mushroom soup, skim milk, and black pepper. Add soup mixture to meat mixture. Mix well to combine. Lower heat, cover, and simmer for 30 minutes or until meat and vegetables are tender, stirring occasionally. Divide into 4 servings.

Each serving equals:

HE: 3 Protein, 2¼ Vegetable, ½ Slider, 7 Optional Calories

244 Calories, 8 gm Fat, 27 gm Protein, 16 gm Carbohydrate, 449 mg Sodium, 110 mg Calcium, 3 gm Fiber

DIABETIC: 3 Meat, 2 Vegetable, ½ Starch/Carbohydrate

Stuffed Beef Rounds

■ ❄ ■

Here's a dish that looks just a bit fancy and would be a terrific choice for your next dinner party. The gravy tastes really rich, even if it did start life as beef broth with veggies and spices. Amazing what you can do with a bit of flour and liquid in a jar, isn't it?

Serves 4

3 tablespoons (¾ ounce) dried
    fine bread crumbs
¼ cup finely chopped onion
¼ cup finely chopped celery
4 (4 ounce) lean minute or cube
    beef steaks

6 tablespoons all-purpose flour ☆
1¾ cups (one 14½-ounce can)
    Swanson Beef Broth ☆
1 teaspoon dried parsley flakes
1 teaspoon prepared mustard

In a large bowl, combine bread crumbs, onion, and celery. Evenly spoon crumb mixture over steaks. Roll up each steak, jelly roll–fashion, and secure with toothpick or tie with string. Place 3 tablespoons flour in a saucer. Roll steaks in flour to coat. Pour 2 tablespoons beef broth into a large skillet. Arrange steaks in same skillet. Cook over medium heat until meat is browned, turning often. In a covered jar, combine remaining beef broth, remaining 3 tablespoons flour, parsley flakes, and mustard. Shake well to blend. Pour broth mixture evenly over meat. Lower heat, cover, and simmer for 20 minutes or until meat is cooked through, stirring occasionally. For each serving, place beef round on a plate and evenly spoon sauce over top.

Each serving equals:
HE: 3 Protein, ¾ Bread, ¼ Vegetable, 9 Optional Calories
227 Calories, 7 gm Fat, 27 gm Protein, 14 gm Carbohydrate, 478 mg Sodium, 24 mg Calcium, 1 gm Fiber 5
DIABETIC: 3 Meat, 1 Starch

Swiss Steak Stew Skillet

■ ❋ ■

There's an expression in music, where a composer creates "variations on a theme," and that's what I had in mind when I stirred up this fresh approach to that much-loved classic dish, Swiss steak. I took the basic flavor but I found a new way to present it—and that's one of the ways we keep from being bored or getting into a healthy food rut.

Serves 4 (1½ cups)

16 ounces lean round steak, cut
    into 24 pieces
2 cups (one 16-ounce can) toma-
    toes, coarsely chopped, and
    undrained
1 (10¾-ounce) can Healthy
    Request Tomato Soup

2 teaspoons dried parsley flakes
⅛ teaspoon black pepper
½ cup chopped onion
1 cup sliced celery
2 cups (10 ounces) diced raw
    potatoes

In a large skillet sprayed with butter-flavored cooking spray, brown meat. Stir in undrained tomatoes, tomato soup, parsley flakes, and black pepper. Add onion, celery, and potatoes. Mix well to combine. Lower heat, cover, and simmer for 30 minutes, or until meat and vegetables are tender, stirring occasionally.

Each serving equals:
HE: 3 Protein, 1¾ Vegetable, ½ Bread, ½ Slider, 5 Optional Calories
275 Calories, 7 gm Fat, 28 gm Protein, 25 gm Carbohydrate, 324 mg Sodium, 41 mg Calcium, 3 gm Fiber
DIABETIC: 3 Meat, 1½ Starch, 1 Vegetable

Pork Via Veneto Skillet

■ ❋ ■

In Beverly Hills, it's Rodeo Drive that makes hearts beat faster, and in Rome, it's definitely the Via Veneto, where the elite go shopping and enjoy all kinds of culinary pleasures! This lean pork dish is a lively way to serve this much-loved meat to your family as part of a healthy lifestyle.   *Serves 4 (1 full cup)*

8 ounces lean pork tenderloin,
   cut into 16 pieces
½ cup chopped onion
½ cup chopped green bell pepper
1 (10¾-ounce) can Healthy
   Request Tomato Soup
¼ cup water

1 teaspoon prepared mustard
⅛ teaspoon black pepper
¾ cup (3 ounces) shredded Kraft
   reduced-fat Cheddar cheese
2 cups hot cooked elbow macaroni, rinsed and drained

In a large skillet sprayed with butter-flavored cooking spray, brown meat, onion, and green pepper. Stir in tomato soup, water, mustard, and black pepper. Add Cheddar cheese and macaroni. Mix well to combine. Lower heat, cover, and simmer for 10 minutes, stirring occasionally.

HINTS: 1. Do not overcook meat as it will become tough.
            2. 1⅓ cups uncooked elbow macaroni usually cooks to about 2 cups.

Each serving equals:
HE: 2½ Protein, 1 Bread, ½ Vegetable, ½ Slider, 5 Optional Calories
288 Calories, 8 gm Fat, 22 gm Protein, 32 gm Carbohydrate, 463 mg Sodium, 171 mg Calcium, 2 gm Fiber
DIABETIC: 2½ Meat, 1½ Starch/Carbohydrate, ½ Vegetable

Rio Bravo Pork Tenders

■ ❄ ■

No, I didn't have John Wayne in mind when I was creating this hearty dish, but I'm inclined to think the great tough-guy movie star would have devoured it with gusto! It's definitely a candidate for my Man-Pleasers Hall of Fame, don't you agree?

Serves 4

3 tablespoons all-purpose flour
2 teaspoons chili seasoning ☆
1 teaspoon dried parsley flakes
4 (4-ounce) lean tenderized pork
   tenderloins
1 cup chopped onion
½ cup chopped green bell pepper

1 (10¾-ounce) can Healthy
   Request Tomato Soup
½ cup (one 2.5-ounce jar) sliced
   mushrooms, undrained
½ cup Land O Lakes no-fat sour
   cream

In a shallow saucer, combine flour, 1 teaspoon chili seasoning, and parsley flakes. Coat tenderloins in flour mixture. Place tenderloins in a large skillet sprayed with olive oil–flavored cooking spray. Brown tenderloins for 3 to 4 minutes on each side. Sprinkle onion and green pepper evenly over meat. In a medium bowl, combine tomato soup, undrained mushrooms, sour cream, remaining 1 teaspoon chili seasoning, and any remaining flour mixture. Evenly spoon soup mixture over meat. Lower heat, cover, and simmer for 20 minutes or until tenderloins are tender. When serving, spoon sauce evenly over meat.

Each serving equals:
HE: 3 Protein, 1 Vegetable, ¼ Bread, ¾ Slider, 15 Optional Calories
275 Calories, 7 gm Fat, 29 gm Protein, 24 gm Carbohydrate, 430 mg Sodium, 78 mg Calcium, 2 gm Fiber
DIABETIC: 3 Meat, 1 Vegetable, 1 Starch/Carbohydrate

Pork Loin Potato Dish

■ ❋ ■

Here's another recipe designed for the meat-and-potato lovers among us, as nutritious as it is scrumptious! You'll love what the lemon pepper does for this Lund family favorite!

Serves 4

4 (4 ounce) lean pork cutlets or
   tenderloins
1 (10¾-ounce) can Healthy
   Request Cream of Mushroom
   Soup
⅓ cup Carnation Nonfat Dry
   Milk Powder

¼ cup water
½ teaspoon lemon pepper
3 cups frozen cut green beans,
   thawed
3 cups (10 ounces) shredded
   loose-packed frozen potatoes

Preheat oven to 350 degrees. Spray an 8-by-8-inch baking dish with butter-flavored cooking spray. In a large skillet sprayed with butter-flavored cooking spray, brown meat for 2 to 3 minutes on each side. Meanwhile, in a large bowl, combine mushroom soup, dry milk powder, water, and lemon pepper. Stir in green beans and potatoes. Spoon mixture into prepared baking dish. Arrange browned meat over top. Cover with foil. Bake for 30 minutes. Uncover and continue baking for 20 to 30 minutes. Place baking dish on a wire rack and let set for 5 minutes. Divide into 4 servings.

HINT: Thaw green beans by placing in a colander and rinsing under hot water for one minute.

Each serving equals:
HE: 3 Protein, 1½ Vegetable, ¾ Bread, ¼ Skim Milk, ½ Slider, 1 Optional Calorie

296 Calories, 8 gm Fat, 30 gm Protein, 26 gm Carbohydrate, 407 mg Sodium, 169 mg Calcium, 3 gm Fiber

DIABETIC: 3 Meat, 1½ Vegetable, 1½ Starch/Carbohydrate

Oktoberfest Pork Tenders

■ ■ ■

This skillet dish will turn your kitchen into the most popular room in the house while this dish is simmering away. Somehow, the combination of apple juice and mustard becomes a kind of aphrodisiac as it cooks with the pork and onion. This is a great supper to serve when you're hoping for some weekend help in the yard!   *Serves 4*

4 (4-ounce) lean tenderized pork
   tenderloins
2½ cups sliced onion
1 cup unsweetened apple juice

2 tablespoons Dijon Country
   Style Mustard
1 teaspoon dried parsley flakes

In a large skillet sprayed with butter-flavored cooking spray, brown meat for 3 to 4 minutes on each side. Evenly layer onion over meat. In a small bowl, combine apple juice, mustard, and parsley flakes. Pour mixture evenly over top. Lower heat, cover, and simmer for 30 minutes. Uncover and continue simmering until most of liquid is absorbed. When serving, place 1 piece of meat on a plate and evenly divide onion mixture over top.

Each serving equals:

HE: 3 Protein, 1¼ Vegetable, ½ Fruit

230 Calories, 6 gm Fat, 27 gm Protein, 17 gm Carbohydrate, 260 mg Sodium, 50 mg Calcium, 2 gm Fiber

DIABETIC: 3 Meat, 1 Vegetable, 1 Fruit

German Pork Stroganoff

■ ■ ■

Sauerkraut lovers, unite! I want you to know that you're among friends here, and that I sympathize with your passion for this particular taste treat. Why else would I keep coming up with recipes that transform traditional dishes into something rather remarkable, all flavored with a hint of caraway seed?

Serves 4

¾ cup finely chopped onion
1½ cups (8 ounces) diced lean
    cooked roast pork
1¾ cups (one 14½-ounce can)
    Frank's Bavarian-style sauer-
    kraut, drained

½ cup Land O Lakes no-fat sour
    cream
2 cups hot cooked noodles,
    rinsed and drained

In a large skillet sprayed with butter-flavored cooking spray, sauté onion for 5 minutes or until tender. Stir in roast pork and sauerkraut. Lower heat and simmer for 10 minutes, stirring occasionally. Add sour cream. Mix well to combine. Continue simmering for 2 to 3 minutes or until mixture is heated through. For each serving, place ½ cup noodles on a plate and spoon ¾ cup pork mixture over noodles.

HINTS: 1. If you don't have leftovers, purchase a chunk of lean cooked roast pork from your local deli.
2. If you can't find Bavarian sauerkraut, use regular sauerkraut, ½ teaspoon caraway seeds, and 1 teaspoon Brown Sugar Twin.
3. 1¾ cups uncooked noodles usually cooks to about 2 cups.

Each serving equals:
HE: 2 Protein, 1¼ Vegetable, 1 Bread, ¼ Slider, 10 Optional Calories
275 Calories, 7 gm Fat, 22 gm Protein, 31 gm Carbohydrate, 761 mg Sodium, 87 mg Calcium, 4 gm Fiber
DIABETIC: 2 Meat, 1½ Starch, 1 Vegetable

Creamy Ham and Vegetables over Toast

■ ■ ■

This cozy skillet dish demonstrates one of my favorite bits of culinary magic—the power of a little evaporated skim milk and flour to thicken into the most luscious sauce you can imagine! This recipe appeals to young children as well as kids of all ages, and is comfort food with a capital "C" for creamy! *Serves 4*

¼ cup water
1½ cups frozen cut green beans,
* thawed*
1½ cups frozen cut carrots,
* thawed*
1½ cups (one 12-fluid-ounce can)
* Carnation Evaporated Skim*
* Milk*

3 tablespoons all-purpose flour
1 full cup (6 ounces) diced
* Dubuque 97% fat-free ham or*
* any extra-lean ham*
2 teaspoons prepared mustard
⅛ teaspoon black pepper
4 slices reduced-calorie bread,
* toasted*

In a medium saucepan, combine water, green beans, and carrots. Bring mixture to a boil. Cover and cook over medium heat for 4 to 5 minutes, or until vegetables are tender, stirring occasionally. In a covered jar, combine evaporated skim milk and flour. Shake well to blend. Pour milk mixture into saucepan with vegetables. Continue cooking until mixture starts to thicken, stirring constantly. Add ham, mustard, and black pepper. Lower heat and simmer for 10 minutes, or until mixture is heated through, stirring occasionally. For each serving, place 1 slice of toast on a plate and spoon a full ¾ cup ham mixture over top.

HINT: Thaw vegetables by placing in a colander and rinsing under hot water for one minute.

Each serving equals:
HE: 1½ Vegetable, 1 Protein, ¾ Skim Milk, ¾ Bread
210 Calories, 2 gm Fat, 18 gm Protein, 30 gm Carbohydrate, 642 mg Sodium, 326 mg Calcium, 4 gm Fiber
DIABETIC: 1½ Vegetable, 1 Meat, 1 Skim Milk, 1 Starch

Layered Green Bean and Ham Casserole

■ ❋ ■

I remember the children's author Dr. Seuss writing about how "Sam I Am" didn't care for green eggs and ham, but maybe we could convince him to try green *beans* and ham instead! The layers in this dish huddle together in a display of deliciousness that is hard to beat. Like Dr. Seuss, I'll rhyme and add that this is truly "good to eat!"

Serves 6

2 cups hot cooked rice

2 cups (one 16-ounce can) French-style green beans, rinsed and drained

1½ cups (9 ounces) diced Dubuque 97% fat-free ham or any extra-lean ham

1 (10¾-ounce) can Healthy Request Cream of Mushroom Soup

¼ cup skim milk

¼ cup (one 2-ounce jar) chopped pimiento, drained

¾ cup (3 ounces) shredded Kraft reduced-fat Cheddar cheese

6 tablespoons (1½ ounces) dried fine bread crumbs

Preheat oven to 350 degrees. Spray an 8-by-8-inch baking dish with butter-flavored cooking spray. Spread rice into prepared baking dish. Layer green beans and ham over rice. In a small bowl, combine mushroom soup, skim milk, pimiento, and Cheddar cheese. Spread soup mixture evenly over ham. Sprinkle bread crumbs evenly over top. Lightly spray crumbs with butter-flavored cooking spray. Bake for 30 minutes. Place baking dish on a wire rack and let set for 5 minutes. Divide into 6 servings.

HINT: 1⅓ cups uncooked rice usually cooks to about 2 cups.

Each serving equals:

HE: 1⅔ Protein, 1 Bread, ⅔ Vegetable, ¼ Slider, 11 Optional Calories

201 Calories, 5 gm Fat, 14 gm Protein, 25 gm Carbohydrate, 742 mg Sodium, 170 mg Calcium, 1 gm Fiber

DIABETIC: 1½ Meat, 1½ Starch, 1 Vegetable

Ham and Potato Hot Dish

■ ❄ ■

If you're the chief cook and bottle washer in your house, I know you'll smile when you spot this tasty recipe for a microwave meal that "dirties" only a single bowl! Not only that, of course, but it brings together so many yummy ingredients in a pretty mélange!

Serves 4 (1¼ cups)

> 1½ cups (9 ounces) finely diced
>   Dubuque 97% fat-free ham or
>   any extra-lean ham
> 3 cups (15 ounces) diced raw
>   potatoes

> 1 cup sliced carrots
> ¾ cup chopped onion
> 1¾ cups (one 14½-ounce can)
>   stewed tomatoes, undrained

In an 8-cup glass measuring bowl, combine ham, potatoes, carrots, onion, and undrained stewed tomatoes. Cover and microwave on HIGH (100% power) for 12 to 15 minutes or until potatoes and carrots are tender, stirring after every 5 minutes. Let set for 2 to 3 minutes. Gently stir again just before serving.

Each serving equals:

HE: 1¾ Vegetable, 1½ Protein, ¾ Bread

178 Calories, 2 gm Fat, 13 gm Protein, 27 gm Carbohydrate, 871 mg Sodium, 76 mg Calcium, 3 gm Fiber

DIABETIC: 2 Vegetable, 1½ Meat, 1 Starch

Ham and Maple Syrup–Stuffed Sweet Potatoes

■ ■ ■

Ever notice how some recipe titles are so irresistible, you almost don't need to prepare them to feel satisfied? This one might make you feel that way, but please, PLEASE, don't stop at reading it—you've got to taste it and learn how right you are! Sweet potatoes are often forgotten except at holiday time, but maybe this dish will bring them around more often.

Serves 4

2 (6-ounce) unpeeled sweet pota-toes

¼ cup Cary's Sugar Free Maple Syrup

1 full cup (6 ounces) finely diced Dubuque 97% fat-free ham or any extra-lean ham

2 tablespoons (½ ounce) chopped pecans

Preheat oven to 375 degrees. Place sweet potatoes in an 8-by-8-inch baking dish. Bake for 45 to 50 minutes or until potatoes are tender. Cut potatoes in half lengthwise and scoop out pulp, leaving ¼-inch shells. Place pulp in a medium bowl and mash well using a potato masher or a fork. Stir in maple syrup. Add ham and pecans. Mix well to combine. Evenly spoon mixture into potato shells. Return potato halves to baking dish and continue baking for 15 minutes or until potatoes are heated through. Serve at once.

Each serving equals:
HE: 1 Bread, 1 Protein, ½ Fat, 10 Optional Calories

160 Calories, 4 gm Fat, 8 gm Protein, 23 gm Carbohydrate, 458 mg Sodium, 27 mg Calcium, 1 gm Fiber

DIABETIC: 1 Starch, 1 Meat, ½ Fat

Baked Ham and Pineapple Loaf

■ ❋ ■

Close your eyes and envision a classic holiday ham, studded with slices of pineapple—*mm-mm*, doesn't it look and smell great? This handy recipe will surprise you with its sweet and tangy richness of taste.   *Serves 6*

2 cups (12 ounces) ground Dubuque 97% fat-free ham or any extra-lean ham
1 cup (one 8-ounce can) crushed pineapple, packed in fruit juice, undrained

½ cup + 1 tablespoon purchased graham cracker crumbs or 9 (2½-inch) graham cracker squares, made into crumbs
1 teaspoon dried onion flakes
1 teaspoon dried parsley flakes

Preheat oven to 350 degrees. Spray an 8-by-8-inch baking dish with butter-flavored cooking spray. In a large bowl, combine ham, undrained pineapple, graham cracker crumbs, onion flakes, and parsley flakes. Mix well to combine. Pat mixture into prepared baking dish. Bake for 45 minutes. Place baking dish on a wire rack and let set for 5 minutes. Cut into 6 servings.

HINTS: 1. Purchase ground ham, if you don't have a grinder.
2. A self-seal sandwich bag works great for crushing graham crackers.

Each serving equals:
HE: 1⅓ Protein, ½ Bread, ⅓ Fruit

131 Calories, 3 gm Fat, 10 gm Protein, 16 gm Carbohydrate, 549 mg Sodium, 10 mg Calcium, 1 gm Fiber

DIABETIC: 1½ Meat, 1 Starch/Carbohydrate

Frankfurter and Sauerkraut Pizza

■ ❄ ■

Gourmet pizza places are sprouting up everywhere across the nation, and each restaurant seems to pride itself on unique combinations of toppings. This German version is so full of great flavor, I wouldn't be surprised if you decided to open up a sidewalk stand and sell it to the neighborhood kids. You're bound to do well!

Serves 8

1 (11-ounce) can Pillsbury refrigerated French loaf
16 ounces Healthy Choice 97%
   fat-free frankfurters, diced
½ cup chopped onion
2 cups (one 16-ounce can) sauerkraut, well drained
1¾ cups (one 15-ounce can)
   Hunt's Tomato Sauce

¼ cup (¾ ounce) grated Kraft
   fat-free Parmesan cheese
1 teaspoon all-purpose meat seasoning
1½ cups (6 ounces) shredded
   Kraft reduced-fat Cheddar
   cheese

Preheat oven to 425 degrees. Unroll French loaf. Pat into jelly-roll pan and up sides of pan to form a rim. Bake for 5 minutes. Meanwhile, in a large skillet sprayed with butter-flavored cooking spray, sauté frankfurters and onion for 5 minutes. Stir in sauerkraut. In a medium bowl, combine tomato sauce, Parmesan cheese, and meat seasoning. Spread sauce mixture evenly over partially baked crust. Evenly sprinkle frankfurter mixture over sauce. Sprinkle Cheddar cheese evenly over top. Continue baking for 15 minutes or until cheese melts and crust is browned. Place pan on a wire rack and let set for 5 minutes. Cut into 8 servings.

Each serving equals:
HE: 2½ Protein, 1½ Vegetable, 1 Bread

246 Calories, 6 gm Fat, 18 gm Protein, 30 gm Carbohydrate, 1778 mg Sodium, 160 mg Calcium, 3 gm Fiber

DIABETIC: 2½ Meat, 1½ Vegetable, 1½ Starch

Corned Beef Toasties

■ ■ ■

What a cozy-warm idea for a brisk afternoon—a luscious combo of cheese and corned beef baked up in a soft bun! This is my idea of a perfect topping sauce, but feel free to play around with it a bit if you favor more pickle relish or less mayo. Enjoy!

Serves 4

1 (2.5-ounce) package Carl Buddig 90% lean corned beef, shredded
½ cup chopped onion
⅓ cup (1½ ounces) shredded Kraft reduced-fat Cheddar cheese

½ cup Kraft fat-free mayonnaise
2 teaspoons prepared mustard
1 tablespoon sweet pickle relish
1 teaspoon dried parsley flakes
4 reduced-calorie hamburger buns

Preheat oven to 425 degrees. In a medium bowl, combine corned beef, onion, and Cheddar cheese. Add mayonnaise, mustard, pickle relish, and parsley flakes. Mix well to combine. Place hamburger bun bottoms on 4 pieces of aluminum foil. Spread about ¼ cup meat mixture over each bun bottom. Arrange top part of bun over meat mixture. Wrap each in foil. Bake for 12 to 15 minutes. Serve warm.

Each serving equals:
HE: 1 Bread, 1 Protein, ¼ Vegetable, ¼ Slider, 1 Optional Calorie
152 Calories, 4 gm Fat, 9 gm Protein, 20 gm Carbohydrate, 677 mg Sodium, 81 mg Calcium, 2 gm Fiber
DIABETIC: 1 Starch, 1 Meat

Potato Reuben Casserole

■ ❋ ■

Just reading the list of ingredients in this recipe might make your mouth water and your eyes sparkle, let me warn you now! This dish is part sweet, part savory, and all hearty. It's a great way to celebrate the flavors of one of America's favorite deli sandwiches in an outrageously easy home-baked casserole you can feast on anytime you like.   *Serves 4*

1¾ cups hot water

1⅓ cups (3 ounces) instant
    potato flakes

1 teaspoon dried parsley flakes

⅓ cup Carnation Nonfat Dry
    Milk Powder

1¾ cups (one 14½-ounce can)
    Frank's Bavarian-style sauer-
    kraut, well drained

¼ cup finely chopped onion

1 cup (2 small) peeled and diced
    cooking apples

2 (2.5-ounce) packages Carl
    Buddig 90% lean corned beef,
    shredded

3 (¾-ounce) slices Kraft reduced-
    fat Swiss cheese, shredded

Preheat oven to 350 degrees. Spray an 8-by-8-inch baking dish with butter-flavored cooking spray. In a large saucepan, bring water to a boil. Remove from heat. Add potato flakes, parsley flakes, and dry milk powder. Mix gently to combine. Stir in sauerkraut, onion, and apples. Spread half of mixture into prepared baking dish. Evenly arrange corned beef and Swiss cheese over potato mixture. Spread remaining potato mixture over top. Bake for 25 to 30 minutes. Place baking dish on a wire rack and let set for 5 minutes. Cut into 4 servings.

HINT: If you can't find Bavarian sauerkraut, use regular sauerkraut, ½ teaspoon caraway seeds, and 1 teaspoon Brown Sugar Twin.

Each serving equals:
HE: 2 Protein, 1 Bread, 1 Vegetable, ½ Fruit, ¼ Skim Milk

219 Calories, 7 gm Fat, 14 gm Protein, 25 gm Carbohydrate, 1451 mg Sodium, 109 mg Calcium, 4 gm Fiber

DIABETIC: 2 Meat, 1 Starch, 1 Vegetable, ½ Fruit

DESSERTS DESIGNED WITH LOVE

■ ■ ■

If your goal is to make the dreamiest desserts around, make sure you stir in the love along with the rest of the ingredients! I admit it, I am one of those millions of people who show their love with food. Of course, I do it with my tastiest, healthiest versions of family favorites!

Here's something I've learned over the years of creating more dessert recipes than I ever thought possible: When you think about the people who are going to eat and enjoy what you're preparing, it makes the process extra-special. I've never made a peach pie or cobbler without thoughts of my daughter, Becky, warming my soul. And each time the can opener whirrs on a can of crushed pineapple, I can almost feel the sweetness of little Zachie's kisses for Grandma.

I'm proud to share my love through food prepared in a particularly healthy way. But just because I made a healthy pie for someone I love doesn't mean I'm *pushing my healthy way of life down anyone's throat along with the cream pie. I also don't do "plate patrol" or watch what everyone eats with an eagle eye. But I do like considering family members' or employees' favorite flavors before creating a dish I want them to enjoy. Picture your loved ones, imagine their pleasure in every bite, then stir the dish up just for them!*

Winning "converts" to this happy style of healthy eating is usually easiest when there's pie on the plate! Or perhaps pudding, or maybe cake, or sundaes, or cheesecake . . . There are enough dessert-dreams-come-true in this section to dazzle everyone in your life, no matter what their favorite tastes might be. Tempt them with *Hawaiian Heavenly Hash,* or capture their hearts with *Orange Marmalade Cheesecake with Blueberry Glaze,* or just make a beloved niece or nephew grin when you serve *German Chocolate Crazy Cake.* Surprise 'em with shortcakes (*Summer Breezes Cream-Filled Shortcakes*), please them with pie (*Pineapple Meringue Pie*), when you delight them daily with DESSERT!

> *"You will show me the path of life;*
> *In your presence is fullness of joy,*
> *At your right hand are pleasures forevermore."*
>
> —PSALM 16:11

Fluffy Raspberry Whip

Blueberry Pineapple Rice Pudding

Strawberries in Pineapple Clouds

Hawaiian Heavenly Hash

Pumpkin-Raisin Custards

Banana Chocolate Crunch Pudding

Chocolate Peanut Butter Pudding

Chocolate and Peanut Butter Layered Dessert

Maximum Chocolate Power Dessert

Turtle Dessert

Heavenly Chocolate and Raspberry Dream Dessert

Baked Apple and Graham Cracker Pudding

Maple-Raisin Sour Cream Tarts

Orange Marmalade Chocolate Cream Pie

Chocolate Fruit Cordial Rocky Road Pie

Banana Peanut Butter Dream Pie

Heavenly Chocolate-Coconut Pie

Banana Fruit Pie

Blueberry Pineapple Layered Pie

Pear and Raspberry Crumb Pie

Ice Cream Mince Pie

Layered Cherry Almond Pie

Perfect Apple Pie

Pineapple Meringue Pie

Cranberry-Walnut Glazed
Cheesecake

White Chocolate–Covered Cherry
Cheesecake

Orange Marmalade Cheesecake
with Blueberry Glaze

Strawberry Banana Pizza Dessert

Coconut Lemon Layer Cream
Cheese Pie

Sour Cream Cakes with Raisin
Cream Topping

Black Forest Cake Roll

Chocolate Brownie Cake with
Raspberry Glaze and White
Chocolate Topping

German Chocolate Crazy Cake

S'More Snack Cake

Applesauce Bars with Crunch
Topping

Pineapple Sheet Bars

Lemon Squares

Apple Dessert Enchiladas

Fruit Cocktail Cobbler

Summer Breezes Cream Filled
Shortcakes

Chocolate Mandarin Orange
Decadence

Bundles of Heaven

Applesauce à la Mode

Peach Melba Sundaes

Fluffy Raspberry Whip

■ ■ ■

Pudding is always wonderful, and custard makes your heart beat faster. But wait till you tempt your tastebuds with a Midwestern favorite, a "whip"! Add the freshest, juiciest fruit you can find, and you've got a dessert that's lighter than air, yet sweet enough to please the most ravenous appetite.   *Serves 4*

1 (4-serving) package JELL-O sugar-free raspberry gelatin
1 cup boiling water
¾ cup cold water

¾ cup Yoplait plain fat-free yogurt
1½ cups fresh raspberries ☆
¼ cup Cool Whip Lite

In a medium bowl, combine dry gelatin and boiling water. Mix well to dissolve gelatin. Stir in cold water. Refrigerate for 45 minutes or until gelatin mixture begins to set. Whip with an electric mixer on HIGH until light and fluffy. Fold in yogurt. Reserve 4 raspberries. Add remaining raspberries to gelatin mixture. Mix gently to combine. Evenly spoon mixture into 4 parfait dishes. Refrigerate for at least 2 hours. When serving, top each with 1 tablespoon Cool Whip Lite and garnish with a reserved raspberry.

Each serving equals:
HE: ½ Fruit, ¼ Skim Milk, ¼ Slider
65 Calories, 1 gm Fat, 4 gm Protein, 10 gm Carbohydrate, 86 mg Sodium, 95 mg Calcium, 2 gm Fiber
DIABETIC: 1 Fruit or 1 Starch/Carbohydrate

Blueberry Pineapple Rice Pudding

■ ■ ■

There's a simply delectable contrast in flavor and texture between the cool, creamy rice pudding and the crisp, fresh blueberries in this old-fashioned dish. So many people in our rush-rush age gobble down their meals, including dessert, but here is a pudding treat that invites you to take your time and enjoy every mouthful.

Serves 4

1 (4-serving) package JELL-O sugar-free vanilla cook-and-serve pudding mix
⅔ cup Carnation Nonfat Dry Milk Powder
1 cup (one 8-ounce can) crushed pineapple, packed in fruit juice, drained, and ½ cup liquid reserved

1½ cups water
1 teaspoon vanilla extract
¼ teaspoon ground nutmeg
1⅓ cups (4 ounces) uncooked Minute Rice
¾ cup fresh blueberries
¼ cup Cool Whip Lite

In a large saucepan, combine dry pudding mix and dry milk powder. Add reserved pineapple liquid and water. Mix well to combine. Cook over medium heat until mixture thickens and starts to boil, stirring constantly. Remove from heat. Stir in vanilla extract, nutmeg, uncooked rice, and pineapple. Cover and let set for 5 minutes. Gently fold in blueberries. Evenly spoon mixture into 4 dessert dishes. Refrigerate for at least 1 hour. When serving, top each with 1 tablespoon Cool Whip Lite.

Each serving equals:
HE: 1 Bread, ¾ Fruit, ½ Skim Milk, ¼ Slider, 8 Optional Calories

185 Calories, 1 gm Fat, 6 gm Protein, 38 gm Carbohydrate, 395 mg Sodium, 153 mg Calcium, 2 gm Fiber

DIABETIC: 1 Starch, 1 Fruit, ½ Skim Milk

Strawberries in Pineapple Clouds

■ ■ ■

Does your heart speed up like mine does when you spot those first ruby red gems each spring? I'm a confessed strawberry fanatic, and let me warn you, it's contagious! I often enjoy a bowl of sliced strawberries all by themselves, but I thought this would be a pretty way to serve my favorite fruit.   *Serves 6*

4 cups fresh strawberries ☆
*¾ cup Yoplait plain fat-free
   yogurt*
*⅓ cup Carnation Nonfat Dry
   Milk Powder*
*Sugar substitute to equal ¼ cup
   sugar*

1 teaspoon coconut extract
½ cup Cool Whip Free
*1 cup (one 8-ounce can) crushed
   pineapple, packed in fruit
   juice, well drained*
1 tablespoon flaked coconut

Reserve 6 whole strawberries. Slice remaining strawberries and evenly divide among 6 dessert dishes. In a medium bowl, combine yogurt and dry milk powder. Add sugar substitute and coconut extract. Mix gently to combine. Fold in Cool Whip Free and pineapple. Spoon about ⅓ cup pineapple mixture over each dish of strawberries. Evenly sprinkle ½ teaspoon coconut over top of each. Serve immediately or refrigerate until ready to serve.

Each serving equals:
HE: 1 Fruit, ⅓ Skim Milk, 17 Optional Calories
96 Calories, 0 gm Fat, 4 gm Protein, 20 gm Carbohydrate, 49 mg Sodium, 122 mg Calcium, 2 gm Fiber
DIABETIC: 1 Fruit, ½ Starch/Carbohydrate

Hawaiian Heavenly Hash

The angel sitting on my shoulder while I was creating this dessert kept encouraging me to add more goodies, and so the gorgeous end result is true ambrosia! Kids of all ages (and yes, my husband and yours) just love the treasure hunt of finding all those tasty bits amid the rice.

Serves 8

2 cups cold cooked rice	*¼ cup Land O Lakes no-fat sour*
1 cup (one 8-ounce can) crushed	*cream*
pineapple, packed in fruit	*¾ cup (1½ ounces) miniature*
juice, drained	*marshmallows*
¼ cup (1 ounce) chopped pecans	*6 maraschino cherries, quartered*
1 cup Cool Whip Free	*2 tablespoons flaked coconut*
1 teaspoon coconut extract	

In a large bowl, combine rice, pineapple, and pecans. Add Cool Whip Free, sour cream, and coconut extract. Mix gently to combine. Fold in marshmallows and cherry pieces. Evenly spoon mixture into 8 dessert dishes. Sprinkle ¾ teaspoon coconut over top of each. Refrigerate for at least 30 minutes.

HINT: 1⅓ cups uncooked rice usually cooks to about 2 cups.

Each serving equals:
HE: ½ Bread, ½ Fat, ¼ Fruit, ½ Slider, 3 Optional Calories
126 Calories, 2 gm Fat, 2 gm Protein, 25 gm Carbohydrate, 22 mg Sodium,
17 mg Calcium, 1 gm Fiber
DIABETIC: 1 Starch/Carbohydrate, ½ Fat

Pumpkin-Raisin Custards

■ ❋ ■

Canned pumpkin is a great staple to keep on your pantry shelf all year long, not just at holiday time. Whether you're creating a moist, fragrant pumpkin bread, or a luscious custard like this one, its unique flavor and texture will soothe and delight.

Serves 6

1 (4-serving) package JELL-O sugar-free vanilla cook-and-serve pudding mix
2 tablespoons Brown Sugar Twin
1½ cups (one 12-fluid-ounce can) Carnation Evaporated Skim Milk

2 cups (one 15-ounce can) pumpkin
1½ teaspoons pumpkin pie spice
½ cup raisins
6 tablespoons Cool Whip Lite

In a large saucepan, combine dry pudding mix, Brown Sugar Twin, and evaporated skim milk. Stir in pumpkin and pumpkin pie spice. Add raisins. Mix well to combine. Cook over medium heat until mixture thickens and starts to boil, stirring often. Evenly spoon mixture into 6 dessert dishes. Refrigerate for at least 1 hour. When serving, top each with 1 tablespoon Cool Whip Lite.

Each serving equals:
HE: ⅔ Fruit, ⅔ Vegetable, ½ Skim Milk, ¼ Slider, 5 Optional Calories
149 Calories, 1 gm Fat, 6 gm Protein, 29 gm Carbohydrate, 299 mg Sodium, 216 mg Calcium, 3 gm Fiber
DIABETIC: 1 Fruit, ½ Skim Milk, ½ Starch/Carbohydrate

Banana Chocolate Crunch Pudding

■ ■ ■

Here I've chosen to distract you from the cool and creamy sensation of banana pudding by adding some chocolate "excitement" along with the fruit. It's so downright delicious, you almost raise your hand to plead for seconds, but then you pause a moment and realize that you're completely satisfied. With desserts this good, moderation isn't hard.

Serves 6

1 (4-serving) package JELL-O
   sugar-free instant banana
   cream pudding mix
⅔ cup Carnation Nonfat Dry
   Milk Powder
1½ cups water
¾ cup Yoplait plain fat-free
   yogurt

½ cup Cool Whip Free
1 teaspoon vanilla extract
2 cups (2 medium) sliced
   bananas
12 (2½-inch) chocolate graham
   cracker squares, coarsely
   crushed

In a large bowl, combine dry pudding mix, dry milk powder, and water. Mix well using a wire whisk. Blend in yogurt, Cool Whip Free, and vanilla extract. Add bananas and crushed chocolate graham crackers. Mix gently to combine. Evenly spoon mixture into 6 dessert dishes. Refrigerate for at least 15 minutes.

HINT: To prevent bananas from turning brown, mix with 1 teaspoon lemon juice or sprinkle with Fruit Fresh.

Each serving equals:
HE: ⅔ Bread, ⅔ Fruit, ½ Skim Milk, ¼ Slider, 7 Optional Calories

145 Calories, 1 gm Fat, 5 gm Protein, 29 gm Carbohydrate, 338 mg Sodium, 151 mg Calcium, 1 gm Fiber

DIABETIC: 1 Fruit, ½ Starch/Carbohydrate, ½ Skim Milk

Chocolate Peanut Butter Pudding

■ ■ ■

Think of how outrageously good a melted peanut butter cup candy bar might taste, and then dig your spoon into this smooth and nutty dish! Chocolate and peanut butter go together as perfectly as, oh, love and marriage? Salt and pepper? Night and day? You decide!

Serves 4

¼ cup Peter Pan reduced-fat peanut butter (chunky or creamy)

2 cups skim milk ☆

1 (4-serving) package JELL-O sugar-free instant chocolate pudding mix

3 (2½-inch) chocolate graham cracker squares, made into crumbs

In a large bowl, combine peanut butter and ¼ cup skim milk. Mix until smooth using a wire whisk. Stir in remaining 1¾ cups skim milk. Add dry pudding mix. Mix well to combine. Evenly spoon mixture into 4 dessert dishes. Sprinkle chocolate graham cracker crumbs evenly over top. Refrigerate for at least 30 minutes.

HINT: A self-seal sandwich bag works great for crushing graham crackers.

Each serving equals:

HE: 1 Protein, 1 Fat, ½ Skim Milk, ¼ Bread, ¼ Slider, 10 Optional Calories

182 Calories, 6 gm Fat, 9 gm Protein, 23 gm Carbohydrate, 485 mg Sodium, 151 mg Calcium, 1 gm Fiber

DIABETIC: 1 Starch/Carbohydrate, ½ Meat, ½ Fat, ½ Skim Milk

Chocolate and Peanut Butter Layered Dessert

■ ■ ■

Remember when the only graham crackers you could buy were the plain ones? Now we've got so many fun flavors to choose from: cinnamon, chocolate, and—be still, my heart—peanut butter! This amazingly rich creation both looks and tastes like a piece of heaven. *Serves 8*

12 (2½-inch) peanut butter or chocolate graham crackers ☆
1 (8-ounce) package Philadelphia fat-free cream cheese
¼ cup Peter Pan reduced-fat peanut butter
¾ cup Cool Whip Free ☆
⅔ cup Carnation Nonfat Dry Milk Powder

1 (4-serving) package JELL-O sugar-free instant chocolate pudding mix
1¼ cups water
1 teaspoon vanilla extract
2 tablespoons (½ ounce) chopped dry-roasted peanuts

Arrange 9 peanut butter graham crackers in bottom of a 9-by-9-inch cake pan. In a medium bowl, stir cream cheese with a spoon until soft. Add peanut butter and ¼ cup Cool Whip Free. Mix well to combine. Carefully spread mixture over graham crackers. In a large bowl, combine dry pudding mix, dry milk powder, and water. Mix well using a wire whisk. Blend in vanilla extract and remaining ½ cup Cool Whip Free. Evenly spread pudding mixture over cream cheese mixture. Refrigerate for 10 minutes. Crush remaining 3 graham crackers. Evenly sprinkle cracker crumbs and peanuts over top. Cover and refrigerate for at least 2 hours. Cut into 8 servings.

HINT: A self-seal sandwich bag works great for crushing graham crackers.

Each serving equals:
HE: 1 Protein, ⅔ Fat, ½ Bread, ¼ Skim Milk, ¼ Slider, 10 Optional Calories
144 Calories, 4 gm Fat, 9 gm Protein, 18 gm Carbohydrate, 441 mg Sodium, 70 mg Calcium, 1 gm Fiber
DIABETIC: 1 Meat, 1 Starch/Carbohydrate, ½ Fat

Maximum Chocolate Power Dessert

■ ■ ■

Yes, I know I tend to preach moderation, but some days you just have to let yourself go—in a healthy way, of course! This utterly intense, oh-so-chocolate-y recipe is an ideal way to celebrate an important occasion, whether it's a birthday, a graduation, or a healthy milestone like a great checkup or a lowered cholesterol count. It's wonderfully rich; and let me warn you, no one will believe you when you insist this dessert is low in fat and low in calories. Just smile and accept the applause you're sure to receive. *Serves 8*

12 (2½-inch) chocolate graham crackers ☆
1 (8-ounce) package Philadelphia fat-free cream cheese
1 (4-serving) package JELL-O sugar-free instant chocolate fudge pudding mix
2 cups Carnation Nonfat Dry Milk Powder ☆

3½ cups water ☆
1 (4-serving) package JELL-O sugar-free instant chocolate pudding mix
1 cup Cool Whip Free ☆
1 (4-serving) package JELL-O sugar-free instant white chocolate pudding mix

Arrange 9 graham crackers in bottom of a 9-by-9-inch cake pan. In a large bowl, stir cream cheese with a spoon until soft. Add dry chocolate fudge pudding mix, ⅔ cup dry milk powder, and 1¼ cups water. Mix well using a wire whisk. Carefully spread mixture over graham crackers. In same bowl, combine dry chocolate pudding mix, another ⅔ cup dry milk powder, and another 1¼ cups water. Mix well using a wire whisk. Blend in ¼ cup Cool Whip Free. Spread mixture evenly over cream cheese layer. Refrigerate while preparing topping. In another large bowl, combine dry white chocolate pudding mix, remaining ⅔ cup dry milk powder, and remaining 1 cup water. Mix well using a wire whisk. Blend in remaining ¾ cup Cool Whip Free. Spread white chocolate mixture evenly over set chocolate layer. Crush remaining 3 graham crackers. Evenly sprinkle cracker crumbs over top. Cover and refrigerate for at least 2 hours. Cut into 8 servings.

HINT: A self-seal sandwich bag works great for crushing graham crackers.

Each serving equals:

HE: ¾ Skim Milk, ½ Bread, ½ Protein, ½ Slider, 15 Optional Calories

169 Calories, 1 gm Fat, 11 gm Protein, 29 gm Carbohydrate, 797 mg Sodium, 209 mg Calcium, 0 gm Fiber

DIABETIC: 1 Skim Milk, 1 Starch/Carbohydrate, ½ Meat

Turtle Dessert

■ ■ ■

I don't know who was the first to create that chocolate-caramel chewy treat named the Turtle, but whoever you are, I salute you! This captivating combination of goodies is fun to eat and fun to prepare, too. And while we're licking our lips over this treat, let's remember the example of the turtle (well, his relative, the tortoise): Slow and steady (as in healthy weight loss) wins the race!

Serves 8

¾ cup purchased graham cracker crumbs or 12 (2½-inch) graham cracker squares, made into crumbs

¼ cup (1 ounce) chopped pecans

2 tablespoons pourable Sugar Twin

2 tablespoons unsweetened apple juice

1 (8-ounce) package Philadelphia fat-free cream cheese

1 (4-serving) package JELL-O sugar-free instant chocolate fudge pudding mix

⅔ cup Carnation Nonfat Dry Milk Powder

1¼ cups water

2 tablespoons caramel syrup

½ cup Cool Whip Lite

Preheat oven to 350 degrees. Spray an 8-by-8-inch baking dish with butter-flavored cooking spray. In a medium bowl, combine graham cracker crumbs, pecans, and Sugar Twin. Add apple juice. Mix well to combine. Evenly pat mixture into prepared baking dish. Bake for 8 to 10 minutes. Place baking dish on a wire rack and allow to cool completely. Meanwhile, in a medium bowl, stir cream cheese with a spoon until soft. Add dry pudding mix, dry milk powder, and water. Mix well using a wire whisk. Evenly spread mixture into cooled crust. Drizzle caramel syrup over top. Refrigerate for at least 1 hour. Cut into 8 servings. When serving, top each piece with 1 tablespoon Cool Whip Lite.

HINT: A self-seal sandwich bag works great for crushing graham crackers.

Each serving equals:
HE: ½ Bread, ½ Protein, ½ Fat, ¼ Skim Milk, ¼ Slider, 14 Optional Calories
152 Calories, 4 gm Fat, 7 gm Protein, 22 gm Carbohydrate, 452 mg Sodium, 76 mg Calcium, 0 gm Fiber
DIABETIC: 1½ Starch, ½ Meat, ½ Fat

Heavenly Chocolate and Raspberry Dream Dessert

■ ■ ■

Since raspberries and chocolate are such a dreamy combination, I decided to turn them into a kind of instant trifle, that beloved English dessert that layers fruit and creamy goodness together. I've also layered the flavors, so you've got really intense almond taste along with double chocolate "yum." *Serves 8*

- 4 individual sponge cake dessert cups
- 1½ cups frozen unsweetened raspberries, thawed and undrained
- 2 (4-serving) packages JELL-O sugar-free instant chocolate pudding mix
- 3 cups water
- 1⅓ cups Carnation Nonfat Dry Milk Powder
- 1 cup Cool Whip Free
- 1 teaspoon almond extract
- 2 tablespoons Hershey's Lite Chocolate Syrup
- 2 tablespoons (½ ounce) slivered almonds

Cut each sponge cake into 6 pieces. Sprinkle cake pieces into an 8-by-8-inch dish. Evenly spoon raspberries over cake pieces. In a large bowl, combine dry pudding mixes, dry milk powder, and water. Mix well using a wire whisk. Pour pudding mixture evenly over raspberries. Refrigerate while preparing topping. In a medium bowl, combine Cool Whip Free and almond extract. Evenly spread topping mixture over chocolate layer. Drizzle chocolate syrup over topping mixture. Sprinkle almonds evenly over top. Cover and refrigerate for at least 1 hour. Divide into 8 servings.

Each serving equals:
HE: ½ Skim Milk, ½ Bread, ¼ Fruit, ½ Slider, 16 Optional Calories
174 Calories, 2 gm Fat, 6 gm Protein, 33 gm Carbohydrate, 467 mg Sodium, 159 mg Calcium, 2 gm Fiber
DIABETIC: 1½ Starch/Carbohydrate, ½ Skim Milk

Baked Apple and Graham Cracker Pudding

■ ■ ■

If you haven't got time for a vacation in Vermont this year, put your feet up and enjoy a piece of this sweet and fragrant New England–style pudding. The scent of the apples and raisins blending with the maple syrup may call to you from the oven while it's baking, but try not to keep opening the oven to inhale!

Serves 8

3 cups (6 small) cored, peeled, and diced cooking apples
½ cup pourable Sugar Twin
1½ cups purchased graham cracker crumbs or 24 (2½-inch) graham cracker squares, made into crumbs

¼ cup raisins
1⅓ cups Carnation Nonfat Dry Milk Powder
1¼ cups water
½ cup Cary's Sugar Free Maple Syrup

Preheat oven to 350 degrees. Spray a 9-by-9-inch cake pan with butter-flavored cooking spray. Layer apples, Sugar Twin, raisins, and graham cracker crumbs in prepared cake pan. In a small bowl, combine dry milk powder, water, and maple syrup. Mix well to combine. Evenly pour mixture over top. Bake for 35 to 45 minutes. Place cake pan on a wire rack and let set for 5 minutes. Cut into 8 servings. Good served warm or cold.

HINT: A self-seal sandwich bag works great for crushing graham crackers.

Each serving equals:
HE: 1 Bread, 1 Fruit, ½ Skim Milk, 16 Optional Calories
178 Calories, 2 gm Fat, 5 gm Protein, 35 gm Carbohydrate, 232 mg Sodium, 149 mg Calcium, 2 gm Fiber
DIABETIC: 1 Fruit, ½ Skim Milk, ½ Starch

Maple-Raisin Sour Cream Tarts

■ ■ ■

I don't know why I often think of raisins and sour cream together—maybe because Cliff has always liked that combination in pie! These treats can be stirred up in minutes, then left to firm up in the fridge while you chat with your guests.   *Serves 6*

1 (4-serving) package JELL-O
    sugar-free instant vanilla pud-
    ding mix
⅔ cup Carnation Nonfat Dry
    Milk Powder
½ cup Cary's Sugar Free Maple
    Syrup

1 cup water
¼ cup Land O Lakes no-fat sour
    cream
½ cup Cool Whip Free
¾ cup raisins
1 (6 single-serve) package
    Keebler graham cracker crusts

In a large bowl, combine dry pudding mix, dry milk powder, maple syrup, and water. Mix well using a wire whisk. Blend in sour cream and Cool Whip Free. Add raisins. Mix gently to combine. Evenly spoon pudding mixture into crusts. Refrigerate for at least 1 hour.

HINT: To plump up raisins without "cooking," place in a glass measuring cup and microwave on HIGH for 20 seconds.

Each serving equals:
HE: 1 Fruit, ½ Bread, ⅓ Skim Milk, 1 Slider, 19 Optional Calories
238 Calories, 6 gm Fat, 4 gm Protein, 42 gm Carbohydrate, 471 mg Sodium,
112 mg Calcium, 1 gm Fiber
DIABETIC: 1½ Starch/Carbohydrate, 1 Fruit, 1 Fat

Orange Marmalade Chocolate Cream Pie

■ ■ ■

A friend recently bemoaned the disappearance of her favorite ice cream parlor, which had served a wonderful Swiss chocolate ice cream blended with the flavor of oranges. I thought I could come up with something to fill that void, and I bet this will do it. Erika, this one's for you!

Serves 8

2 (4-serving) packages JELL-O sugar-free instant chocolate pudding mix
1⅓ cups Carnation Nonfat Dry Milk Powder
2 cups water
1 (6-ounce) Keebler chocolate piecrust

½ cup orange marmalade spreadable fruit
1 cup Cool Whip Free ☆
1 tablespoon (¼ ounce) mini chocolate chips

In a large bowl, combine dry pudding mixes, dry milk powder, and water. Mix well using a wire whisk. Pour half of mixture into piecrust. Refrigerate while preparing next layer. In a small bowl, stir spreadable fruit until softened. Stir in ½ cup Cool Whip Free. Spread fruit mixture evenly over chocolate filling. Fold remaining ½ cup Cool Whip Free into remaining pudding mixture. Gently spread topping mixture evenly over marmalade filling. Evenly sprinkle chocolate chips over top. Refrigerate for at least 1 hour. Cut into 8 servings.

Each serving equals:
HE: 1 Fruit, ½ Skim Milk, ½ Bread, 1 Slider, 19 Optional Calories
237 Calories, 5 gm Fat, 6 gm Protein, 42 gm Carbohydrate, 497 mg Sodium, 139 mg Calcium, 1 gm Fiber
DIABETIC: 1 Fruit, 1 Starch/Carbohydrate, 1 Fat, ½ Skim Milk

Chocolate Fruit Cordial Rocky Road Pie

■ ■ ■

This dessert features a veritable buried treasure of "forbidden fruit," but you can enjoy it without a smidgen of guilt. I've included a bit of brandy extract, which is a non-alcoholic flavoring, but if you don't love that "liqueur" taste, you can substitute vanilla or almond extract instead. *Serves 8*

1 (4-serving) package JELL-O sugar-free chocolate cook-and-serve pudding mix

⅔ cup Carnation Nonfat Dry Milk Powder

1 cup (one 8-ounce can) crushed pineapple, packed in fruit juice, undrained

2 cups (one 16-ounce can) tart red cherries, packed in water, drained, and ½ cup liquid reserved

1 teaspoon brandy extract

2 tablespoons (½ ounce) chopped pecans

1 (6-ounce) Keebler chocolate piecrust

1 cup Cool Whip Lite

½ cup (1 ounce) miniature marshmallows

2 tablespoons (½ ounce) mini chocolate chips

In a large saucepan, combine dry pudding mix, dry milk powder, undrained pineapple, and reserved cherry liquid. Stir in cherries. Cook over medium heat until mixture thickens and starts to boil, stirring often, and being careful not to crush cherries. Remove from heat. Add brandy extract and pecans. Mix gently to combine. Pour mixture into piecrust. Refrigerate for at least 2 hours. In a small bowl, gently combine Cool Whip Lite and marshmallows. Evenly spread topping mixture over set filling. Sprinkle chocolate chips evenly over top. Refrigerate for at least 15 minutes. Cut into 8 pieces.

Each serving equals:

HE: ¾ Fruit, ½ Bread, ¼ Skim Milk, ¼ Fat, 1 Slider, 18 Optional Calories

232 Calories, 8 gm Fat, 4 gm Protein, 36 gm Carbohydrate, 192 mg Sodium, 81 mg Calcium, 2 gm Fiber

DIABETIC: 1½ Starch/Carbohydrate, 1 Fruit, 1 Fat

Banana Peanut Butter Dream Pie

■ ■ ■

Each layer of this tummy-pleasing extravaganza has its own special joys, and each forkful of pie provides a taste memory you're sure to relish. It's kind of a "double your pleasure" pie, as it features double doses of great flavors like bananas, chocolate, and peanut!

Serves 8

2 cups (2 medium) diced
  bananas
1 (6-ounce) Keebler chocolate
  piecrust
1 (4-serving) package JELL-O
  sugar-free instant banana
  cream pudding mix
1⅓ cups Carnation Nonfat Dry
  Milk Powder ☆

2⅓ cups water ☆
¼ cup Peter Pan reduced-fat
  peanut butter
1 (4-serving) package JELL-O
  sugar-free instant chocolate
  pudding mix
½ cup Cool Whip Free
1 tablespoon (¼ ounce) chopped
  dry-roasted peanuts

Layer bananas in bottom of piecrust. In a large bowl, combine dry banana cream pudding mix, ⅔ cup dry milk powder, and 1⅓ cups water. Mix well using a wire whisk. Blend in peanut butter. Spread pudding mixture evenly over bananas. Refrigerate while preparing topping. In a large bowl, combine dry chocolate pudding mix, remaining ⅔ cup dry milk powder, and remaining 1 cup water. Mix well using a wire whisk. Blend in Cool Whip Free. Spread topping mixture evenly over set filling. Evenly sprinkle peanuts over top. Refrigerate for at least 1 hour. Cut into 8 servings.

HINT: To prevent bananas from turning brown, mix with 1 teaspoon lemon juice or sprinkle with Fruit Fresh.

Each serving equals:
HE: ½ Skim Milk, ½ Bread, ½ Protein, ½ Fruit, ½ Fat, 1 Slider, 5 Optional Calories

268 Calories, 8 gm Fat, 8 gm Protein, 41 gm Carbohydrate, 537 mg Sodium, 142 mg Calcium, 2 gm Fiber

DIABETIC: 1½ Starch/Carbohydrate, 1 Fat, ½ Skim Milk, ½ Fruit, or 2 Starch/Carbohydrate, 1 Fat, ½ Skim Milk

Heavenly Chocolate-Coconut Pie

■ ■ ■

Just think of it this way: Coconuts come from palm trees that grow in the world's paradises, so anytime you find those sweet and chewy bits in your dessert, you'll be transported to a land of tropical breezes. Invite every coconut lover you know over for coffee and a piece of pie! *Serves 8*

2 (4-serving) packages JELL-O sugar-free instant chocolate pudding mix
1¼ cups Carnation Nonfat Dry Milk Powder
2½ cups water
1½ teaspoons coconut extract ☆

3 tablespoons flaked coconut ☆
1 (6-ounce) Keebler chocolate piecrust
¾ cup Cool Whip Free
6 (2½-inch) chocolate graham cracker squares, made into fine crumbs

In a large bowl, combine dry pudding mixes, dry milk powder, and water. Mix well using a wire whisk. Blend in ½ teaspoon coconut extract and 2 tablespoons coconut. Spread mixture evenly into piecrust. Refrigerate while preparing topping. In a medium bowl, combine Cool Whip Free and remaining 1 teaspoon coconut extract. Fold in graham cracker crumbs. Spread topping mixture evenly over set filling. Sprinkle remaining 1 tablespoon coconut over top. Refrigerate for at least 1 hour. Cut into 8 servings.

HINT: A self-seal sandwich bag works great for crushing graham crackers.

Each serving equals:
HE: ¾ Bread, ½ Skim Milk, 1 Slider, 17 Optional Calories
190 Calories, 6 gm Fat, 5 gm Protein, 29 gm Carbohydrate, 352 mg Sodium, 139 mg Calcium, 1 gm Fiber
DIABETIC: 1½ Starch/Carbohydrate, 1 Fat, ½ Skim Milk

Banana Fruit Pie

There's a great country song that goes something like "Too much is not enough," and that's just how I felt when I was creating this joyfully abundant mixed-fruit pie! Actually, of course, it's not too much, just enough, but in this case "enough" is quite a lot.

Serves 8

- 2 cups (2 medium) diced bananas
- 1 cup (one 11-ounce can) mandarin oranges, rinsed and drained
- 1 (6-ounce) Keebler graham cracker piecrust
- 1 (4-serving) package JELL-O sugar-free instant banana cream pudding mix
- ⅔ cup Carnation Nonfat Dry Milk Powder
- 1 cup (one 8-ounce can) crushed pineapple, packed in fruit juice, drained, and ¼ cup liquid reserved
- 1 cup water
- 1 cup Cool Whip Free ☆
- 1 teaspoon coconut extract
- 2 tablespoons flaked coconut

Layer bananas and mandarin oranges in bottom of piecrust. In a large bowl, combine dry pudding mix, dry milk powder, reserved pineapple liquid, and water. Mix well using a wire whisk. Blend in ¼ cup Cool Whip Free. Spread pudding mixture evenly over fruit. Refrigerate while preparing topping. In a small bowl, combine remaining ¾ cup Cool Whip Free, coconut extract, and pineapple. Spread topping mixture evenly over set filling. Evenly sprinkle coconut over top. Refrigerate for at least 2 hours. Cut into 8 servings.

HINT: To prevent bananas from turning brown, mix with 1 teaspoon lemon juice or sprinkle with Fruit Fresh.

Each serving equals:

HE: 1 Fruit, ½ Bread, ¼ Skim Milk, 1 Slider, 1 Optional Calorie

225 Calories, 5 gm Fat, 4 gm Protein, 41 gm Carbohydrate, 346 mg Sodium, 79 mg Calcium, 2 gm Fiber

DIABETIC: 1½ Starch/Carbohydrate, 1 Fruit, 1 Fat

Blueberry Pineapple Layered Pie

■ ■ ■

Last summer, the Healthy Exchanges gang ate all the fresh blueberries we could find here in DeWitt, and believe me, we found quite a few! This recipe was much loved by all our testers who got a taste, and I think your own "testers" will enjoy giving this luscious dessert their seal of approval. *Serves 8*

1 (8-ounce) package Philadelphia fat-free cream cheese

1 (4-serving) package JELL-O sugar-free instant vanilla pudding mix

⅔ cup Carnation Nonfat Dry Milk Powder

1 cup Diet 7-Up

1 (6-ounce) Keebler shortbread piecrust

1 cup water

1 cup (one 8-ounce can) crushed pineapple, packed in fruit juice, drained, and ¼ cup liquid reserved

2 tablespoons cornstarch

¼ cup pourable Sugar Twin

1½ cups fresh blueberries

1 teaspoon lemon juice

1 cup Cool Whip Free

1 teaspoon coconut extract

2 tablespoons flaked coconut

In a large bowl, stir cream cheese with a spoon until soft. Add dry pudding mix, dry milk powder, and Diet 7-Up. Mix well using a wire whisk. Spread mixture evenly into piecrust. In a medium saucepan, combine reserved pineapple liquid, water, cornstarch, and Sugar Twin. Cook over medium heat until mixture thickens and starts to boil, stirring constantly. Remove from heat. Gently fold in blueberries and lemon juice. Place saucepan on wire rack and let set for 10 minutes. Gently spoon cooled blueberry mixture over cream cheese mixture. Refrigerate for 30 minutes. In a medium bowl, combine Cool Whip Free and coconut extract. Stir in pineapple. Evenly spread topping mixture over cooled blueberry layer. Sprinkle coconut evenly over top. Refrigerate for at least 1 hour. Cut into 8 servings.

Each serving equals:

HE: ½ Bread, ½ Protein, ½ Fruit, ¼ Skim Milk, 1 Slider, 12 Optional Calories

217 Calories, 5 gm Fat, 7 gm Protein, 36 gm Carbohydrate, 474 mg Sodium, 75 mg Calcium, 2 gm Fiber

DIABETIC: 1½ Starch/Carbohydrate, 1 Fat, ½ Fruit

Pear and Raspberry Crumb Pie

■ ■ ■

It's great when you can bring home fresh fruit from your garden or the local farm stand to make pie, but what about those colder months when it's not as easy to find? I certainly don't want you to deny yourself the pleasures of fruit pies, so here's a splendid one that features fruit picked "fresh" from your pantry and freezer.

Serves 8

1 (4-serving) package JELL-O sugar-free vanilla cook-and-serve pudding mix

2 cups (one 16-ounce can) pears, packed in fruit juice, drained, coarsely chopped, and ¼ cup liquid reserved

1 cup water

1 teaspoon almond extract

1½ cups frozen unsweetened raspberries, thawed and undrained

1 (6-ounce) Keebler graham cracker piecrust

6 tablespoons purchased graham cracker crumbs or 6 (2½-inch) graham cracker squares, made into crumbs

2 tablespoons pourable Sugar Twin

2 teaspoons reduced-calorie margarine

2 tablespoons (½ ounce) slivered almonds

Preheat oven to 350 degrees. In a medium saucepan, combine dry pudding mix, reserved pear liquid, and water. Cook over medium heat until mixture thickens and starts to boil, stirring often. Remove from heat. Add almond extract. Mix well to combine. Gently stir in pears and undrained raspberries. Spoon hot mixture into piecrust. In a small bowl, combine graham cracker crumbs, Sugar Twin, and margarine. Mix with a fork until crumbly. Stir in almonds. Sprinkle crumb mixture evenly over top. Bake for 12 to 15 minutes. Place pie plate on a wire rack and allow to cool completely. Cut into 8 servings.

HINT: A self-seal sandwich bag works great for crushing graham crackers.

Each serving equals:
HE: ¾ Bread, ¾ Fruit, ¼ Fat, ¾ Slider, 5 Optional Calories

207 Calories, 7 gm Fat, 2 gm Protein, 34 gm Carbohydrate, 342 mg Sodium, 14 mg Calcium, 3 gm Fiber

DIABETIC: 1 Starch, 1 Fruit, 1 Fat

Ice Cream Mince Pie

■ ❄ ■

Mmm-mmm, ice cream pie—it does sound like a dangerous splurge, doesn't it? But when you combine lots of good-for-you ingredients with your favorite brand of fat- and sugar-free ice cream, you'll be thrilled by just how delicious a little "danger" can taste!   *Serves 8*

*1 (4-serving) package JELL-O
    sugar-free vanilla cook-and-
    serve pudding mix*
*1 (4-serving) package JELL-O
    sugar-free lemon gelatin*
1 teaspoon apple pie spice
½ cup unsweetened apple juice
½ cup water
*1½ cups (3 small) cored, peeled,
    and diced cooking apples*

½ cup raisins
1 teaspoon rum extract
*2 tablespoons (½ ounce) chopped
    pecans*
*2 cups Wells' Blue Bunny sugar-
    and fat-free vanilla ice cream
    or any sugar- and fat-free ice
    cream*
*1 (6-ounce) Keebler graham
    cracker piecrust*

In a large saucepan, combine dry pudding mix, dry gelatin, apple pie spice, apple juice, and water. Stir in apples and raisins. Cook over medium heat until mixture thickens and apples soften, stirring often. Remove from heat. Stir in rum extract and pecans. Place saucepan on a wire rack and let set for 5 minutes. Add ice cream. Mix well to combine. Spread mixture evenly into piecrust. Cover and freeze for at least 2 hours. Remove from freezer 20 minutes before serving. Cut into 8 servings.

Each serving equals:
HE: 1 Fruit, ½ Bread, ¼ Fat, 1 Slider, 15 Optional Calories

226 Calories, 6 gm Fat, 4 gm Protein, 39 gm Carbohydrate, 354 mg Sodium, 68 mg Calcium, 1 gm Fiber

DIABETIC: 1½ Starch/Carbohydrate, 1 Fruit, 1 Fat

Layered Cherry Almond Pie

■ ❅ ■

I was thinking about cherry almond cheesecake, but then I discovered I had only one package of fat-free cream cheese on hand. True, I could have run to the store for more, but I decided to be inventive instead. This is such a gorgeous-looking dessert, I'd serve it for a special occasion—maybe Valentine's Day or on your anniversary!

Serves 8

2 cups (one 16-ounce can) tart red cherries, packed in water, drained, and ½ cup liquid reserved
¾ cup water
1 (4-serving) package JELL-O sugar-free cherry gelatin
1 (4-serving) package JELL-O sugar-free instant vanilla pudding mix

1½ teaspoons almond extract ☆
1 (8-ounce) package Philadelphia fat-free cream cheese
¼ cup pourable Sugar Twin
1 cup Cool Whip Lite ☆
1 (6-ounce) Keebler graham cracker piecrust
3 to 4 drops red food coloring
¼ cup (1 ounce) sliced almonds

In a medium saucepan, combine reserved cherry liquid and water. Bring mixture just to a boil. Remove from heat. Add dry gelatin. Mix well to dissolve gelatin. Place saucepan on a wire rack and allow mixture to cool completely. Add dry pudding mix. Mix well using a wire whisk. Stir in 1 teaspoon almond extract and cherries. Set aside. In a medium bowl, stir cream cheese with a spoon until soft. Add Sugar Twin, ¼ cup Cool Whip Lite, and remaining ½ teaspoon almond extract. Mix well to combine. Spread cream cheese mixture evenly into piecrust. Spread cherry mixture over top. Refrigerate for at least 2 hours. In a small bowl, combine remaining ¾ cup Cool Whip Lite and red food coloring. Spread mixture evenly over cherry layer. Evenly sprinkle almonds over top. Refrigerate for at least 15 minutes. Cut into 8 servings.

Each serving equals:
HE: ⅔ Protein, ½ Bread, ½ Fruit, ¼ Fat, 1 Slider, 11 Optional Calories

208 Calories, 8 gm Fat, 7 gm Protein, 27 gm Carbohydrate, 502 mg Sodium, 16 mg Calcium, 1 gm Fiber

DIABETIC: 1 Starch/Carbohydrate, 1 Fat, ½ Meat, ½ Fruit

Perfect Apple Pie

Okay, so nothing is absolutely perfect, but this apple pie comes oh-so-very-close! The best desserts are often the simplest, and this one certainly requires very little effort, experience, or skill. Even if your grandma never made a pie from scratch, you can approach a kind of culinary perfection by putting this on the menu!

Serves 8

1 Pillsbury refrigerated unbaked 9-inch piecrust
½ cup + 1 tablespoon pourable Sugar Twin ☆
1 tablespoon all-purpose flour
1½ teaspoons apple pie spice
4 cups (8 small) cored, peeled, and sliced tart cooking apples

Let piecrust sit at room temperature for 20 minutes, then cut piecrust in half on the folded line. Gently roll each half into a ball. Wipe counter with a wet cloth and place a sheet of waxed paper over damp spot. Place one of the balls on the waxed paper. Cover with another piece of waxed paper and roll out with rolling pin. Carefully remove waxed paper on one side and place into an 8-inch pie plate. Remove other piece of waxed paper. In a large bowl, combine ½ cup Sugar Twin, flour, and apple pie spice. Add apples. Mix well to combine. Evenly arrange apple mixture in prepared piecrust. Repeat process of rolling out remaining piecrust half. Place on top of pie. Flute edges. Lightly spray top crust with butter-flavored cooking spray and sprinkle remaining 1 tablespoon Sugar Twin evenly over top. Make about 8 slashes with a knife to allow steam to escape. Bake at 400 degrees for 45 to 50 minutes or until crust is golden brown and apples are tender. Place pie plate on a wire rack and allow to cool. Cut into 8 servings.

HINT: Place piece of uncooked elbow macaroni upright in center of pie to keep filling from cooking out of crust.

Each serving equals:
HE: 1 Fruit, ½ Bread, ¾ Slider, 1 Optional Calorie
151 Calories, 7 gm Fat, 0 gm Protein, 22 gm Carbohydrate, 100 mg Sodium, 4 mg Calcium, 1 gm Fiber
DIABETIC: 1 Fruit, 1 Fat, ½ Starch

Pineapple Meringue Pie

■ ■ ■

If there's a classic American dessert that attracts all eyes to the revolving glass case at the diner, it's got to be the meringue pie! The traditional version is lemon, but I made this one with my pineapple-loving grandkids in mind! Meringue is somewhat mysterious, all that fluff from just a few egg whites, but it's also hard to resist.

Serves 8

1 (4-serving) package JELL-O sugar-free vanilla cook-and-serve pudding mix

1 (4-serving) package JELL-O sugar-free lemon gelatin

2 cups (two 8-ounce cans) crushed pineapple, packed in fruit juice, drained, and ½ cup liquid reserved

½ cup water

1 (6-ounce) Keebler graham cracker piecrust

6 egg whites

6 tablespoons pourable Sugar Twin

1 teaspoon coconut extract

2 tablespoons flaked coconut

Preheat oven to 425 degrees. In a medium saucepan, combine dry pudding mix and dry gelatin. Add reserved pineapple liquid, water, and pineapple. Mix well to combine. Cook over medium heat until mixture thickens and starts to boil, stirring constantly. Spoon pineapple mixture evenly into piecrust. In a large bowl, beat egg whites with an electric mixer on HIGH until soft peaks form. Add Sugar Twin and coconut extract. Continue beating on HIGH until stiff peaks form. Spread meringue mixture evenly over filling mixture, being sure to seal to edges of piecrust. Evenly sprinkle coconut over top. Bake for 6 to 8 minutes or until meringue starts to turn brown. Place pie plate on a wire rack and allow to cool completely. Cut into 8 servings.

HINTS: 1. Egg whites beat best at room temperature.
2. Meringue pie cuts easily if you dip a sharp knife in warm water before slicing.

Each serving equals:

HE: ½ Bread, ½ Fruit, ¼ Protein, ¾ Slider, 13 Optional Calories

177 Calories, 5 gm Fat, 5 gm Protein, 28 gm Carbohydrate, 264 mg Sodium, 10 mg Calcium, 1 gm Fiber

DIABETIC: 1½ Starch/Carbohydrate, 1 Fat, ½ Fruit

Cranberry-Walnut Glazed Cheesecake

■ ❋ ■

I can't imagine a more glorious centerpiece for your next Christmas buffet table than this truly magnificent dessert! The blend of flavors and textures is something special, sweet and tart and creamy all at once. Here's a thought: If you've been a little naughty this year instead of always nice, maybe you should leave a piece for Santa—just in case!   *Serves 8*

2 (8-ounce) packages Philadelphia fat-free cream cheese

1 (4-serving) package JELL-O sugar-free instant vanilla pudding mix

⅔ cup Carnation Nonfat Dry Milk Powder

1 cup water

¼ cup Cool Whip Free

1 (6-ounce) Keebler graham cracker piecrust

1 (4-serving) package JELL-O sugar-free vanilla cook-and serve pudding mix

1 cup Ocean Spray reduced-calorie cranberry juice cocktail

1 cup fresh or frozen cranberries

¼ cup (1 ounce) chopped walnuts

In a large bowl, stir cream cheese with a spoon until soft. Add dry instant pudding mix, dry milk powder, and water. Mix well using a wire whisk. Blend in Cool Whip Free. Spread mixture into piecrust. Refrigerate while preparing topping. In a medium saucepan, combine dry cook-and-serve pudding mix and cranberry juice cocktail. Stir in cranberries. Cook over medium heat until cranberries soften, stirring often. Add walnuts. Mix well to combine. Remove from heat. Place saucepan on a wire rack and allow to cool for 15 minutes, stirring occasionally. Evenly spoon cranberry mixture over filling. Refrigerate for at least 1 hour. Cut into 8 servings.

Each serving equals:

HE: 1 Protein, ½ Bread, ¼ Skim Milk, ¼ Fruit, ¼ Fat, 1 Slider, 4 Optional Calories

227 Calories, 7 gm Fat, 12 gm Protein, 29 gm Carbohydrate, 734 mg Sodium, 73 mg Calcium, 1 gm Fiber

DIABETIC: 1½ Starch/Carbohydrate, 1 Meat, 1 Fat

White Chocolate–Covered Cherry Cheesecake

■ ❋ ■

White chocolate has a more delicate flavor than the darker kinds, but for those of us who adore its subtle joys, this is a lovely way to enjoy it! Even if you're not a confident "garnisher," just take your time assembling the topping. It'll be beautiful, I know.

Serves 8

2 (8-ounce) packages
  Philadelphia fat-free cream
  cheese
1 (4-serving) package JELL-O
  sugar-free instant white chocolate pudding mix
⅔ cup Carnation Nonfat Dry
  Milk Powder

1 cup water
¾ cup Cool Whip Lite ☆
6 maraschino cherries,
  quartered ☆
1 (6-ounce) Keebler chocolate
  piecrust
2 tablespoons (½ ounce) mini
  chocolate chips

In a large bowl, stir cream cheese with a spoon until soft. Add dry pudding mix, dry milk powder, and water. Mix well using a wire whisk. Blend in ¼ cup Cool Whip Lite. Reserve 8 cherry pieces for garnish. Gently stir remaining cherry pieces into cream cheese mixture. Spread mixture evenly into piecrust. Drop remaining ½ cup Cool Whip Lite by tablespoonful over top of filling to form 8 mounds. Evenly arrange a cherry piece in center of each mound. Sprinkle chocolate chips evenly over top. Refrigerate for at least 1 hour. Cut into 8 servings.

Each serving equals:
HE: 1 Protein, ½ Bread, ¼ Skim Milk, 1 Slider, 19 Optional Calories

211 Calories, 7 gm Fat, 11 gm Protein, 26 gm Carbohydrate, 636 mg Sodium, 70 mg Calcium, 1 gm Fiber 5

DIABETIC: 1½ Starch/Carbohydrate, 1 Meat, 1 Fat

Orange Marmalade Cheesecake
with Blueberry Glaze

■ ■ ■

One of the special pleasures of orange marmalade is the intensity of orange flavor it provides in just a single spoonful. Make this dessert if you love that tart-sweet flavor, or maybe if your favorite team's colors are orange and blue like the New York Mets. Or simply make it because you love trying new and different combinations of tastes. I must confess that I was never an orange marmalade lover until I started using it in my recipes. It adds such intense flavor, especially when coupled with blueberries. Truly, the end result is so much more than the sum of its parts.

Serves 8

1 (4-serving) package JELL-O sugar-free vanilla cook-and-serve pudding mix
1 (4-serving) package JELL-O sugar-free lemon gelatin
1¾ cups water ☆
1½ cups fresh blueberries
1 (8-ounce) package Philadelphia fat-free cream cheese
1 (4-serving) package JELL-O sugar-free instant vanilla pudding mix

⅔ cup Carnation Nonfat Dry Milk Powder
¾ cup Cool Whip Lite ☆
¼ cup orange marmalade spreadable fruit
1 (6-ounce) Keebler graham cracker piecrust
2 tablespoons (½ ounce) chopped pecans

In a medium saucepan, combine dry cook-and-serve pudding mix, dry gelatin, and 1 cup water. Cook over medium heat until mixture thickens and starts to boil, stirring often. Remove from heat. Fold in blueberries. Place saucepan on a wire rack and allow to cool, stirring occasionally. Meanwhile, in a large bowl, stir cream cheese with a spoon until soft. Add dry instant pudding mix, dry milk powder, and remaining ¾ cup water. Mix well using a wire whisk. Blend in ¼ cup Cool Whip Lite and orange marmalade. Spread mixture into piecrust. Refrigerate until blueberry mixture has cooled. Spread cooled blueberry mixture evenly over cream cheese filling. Drop remaining ½ cup Cool Whip Lite by tablespoonful over top to form 8 mounds. Evenly sprinkle pecans over mounds. Refrigerate for at least 1 hour. Cut into 8 servings.

HINTS: You can make this recipe with frozen berries if you like. Just remember to thaw and drain well, and have the berry juice as part of the liquid called for in the recipe.

HE: ¾ Fruit, ½ Bread, ½ Protein, ¼ Skim Milk, ¼ Fat, 1 Slider, 13 Optional Calories

255 Calories, 7 gm Fat, 12 gm Protein, 36 gm Carbohydrate, 757 mg Sodium, 72 mg Calcium, 1 gm Fiber

DIABETIC: 1 Meat, 1 Fruit, 1 Starch/Carbohydrate, 1 Fat

Strawberry Banana Pizza Dessert

■ ■ ■

Kids of all ages love pizza, whether it's the traditional main-dish, tomato-and-cheese-topped kind, or a sweet and fruity dessert pie that is as colorful as it is delicious! I'd serve this for a teenager's graduation party or when the family is gathered to watch the basketball playoffs. Whenever you do bring it out, you're bound to hear cheers!

Serves 8

¾ cup all-purpose flour
½ cup pourable Sugar Twin
1 teaspoon baking powder
½ teaspoon baking soda
⅓ cup (1 ripe medium) mashed banana
⅓ cup Yoplait plain fat-free yogurt
¼ cup Kraft fat-free mayonnaise
3 cups water ☆
2 teaspoons vanilla extract
1 (8-ounce) package Philadelphia fat-free cream cheese

1 (4-serving) package JELL-O sugar-free instant banana cream pudding mix
⅔ cup Carnation Nonfat Dry Milk Powder
2 cups sliced fresh strawberries
1 cup (1 medium) sliced banana
1 (4-serving) package JELL-O sugar-free vanilla cook-and-serve pudding mix
1 (4-serving) package JELL-O sugar-free strawberry gelatin

Preheat oven to 375 degrees. Spray a 12-inch pizza pan with butter-flavored cooking spray. In a large bowl, combine flour, Sugar Twin, baking powder, and baking soda. In a small bowl, combine mashed banana, yogurt, mayonnaise, ½ cup water, and vanilla extract. Add banana mixture to flour mixture. Mix gently just to combine. Spread mixture onto prepared pizza pan. Bake for 15 minutes or until crust springs back when lightly touched in center. Place pizza pan on a wire rack and allow to cool for 10 minutes. In a large bowl, stir cream cheese with a spoon until soft. Add dry banana cream pudding mix, dry milk powder, and 1¼ cups water. Mix well using a wire whisk. Spread mixture evenly over cooled crust. Evenly arrange sliced strawberries and banana over top. In a medium saucepan, combine dry cook-and-serve pudding mix, dry gelatin, and remaining 1¼ cups water. Cook over medium heat until mixture thickens and starts to boil, stirring often. Remove from heat and place saucepan on a wire rack for 2 to 3 minutes. Drizzle partially cooled mixture evenly over fruit. Refrigerate for at least 1 hour. Cut into 8 wedges.

HINT: If you have difficulty finding cook-and-serve pudding for this and other recipes, please check my tips on pages 55 and 56.

Each serving equals:

HE: ¾ Fruit, ½ Bread, ½ Protein, ¼ Skim Milk, ½ Slider, 2 Optional Calories

156 Calories, 0 gm Fat, 9 gm Protein, 30 gm Carbohydrate, 668 mg Sodium, 131 mg Calcium, 2 gm Fiber

DIABETIC: 1 Fruit, 1 Starch/Carbohydrate

Coconut Lemon Layer Cream Cheese Pie

■ ■ ■

Did you worry that living a healthy lifestyle meant you'd never get to feast on a piece of coconut layer cake or lemon cream pie again? You can sigh with relief now, then dive into this fabulous and festive dessert that takes some of the best of both and joins hands!

Serves 8

1 (8-ounce) package
  Philadelphia fat-free cream
  cheese
1 teaspoon coconut extract
¼ cup pourable Sugar Twin
¾ cup Cool Whip Lite ☆
1 (6-ounce) Keebler shortbread
  piecrust
1 (4-serving) package JELL-O
  sugar-free lemon gelatin

1 (4-serving) package JELL-O
  sugar-free vanilla cook-and-
  serve pudding mix
⅔ cup Carnation Nonfat Dry
  Milk Powder
1 cup water
2 tablespoons flaked coconut

In a large bowl, stir cream cheese with a spoon until soft. Add coconut extract, Sugar Twin, and ¼ cup Cool Whip Lite. Mix gently to combine. Spread mixture evenly into piecrust. Refrigerate. Meanwhile, in a medium saucepan, combine dry pudding mix, dry gelatin, dry milk powder, and water. Cook over medium heat until mixture thickens and starts to boil, stirring often. Remove from heat. Place pan on a wire rack and allow to cool for 15 minutes, stirring occasionally. Evenly spread cooled lemon mixture over cream cheese layer. Sprinkle coconut evenly over top. Refrigerate for at least 1 hour. Cut into 8 servings. When serving, top each piece with 1 tablespoon Cool Whip Lite.

Each serving equals:
HE: ½ Bread, ½ Protein, ¼ Skim Milk, 1 Slider, 7 Optional Calories
165 Calories, 5 gm Fat, 7 gm Protein, 23 gm Carbohydrate, 383 mg Sodium, 69 mg Calcium, 1 gm Fiber
DIABETIC: 1½ Starch/Carbohydrate, 1 Fat, ½ Meat

Sour Cream Cakes with Raisin Cream Topping

■ ■ ■

Here's a luscious way to end a meal with a little extra excitement. These rich and creamy treats are wonderfully easy, and Cliff was a particular fan of the yummy topping.

Serves 4

½ cup Land O Lakes no-fat sour cream ☆

½ cup Cool Whip Free

¾ teaspoon ground nutmeg ☆

¼ cup raisins

¾ cup Bisquick Reduced Fat Baking Mix

2 tablespoons pourable Sugar Twin

⅓ cup Carnation Nonfat Dry Milk Powder

⅓ cup water

Preheat oven to 350 degrees. Spray 4 (12-ounce) custard cups with butter-flavored cooking spray. In a medium bowl, combine ¼ cup sour cream, Cool Whip Free, and ¼ teaspoon nutmeg. Stir in raisins. Set aside. In a medium bowl, combine baking mix, Sugar Twin, remaining ½ teaspoon nutmeg, and dry milk powder. Add water and remaining ¼ cup sour cream. Mix well to combine. Evenly spoon batter into prepared custard cups. Bake for 20 to 25 minutes or until a toothpick inserted in center comes out clean. Place custard cups on a wire rack and cool completely. Frost each with about 2 tablespoons raisin cream topping.

Each serving equals:
HE: 1 Bread, ½ Fruit, ¼ Skim Milk, ½ Slider, 13 Optional Calories
178 Calories, 2 gm Fat, 5 gm Protein, 35 gm Carbohydrate, 338 mg Sodium, 125 mg Calcium, 0 gm Fiber
DIABETIC: 1½ Starch/Carbohydrate, ½ Fruit

Black Forest Cake Roll

■　■　■

This delectable dessert takes a little bit of effort, but the result is so dazzling, it's worth it! My son James is a big fan of the chocolate-cherry combination that is always identified with the "Black Forest" name, so I made sure I was testing this on a weekend when he and Pam brought my grandchildren for a visit. The boys love to cook with Gamma. . . .　　　　　　　　　　　　　　　　*Serves 8*

¾ cup all-purpose flour

1 teaspoon baking powder

¼ cup unsweetened cocoa

½ cup pourable Sugar Twin

3 eggs or equivalent in egg substitute

¼ cup Kraft fat-free mayonnaise

1 (4-serving) package JELL-O sugar-free vanilla cook-and-serve pudding mix

1 (4-serving) package JELL-O sugar-free cherry gelatin

2 cups (one 16-ounce can) tart red cherries, packed in water, drained, and ⅓ cup liquid reserved

¼ cup water

1 cup Cool Whip Lite

¼ cup (1 ounce) chopped walnuts

Preheat oven to 400 degrees. Line a 15½-by-10½-by-1-inch pan with waxed paper and spray paper with butter-flavored cooking spray. In a large bowl, combine flour, baking powder, cocoa, and Sugar Twin. Add eggs and mayonnaise. Mix well to combine. Spread batter into prepared pan. Bake for 6 to 8 minutes or until a toothpick inserted in center comes out clean. Place pan on a wire rack and let set for 5 minutes. Place a clean cloth over top, turn pan over and gently remove cake from pan. Carefully peel waxed paper off of cake. Starting at narrow end, roll cake with towel inside. Cool for 30 minutes. Meanwhile, in a large saucepan, combine dry pudding mix, dry gelatin, reserved cherry liquid, and water. Stir in cherries. Cook over medium heat until mixture thickens and starts to boil, stirring often, and being careful not to crush cherries. Remove from heat. Place saucepan on a wire rack and let set for 5 minutes. Gently unroll cooled cake and carefully remove the towel. Spread cherry mixture evenly over top. Reroll and refrigerate for at least 1 hour. Cut into 8 pieces. For each serving, place 1 piece of cake roll on a dessert plate, top with 2 tablespoons Cool Whip Lite, and garnish with 1½ teaspoons walnuts.

HINTS: If you have trouble finding canned tart cherries packed in water,
1. Ask your grocer to contact the manufacturer directly. In DeWitt, I have two brands available, Comstock and ShurFine.
2. You can use frozen unsweetened tart cherries, but thaw and drain them well. Also, you'll need to add water to equal the amount of reserved liquid you would have used in this recipe.
3. If carbohydrates and calories are not a problem for you, you can skip making the pie "filling" and just use Comstock Light Cherry Pie Filling. Just scoop out and discard ¼ to ⅓ cup of sauce, or your dessert will be too "loose."

Each serving equals:
HE: ½ Bread, ½ Protein (⅓ limited), ½ Fruit, ¼ Fat, ½ Slider, 14 Optional Calories

161 Calories, 5 gm Fat, 6 gm Protein, 23 gm Carbohydrate, 240 mg Sodium, 58 mg Calcium, 2 gm Fiber

DIABETIC: 1 Starch/Carbohydrate, 1 Fat, ½ Fruit

Chocolate Brownie Cake with Raspberry Glaze and White Chocolate Topping

■ ■ ■

Every month at Healthy Exchanges, we have one giant birthday party for everyone whose birthday falls during that month. And yes, of course, there is ALWAYS cake—or pie! This particular party-on-a-plate was so popular, some of my staff asked if we could have it again the following month. *Serves 8*

1½ cups all-purpose flour
¼ cup unsweetened cocoa
½ cup pourable Sugar Twin
1 teaspoon baking powder
½ teaspoon baking soda
½ cup Yoplait plain fat-free yogurt
⅓ cup Kraft fat-free mayonnaise
1 teaspoon vanilla extract
1¾ cups water ☆

½ cup raspberry spreadable fruit
1 (4-serving) package JELL-O sugar-free instant white chocolate pudding mix
⅔ cup Carnation Nonfat Dry Milk Powder
½ cup Cool Whip Free
2 tablespoons (½ ounce) mini chocolate chips

Preheat oven to 350 degrees. Spray a 9-by-9-inch cake pan with butter-flavored cooking spray. In a large bowl, combine flour, cocoa, Sugar Twin, baking powder, and baking soda. In a medium bowl, combine yogurt, mayonnaise, vanilla extract, and ¾ cup water. Add yogurt mixture to flour mixture. Mix gently just to combine. Spread batter into prepared cake pan. Bake for 25 to 30 minutes or until a toothpick inserted in center comes out clean. Place cake pan on a wire rack and let set 5 minutes. In a small bowl, stir spreadable fruit with a spoon until soft. Evenly spread spreadable fruit over partially cooled cake. Continue cooling for 15 minutes. In a large bowl, combine dry pudding mix, dry milk powder, and remaining 1 cup water. Mix well using a wire whisk. Blend in Cool Whip Free. Evenly spread topping mixture over completely cooled cake. Sprinkle chocolate chips evenly over top. Cut into 8 servings. Refrigerate leftovers.

HINT: This is a heavy, moist cake.

Each serving equals:

HE: 1 Bread, 1 Fruit, ⅓ Skim Milk, ½ Slider, 15 Optional Calories

193 Calories, 1 gm Fat, 6 gm Protein, 40 gm Carbohydrate, 436 mg Sodium, 139 mg Calcium, 2 gm Fiber

DIABETIC: 1½ Starch/Carbohydrate, 1 Fruit

German Chocolate Crazy Cake

■ ❋ ■

I've tried all kinds of ways to make low-fat cakes taste as irresistibly good as the real thing, and over the years I've found some surprising ways to perform this culinary abracadabra! This looks so rich, you may find your credibility questioned when you assure your guests that the cake they're devouring has fewer than 200 calories per serving!

Serves 8

1½ cups all-purpose flour
¼ cup unsweetened cocoa
½ cup pourable Sugar Twin
1 teaspoon baking soda
½ cup unsweetened applesauce
1¾ cups water ☆
1 tablespoon white vinegar
2 teaspoons vanilla extract

1 (4-serving) package JELL-O sugar-free vanilla cook-and-serve pudding mix
2 tablespoons Brown Sugar Twin
⅔ cup Carnation Nonfat Dry Milk Powder
1½ teaspoons coconut extract
¼ cup (1 ounce) chopped pecans
¼ cup flaked coconut

Preheat oven to 350 degrees. Spray a 9-by-9-inch cake pan with butter-flavored cooking spray. In a large bowl, combine flour, cocoa, Sugar Twin, and baking soda. In a small bowl, combine applesauce, ¾ cup water, vinegar, and vanilla extract. Add applesauce mixture to flour mixture. Mix gently to combine. Pour batter into prepared cake pan. Bake for 20 to 25 minutes or until a toothpick inserted in center comes out clean. Place cake pan on a wire rack and allow to cool. Meanwhile, in a medium saucepan, combine dry pudding mix, Brown Sugar Twin, dry milk powder, and remaining 1 cup water. Cook over medium heat until mixture thickens and starts to boil, stirring constantly. Remove from heat. Stir in coconut extract. Add pecans and coconut. Mix well to combine. Spread hot mixture evenly over partially cooled cake. Allow to cool completely. Cut into 8 servings.

Each serving equals:
HE: 1 Bread, ½ Fat, ¼ Skim Milk, ½ Slider

168 Calories, 4 gm Fat, 5 gm Protein, 28 gm Carbohydrate, 253 mg Sodium, 78 mg Calcium, 2 gm Fiber

DIABETIC: 1½ Starch/Carbohydrate, 1 Fat

S'More Snack Cake

■ ■ ■

No campfire. No sleeping bags. No hooting of owls in the trees as the stars twinkle overhead. But if you close your eyes and take a bite, you may just be transported to those happy days of gobbling s'mores with your Scout troop! What could be yummier than blending the chocolate, marshmallow, and graham cracker combo into a wonderful cake? *Serves 8*

¾ cup all-purpose flour
¾ cup purchased graham cracker crumbs or 12 (2½-inch) graham cracker squares, made into crumbs
½ cup pourable Sugar Twin
1 teaspoon baking powder
½ teaspoon baking soda
½ cup (1 ounce) miniature marshmallows
¼ cup (1 ounce) mini chocolate chips

⅓ cup Yoplait plain fat-free yogurt
¼ cup Kraft fat-free mayonnaise
2 teaspoons vanilla extract ☆
1¾ cups water ☆
1 (4-serving) package JELL-O sugar-free instant chocolate pudding mix
⅔ cup Carnation Nonfat Dry Milk Powder
½ cup Cool Whip Free

Preheat oven to 350 degrees. Spray a 9-by-9-inch cake pan with butter-flavored cooking spray. In a large bowl, combine flour, graham cracker crumbs, Sugar Twin, baking powder, and baking soda. Stir in marshmallows and chocolate chips. In a small bowl, combine yogurt, mayonnaise, 1 teaspoon vanilla extract, and ¾ cup water. Add yogurt mixture to flour mixture. Mix gently to combine. Spread batter into prepared cake pan. Bake for 25 to 30 minutes or until a toothpick inserted in center comes out clean. Place cake pan on a wire rack and allow to cool completely. In a large bowl, combine dry pudding mix, dry milk powder, and remaining 1 cup water. Mix well using a wire whisk. Fold in Cool Whip Free and remaining 1 teaspoon vanilla extract. Spread mixture evenly over cooled cake. Cut into 8 servings.

Each serving equals:
HE: 1 Bread, ¼ Skim Milk, ¾ Slider, 2 Optional Calories

170 Calories, 2 gm Fat, 5 gm Protein, 33 gm Carbohydrate, 480 mg Sodium, 127 mg Calcium, 1 gm Fiber

DIABETIC: 2 Starch/Carbohydrate

Applesauce Bars with Crunch Topping

■ ■ ■

There's nothing like applesauce to make baked goodies remarkably moist and sweet, don't you agree? But why stop at good when you can have something truly great tasting? (That's what I asked myself when I was writing down this recipe!) I grabbed the nuts, chips, and coconut and went a little wild (in moderation, of course)!

Serves 8 (2 each)

1½ cups all-purpose flour
1 cup pourable Sugar Twin ☆
1 teaspoon baking powder
½ teaspoon baking soda
2 cups unsweetened applesauce
1 egg or equivalent in egg substitute

1 teaspoon coconut extract
¼ cup Brown Sugar Twin
¼ cup (1 ounce) chopped walnuts
¼ cup (1 ounce) mini chocolate chips
2 tablespoons flaked coconut

Preheat oven to 300 degrees. Spray a 9-by-13-inch cake pan with butter-flavored cooking spray. In a large bowl, combine flour, ¾ cup Sugar Twin, baking powder, and baking soda. Add applesauce, egg, and coconut extract. Mix well to combine. Spread batter into prepared cake pan. In a medium bowl, combine remaining ¼ cup Sugar Twin, Brown Sugar Twin, walnuts, chocolate chips, and coconut. Evenly sprinkle mixture over top of batter. Bake for 45 to 55 minutes or until a toothpick inserted in center comes out clean. Place cake pan on a wire rack and allow to cool. Cut into 16 bars.

Each serving equals:
HE: 1 Bread, ½ Fruit, ¼ Protein, ¼ Fat, ¼ Slider, 17 Optional Calories
164 Calories, 4 gm Fat, 4 gm Protein, 28 gm Carbohydrate, 271 mg Sodium, 47 mg Calcium, 2 gm Fiber
DIABETIC: 1 Starch, ½ Fruit, ½ Fat

Pineapple Sheet Bars

■ ■ ■

For your next family gathering, when what you really need are fruity, flavorful little cakes to serve a crowd, why not dazzle your near and dear with these scrumptious delights? Be sure not to jump the gun while waiting for the bars to cool, or your topping will lose its charm. *Serves 8 (2 each)*

1½ cups all-purpose flour
1½ teaspoons baking soda
1 (4-serving) package JELL-O sugar-free instant vanilla pudding mix
¼ cup pourable Sugar Twin
¼ cup (1 ounce) chopped walnuts
2 cups (two 8-ounce cans) crushed pineapple, packed in fruit juice, undrained

1 teaspoon vanilla extract
1 egg or equivalent in egg substitute
1 (8-ounce) package Philadelphia fat-free cream cheese
¾ cup Cool Whip Free
1 teaspoon coconut extract
2 tablespoons flaked coconut

Preheat oven to 375 degrees. Spray a 12-by-15-inch rimmed baking sheet with butter-flavored cooking spray. In a large bowl, combine flour, baking soda, dry pudding mix, Sugar Twin, and walnuts. Add undrained pineapple, vanilla extract, and egg. Mix well to combine. Spread batter into prepared baking sheet. Bake for 15 to 18 minutes or until a toothpick inserted in center comes out clean. Place baking sheet on a wire rack and allow to cool for about 20 minutes. In a medium bowl, stir cream cheese with a spoon until soft. Add Cool Whip Free and coconut extract. Mix well to combine. Spread cream cheese mixture evenly over cooled cake. Evenly sprinkle flaked coconut over top. Cut into 16 bars. Refrigerate leftovers.

Each serving equals:
HE: 1 Bread, ¾ Protein, ½ Fruit, ¼ Fat, ¼ Slider, 14 Optional Calories
203 Calories, 3 gm Fat, 8 gm Protein, 36 gm Carbohydrate, 587 mg Sodium, 19 mg Calcium, 1 gm Fiber
DIABETIC: 1½ Starch/Carbohydrate, ½ Meat, ½ Fruit, ½ Fat

Lemon Squares

■ ❋ ■

Sometimes, after a very hearty and filling meal, all you want is a delicate little sweet. I suggest these tart and pretty little cake squares that will perfectly hit the spot. If you want to make a true hostess-with-the-mostest impression, try sprinkling powdered sugar on top through a paper doily to make a lacy pattern!

Serves 8 (2 each)

¾ cup all-purpose flour
¼ cup pourable Sugar Twin
⅓ cup reduced-calorie margarine, melted
1 (4-serving) package JELL-O sugar-free lemon gelatin
¾ cup Land O Lakes no-fat sour cream

¾ teaspoon baking powder
2 eggs or equivalent in egg substitute
2 tablespoons powdered sugar (optional)

Preheat oven to 350 degrees. Spray a 9-by-9-inch cake pan with butter-flavored cooking spray. In a medium bowl, combine flour, Sugar Twin, and margarine. Press mixture evenly into bottom of prepared cake pan. In a large bowl, combine dry gelatin, sour cream, and baking powder. Add eggs. Beat with an electric mixer on HIGH for 3 minutes or until light and fluffy. Pour lemon mixture evenly over crust. Bake for 20 to 25 minutes or until the center is firm. Place cake pan on a wire rack and let set for 10 minutes. Evenly sprinkle powdered sugar over top, if desired. Continue cooling. Cut into 16 squares.

Each serving equals:
HE: 1 Fat, ½ Bread, ¼ Protein (limited), ¼ Slider, 3 Optional Calories

104 Calories, 4 gm Fat, 4 gm Protein, 13 gm Carbohydrate, 155 mg Sodium, 57 mg Calcium, 0 gm Fiber

DIABETIC: 1 Fat, 1 Starch

Apple Dessert Enchiladas

■ ❄ ■

Lots of culinary traditions feature a version of a warm, fruit-filled pancake or crepe, so I decided to create a south-of-the-border version to wrap up your very next spicy feast. Remember that the best apples for cooking are usually not the ones you choose to eat raw for snacks, so try to find the ones that hold their shape and flavor best while cooking.

Serves 6

2 (4-serving) packages JELL-O
    sugar-free vanilla cook-and-
    serve pudding mix ☆
1 (4-serving) package JELL-O
    sugar-free lemon gelatin
1½ teaspoons apple pie spice ☆
2 cups water ☆
½ cup unsweetened apple juice

1½ cups (3 small) cored, peeled,
    and diced cooking apples
¼ cup raisins
6 (6-inch) flour tortillas
⅔ cup Carnation Nonfat Dry
    Milk Powder
1 tablespoon reduced-calorie
    margarine

Preheat oven to 350 degrees. Spray an 8-by-8-inch baking dish with butter-flavored cooking spray. In a large saucepan, combine 1 package dry pudding mix, dry gelatin, 1 teaspoon apple pie spice, ½ cup water, and apple juice. Stir in apples and raisins. Cook over medium heat until mixture thickens and apples soften, stirring often. Remove from heat. Spoon about ⅓ cup apple mixture in center of each tortilla and roll up. Place "enchiladas" into prepared baking dish, seam side down. In a medium saucepan, combine remaining package dry pudding mix, dry milk powder, and remaining 1½ cups water. Cook over medium heat until mixture thickens and starts to boil, stirring constantly. Remove from heat. Stir in margarine and remaining ½ teaspoon apple pie spice. Evenly spoon sauce mixture over "enchiladas." Cover and bake for 30 minutes. Let set for 5 minutes. Divide into 6 servings.

HINT: Good served with sugar- and fat-free vanilla ice cream.

Each serving equals:
HE: 1 Bread, 1 Fruit, ⅓ Skim Milk, ¼ Fat, ¼ Slider, 13 Optional Calories
190 Calories, 2 gm Fat, 6 gm Protein, 37 gm Carbohydrate, 396 mg Sodium, 108 mg Calcium, 1 gm Fiber
DIABETIC: 1½ Starch/Carbohydrate, 1 Fruit

Fruit Cocktail Cobbler

■ ❋ ■

Company's coming and you've got nothing to serve with coffee? This quick and tasty pantry pleaser can easily save the day. All you need are some basic ingredients—and it's ready to serve in less than an hour. Don't you feel like a genius in the kitchen?

Serves 8

1½ cups Bisquick Reduced Fat
   Baking Mix
2 tablespoons pourable Sugar
   Twin
1 tablespoon + 1 teaspoon
   reduced-calorie margarine,
   melted

⅔ cup skim milk
2 cups (one 16-ounce can) fruit
   cocktail, packed in fruit juice,
   undrained

Preheat oven to 400 degrees. Spray a 9-by-9-inch cake pan with butter-flavored cooking spray. In a large bowl, combine baking mix and Sugar Twin. Add skim milk and melted margarine. Mix well to combine. Spread mixture evenly into prepared cake pan. Pour undrained fruit cocktail evenly over top of batter. Bake for 25 to 30 minutes. Place cake pan on a wire rack and let cool for at least 10 minutes. Cut into 8 servings. Good warm or cold.

HINT: Great served with Wells' Blue Bunny sugar- and fat-free vanilla ice
      cream, but don't forget to count the additional calories.

Each serving equals:
HE: 1 Bread, ½ Fruit, ¼ Fat, 9 Optional Calories

122 Calories, 2 gm Fat, 2 gm Protein, 24 gm Carbohydrate, 283 mg Sodium, 48 mg Calcium, 1 gm Fiber

DIABETIC: 1 Starch/Carbohydrate, ½ Fruit

Summer Breezes Cream-Filled Shortcakes

■ ■ ■

What more old-fashioned and lovely tradition for a picnic supper could there be than a dessert of shortcakes just shimmering with bright fresh fruit? This is a perfect Fourth of July spectacular, but you don't need a national holiday or a parade to enjoy its wonderful flavors.   *Serves 4*

¾ cup Bisquick Reduced Fat
   Baking Mix
⅓ cup Carnation Nonfat Dry
   Milk Powder
2 tablespoons pourable Sugar
   Twin
¼ cup Kraft fat-free mayonnaise
¼ cup Diet Mountain Dew

1 (4-serving) package JELL-O
   sugar-free instant vanilla pudding mix
2 cups skim milk
½ cup Cool Whip Lite ☆
2¼ cups fresh raspberries
¾ cup fresh blueberries

Preheat oven to 415 degrees. Spray a baking sheet with butter-flavored cooking spray. In a medium bowl, combine baking mix, dry milk powder, and Sugar Twin. Add mayonnaise and Diet Mountain Dew. Mix well to combine. Drop batter by tablespoonful onto prepared baking sheet to form 4 shortcakes. Bake for 8 to 12 minutes or until golden brown. Place baking sheet on a wire rack and allow to cool. Meanwhile, in a large bowl, combine dry pudding mix and skim milk. Mix well using a wire whisk. Blend in ¼ cup Cool Whip Lite. In a medium bowl, combine raspberries and blueberries. For each serving, cut a shortcake in half, place bottom half in a dessert dish, spoon full ½ cup pudding mixture and ¾ cup fruit mixture over shortcake, arrange top half over fruit, and garnish with 1 tablespoon Cool Whip Lite.

Each serving equals:
HE: 1 Bread, 1 Fruit, ¾ Skim Milk, ½ Slider, 18 Optional Calories

247 Calories, 3 gm Fat, 9 gm Protein, 46 gm Carbohydrate, 819 mg Sodium, 255 mg Calcium, 4 gm Fiber

DIABETIC: 1½ Starch/Carbohydrate, 1 Fruit, 1 Skim Milk

Chocolate Mandarin Orange Decadence

■ ■ ■

"Decadence" is the right name for a dessert so impossibly good it just ought to be bad! This spirited blend of tastes and textures takes a bit of work to assemble, but the end result is simply dazzling! *Serves 12 (¾ cup)*

1½ cups all-purpose flour
¼ cup unsweetened cocoa
¾ cup pourable Sugar Twin
1½ teaspoons baking soda
¾ cup Kraft fat-free mayonnaise
2 teaspoons vanilla extract
1 cup unsweetened orange juice ☆
2¾ cups water ☆
2 (4-serving) packages JELL-O sugar-free instant chocolate fudge pudding mix

1⅓ cups Carnation Nonfat Dry Milk Powder
2 cups Cool Whip Free ☆
2 cups (two 11-ounce cans) mandarin oranges, rinsed and drained ☆
12 (2½-inch) chocolate graham cracker squares, made into crumbs ☆
2 tablespoons (½ ounce) mini chocolate chips

Preheat oven to 350 degrees. Spray a 9-by-9-inch cake pan with butter-flavored cooking spray. In a large bowl, combine flour, cocoa, Sugar Twin, and baking soda. In a small bowl, combine mayonnaise, vanilla extract, ½ cup orange juice, and ¼ cup water. Add liquid mixture to flour mixture. Mix gently just to combine. Spread batter into prepared cake pan. Bake for 18 to 22 minutes or until a toothpick inserted in center comes out clean. Place cake pan on a wire rack and allow to cool completely. Cut cake into 36 pieces. In a large bowl, combine dry pudding mixes, dry milk powder, remaining 2½ cups water, and remaining ½ cup orange juice. Mix well using a wire whisk. Blend in 1 cup Cool Whip Free. To assemble, layer half of cake pieces in the bottom of a glass trifle dish, layer half of pudding mixture, half of mandarin oranges, and half of graham cracker crumbs over top. Repeat layers. Spread remaining 1 cup Cool Whip Free over top. Garnish with chocolate chips. Refrigerate for at least 1 hour.

Each serving equals:

HE: 1 Bread, ½ Fruit, ⅓ Skim Milk, ½ Slider, 19 Optional Calories

189 Calories, 1 gm Fat, 6 gm Protein, 39 gm Carbohydrate, 581 mg Sodium, 104 mg Calcium, 2 gm Fiber

DIABETIC: 1½ Starch/Carbohydrate, ½ Fruit, ½ Skim Milk

Bundles of Heaven

■ ■ ■

Now that we can easily find specialty products from all the different traditions that make up our American melting pot, I enjoy creating new recipes that feature them. Once you track down the sheets of phyllo dough, which I've seen all over the country, you're ready to "bundle" up these sweet surprises. Invite your guests to go hunting for buried treasure when they nibble on these!

Serves 8 (1 each)

¼ cup raisins

¼ cup (1 ounce) chopped walnuts

2 tablespoons (½ ounce) mini chocolate chips

8 sheets (16½-inch by 12-inch) phyllo dough, thawed

1 (4-serving) package JELL-O sugar-free chocolate cook-and-serve pudding mix

⅔ cup Carnation Nonfat Dry Milk Powder

1½ cups water

¼ cup (½ ounce) miniature marshmallows

1 teaspoon vanilla extract

2 tablespoons reduced-calorie margarine

Preheat oven to 350 degrees. Spray a baking sheet with butter-flavored cooking spray. In a small bowl, combine raisins, walnuts, and chocolate chips. On a clean working surface, lay out one sheet of phyllo dough and lightly spray with butter-flavored cooking spray. Evenly spoon about 1 full tablespoon of raisin mixture in center of each phyllo dough section. Begin folding dough strip in triangles, "flag style," to completely seal in filling. Place on prepared baking sheet. Repeat process until all 8 sheets of dough have been used. Lightly spray tops with butter-flavored cooking spray. Bake for 6 to 10 minutes or until golden brown. Meanwhile, in a medium saucepan, combine dry pudding mix, dry milk powder, and water. Cook over medium heat until mixture thickens and starts to boil. Remove from heat. Stir in marshmallows, vanilla extract, and margarine. For each serving, place a warm bundle on a dessert plate and spoon about ¼ cup warm chocolate sauce over top.

HINTS: "Flag style" means taking one corner of the phyllo sheet and folding it over until it touches the other side, the way you fold an American flag on a ceremonial occasion. You keep folding those triangles over until your "bundle" is all wrapped up.

HINT: For true decadence, top each serving with ¼ cup sugar- and fat-free vanilla ice cream.

Each serving equals:

HE: ½ Bread, ½ Fat, ¼ Skim Milk, ¼ Fruit, ¼ Slider, 13 Optional Calories

144 Calories, 4 gm Fat, 4 gm Protein, 23 gm Carbohydrate, 193 mg Sodium, 77 mg Calcium, 1 gm Fiber

DIABETIC: 1 Starch, ½ Skim Milk, ½ Fat

Applesauce à la Mode

■ ■ ■

Not long ago, all you had to serve for dessert was some naked vanilla ice cream, which wasn't very exciting. But after calling on that superstar of kitchen appliances, your microwave, you can be ready to celebrate in about two minutes! Zach and Josh, my ever-growing grandbabies, just loved this one.   *Serves 4*

2 cups unsweetened applesauce
1 teaspoon apple pie spice
1 teaspoon lemon juice
*1 tablespoon pourable Sugar
    Twin*

*2 cups Wells' Blue Bunny sugar-
    and fat-free vanilla ice cream
    or any sugar- and fat-free ice
    cream*

In a 4-cup glass measure, combine applesauce, apple pie spice, lemon juice, and Sugar Twin. Microwave on HIGH (100% power) for 2 minutes. For each serving, place ½ cup ice cream in a dessert dish and spoon about ½ cup hot applesauce mixture over top. Serve at once.

HINT: ¼ cup raisins may be added to applesauce mixture before microwaving.

Each serving equals:
HE: 1 Fruit, ¾ Slider, 2 Optional Calories
140 Calories, 0 gm Fat, 4 gm Protein, 31 gm Carbohydrate, 53 mg Sodium, 124 mg Calcium, 1 gm Fiber
DIABETIC: 1 Fruit, 1 Starch/Carbohydrate

Peach Melba Sundaes

■ ■ ■

Here's another great dessert topping you can whip up in your microwave in no time at all. Just put on your chef's cap and pretend you're creating a grand finale in your celebrity-filled restaurant. This simple preparation could make you a star! (Since my daughter, Becky, loves peaches, I sent her husband, John, the family dessert maker, a copy of this recipe as soon as it was typed.)   *Serves 4*

*2 cups Wells' Blue Bunny sugar-
and fat-free vanilla ice cream
or any sugar- and fat-free ice
cream*
*1 cup (one 8-ounce can) sliced
peaches, packed in fruit juice,
drained, and 2 tablespoons
liquid reserved*

*2 tablespoons raspberry spread-
able fruit*
¼ cup Cool Whip Lite
*1 tablespoon (1/4 ounce)
chopped pecans*

Evenly spoon ½ cup ice cream into 4 dessert dishes and spoon peaches evenly over top of each. In a 1-cup glass measuring cup, combine reserved peach liquid and spreadable fruit. Microwave on HIGH (100% power) for 60 seconds. For each serving, drizzle a full tablespoon hot sauce over peaches, top with 1 table-spoon Cool Whip Lite, and garnish with ¾ teaspoon pecans. Serve at once.

Each serving equals:
HE: 1 Fruit, ¼ Fat, ¾ Slider

149 Calories, 1 gm Fat, 4 gm Protein, 31 gm Carbohydrate, 53 mg Sodium, 124 mg Calcium, 1 gm Fiber

DIABETIC: 1 Fruit, 1 Starch/Carbohydrate

A JOYFUL
ABUNDANCE:
THIS AND THAT

■ ■ ■

Think for a moment about what abundance means, especially when it comes to living healthy. I like to define it as choosing to live more fully, doing it the best you can, and making every meal as tasty as possible.

This section of recipes demonstrates yet again that "just good enough" will never be good enough for Healthy Exchanges. Those wonderful little extras in life have a spiritual element, making us feel energized and inspired to live the rest of our lives more completely. Sure, you could drink a glass of diet soda at your next dinner party, but wouldn't a festive and colorful blended drink be more fun?

I know how it feels to stand at a party, avoiding the buffet and the bar, being afraid to partake of the culinary pleasures available because I feared what enjoying myself would mean to my waistline. But living with that "deprivation situation" only made things worse. I've learned to welcome abundance into my life in every

*area, including food, as long as I make tasty, healthy choices that satisfy my stom-
ach and my soul. And I have confidence that you can do it too!*

I'm giving you all the tools you'll need to make life sparkle at every meal, from
breakfast and brunches to late suppers and midnight snacks. How can it be a
disappointing day when you start with *Bacon and Egg Pizza*? You're bound to
bounce back from a rough morning at work when you gobble down *Pumpkin
Chocolate Chip Muffins* with your coffee. And when the gang is gathered for a
playoff party, you won't care which team wins if you're enjoying *Heartland
Deviled Eggs, Italian Baked Onion Rings,* and *Mexican Mocha Floats!*

> *"Go eat your bread with joy,*
> *And drink your wine with a merry heart;*
> *For God has already accepted your works."*
> —ECCLESIASTES 9:7

Eggs Baked in Toast Cups

Mexican Scrambled Eggs

Denver-Style Scrambled Eggs

Bacon and Egg Pizza

Blueberry Pancakes with Strawberry
  Topping

Peach Melba Pancakes

Italian Tomato-Cheese Muffins

Pumpkin Chocolate Chip Muffins

Three-Way Apple Raisin Bread

Sour Cream Blueberry Banana Bread

Chocolate Zucchini Bread

Cranberry-Orange Bread

Nutty Chicken Dip

Calico Ham Dip

Carrot-Stuffed Celery

Italian Baked Onion Rings

Dilly Deviled Eggs

Heartland Deviled Eggs

Easy Refrigerator Shake Pickles

Munch Mix

Maple Peanut Brittle

Cinnamon-Orange Maple Syrup

Plymouth Rock Floats

Mexican Mocha Float

Berry Bash Slush

Chocolate Brandy Alexander

Eggs Baked in Toast Cups

So many people who are trying to live healthy tell me they get so bored with the same morning routine, eating bran flakes and skim milk, or grabbing a piece of toast and a chunk of reduced-fat cheese. I agree that it's important to feel you've got choices at every meal, so you don't get in a "same-old, same-old" rut and grab a doughnut instead. This breakfast dish is easy to make but takes more time than many of us have on weekdays. But isn't it fun knowing you've got a treat to look forward to?

Serves 4

8 slices reduced-calorie bread
6 eggs or equivalent in egg substi-
    tute
¼ teaspoon lemon pepper

1 teaspoon dried parsley flakes
3 tablespoons (¾ ounce) shred-
    ded Kraft reduced-fat Cheddar
    cheese

Preheat oven to 350 degrees. Spray 8 wells of a 12-hole muffin pan with butter-flavored cooking spray. Trim crusts from bread. Gently fit bread slices into prepared muffin wells. Lightly spray bread with butter-flavored cooking spray. Bake for 10 to 15 minutes or until bread is lightly browned. In a medium bowl, beat eggs with a fork. Stir in lemon pepper, parsley flakes, and Cheddar cheese. Evenly spoon egg mixture into toast cups. Continue baking for 15 to 20 minutes or until eggs are set to desired doneness.

HINT: Fill unused muffin wells with water. It protects the muffin tin and ensures even baking.

Each serving equals:
HE: 1 ¾ Protein (1½ limited), 1 Bread

217 Calories, 9 gm Fat, 15 gm Protein, 19 gm Carbohydrate, 370 mg Sodium, 108 mg Calcium, 5 gm Fiber

DIABETIC: 2 Meat, 1 Starch

Mexican Scrambled Eggs

■ ■ ■

Not everyone is ready for "spicy" first thing in the morning, but if you've got the courage, why not wake up your mouth with this sunny blend of flavors? At our house, eggs are also popular for a late-night supper after a day on the road, so keep this in mind for anytime! *Serves 4*

6 eggs or equivalent in egg substitute
2 tablespoons skim milk
½ teaspoon chili seasoning
¼ teaspoon lemon pepper
1 cup (one 8-ounce can) whole-kernel corn, rinsed and drained

¼ cup (1 ounce) sliced ripe olives
1 cup chunky salsa (mild, medium, or hot)
¼ cup Land O Lakes no-fat sour cream

In a medium bowl, combine eggs, skim milk, chili seasoning, and lemon pepper. Mix well using a wire whisk. Stir in corn and olives. Pour mixture into a large skillet sprayed with butter-flavored cooking spray. Cook over medium heat until eggs are set, stirring occasionally. For each serving, place about ¾ cup egg mixture on a plate, spoon ¼ cup salsa over top, and garnish with 1 tablespoon sour cream.

Each serving equals:
HE: 1½ Protein (limited), ½ Bread, ½ Vegetable, ¼ Fat, 18 Optional Calories
176 Calories, 8 gm Fat, 11 gm Protein, 15 gm Carbohydrate, 414 mg Sodium, 150 mg Calcium, 1 gm Fiber
DIABETIC: 1½ Meat, 1 Starch/Carbohydrate

Denver-Style Scrambled Eggs

■ ■ ■

A traditional Denver omelet usually includes veggies and ham, but I took the idea of the "mile-high" city to heart when I stirred up this tangy-creamy version served over muffin halves. I've tested all my egg recipes with both egg substitute and the real thing, so you can be confident in choosing the alternative if you're watching your egg intake.

Serves 4

¼ cup chopped green bell pepper
¼ cup chopped onion
1 full cup (6 ounces) diced
    Dubuque 97% fat-free ham or
    any extra lean ham
6 eggs or equivalent in egg substitute

2 tablespoons Land O Lakes
    no-fat sour cream
1 teaspoon prepared mustard
⅓ teaspoon lemon pepper
2 English muffins, split and
    toasted

In a large skillet sprayed with butter-flavored cooking spray, sauté green pepper, onion, and ham for 5 minutes or until vegetables are tender. Meanwhile, in a large bowl, combine eggs, sour cream, mustard, and lemon pepper. Mix well using a wire whisk. Add egg mixture to ham mixture. Mix gently to combine. Lower heat and continue cooking until eggs are set, gently stirring occasionally. For each serving, place a muffin half on a plate and spoon about ½ cup egg mixture over top. Serve at once.

Each serving equals:

HE: 2½ Protein (1½ limited), 1 Bread, ¼ Vegetable, 8 Optional Calories
225 Calories, 9 gm Fat, 19 gm Protein, 17 gm Carbohydrate, 613 mg Sodium, 98 mg Calcium, 1 gm Fiber
DIABETIC: 2½ Meat, 1 Starch

Bacon and Egg Pizza

■ ■ ■

Could your kids eat pizza morning, noon, and night? I thought so! Well, I've already provided some great lunch, dinner, and dessert choices, so let me complete the menu with this easy and yummy breakfast dish. I've suggested Cheddar cheese in this recipe, but if your family prefers reduced-fat mozzarella, go for it!

Serves 6

1 (7.5-ounce) can Pillsbury refrigerated buttermilk biscuits
3 eggs, beaten, or equivalent in egg substitute
1 tablespoon skim milk
1 teaspoon dried onion flakes
¼ cup Hormel Bacon Bits
1 full cup (4½ ounces) shredded Kraft reduced-fat Cheddar cheese

Preheat oven to 350 degrees. Spray a 12-inch pizza pan with butter-flavored cooking spray. Separate and flatten biscuits onto prepared pizza pan to form a crust. In a medium bowl, combine eggs, skim milk, and onion flakes. Pour mixture evenly over biscuit crust. Evenly sprinkle bacon bits and Cheddar cheese over top. Bake for 16 to 22 minutes or until crust is golden and eggs are set. Place pizza pan on a wire rack and let set for 5 minutes. Cut into 6 wedges.

Each serving equals:
HE: 1½ Protein (½ limited), 1¼ Bread, 18 Optional Calories
196 Calories, 8 gm Fat, 13 gm Protein, 18 gm Carbohydrate, 682 mg Sodium, 156 mg Calcium, 2 gm Fiber
DIABETIC: 1½ Meat, 1 Starch

Blueberry Pancakes with Strawberry Topping

■ ■ ■

I could dedicate this dish to movie goddess Mae West, famous for reminding us that "too much of a good thing is wonderful!" Making homemade blueberry pancakes is surprisingly easy with today's great low-fat mixes, and when you top them off with cozy-warm strawberries—wow! What a way to say "I love you" on a birthday morning!

Serves 4

3 cups sliced fresh strawberries ☆
1 cup water ☆
1 (4-serving) package JELL-O sugar-free vanilla cook-and-serve pudding mix

1½ cups Aunt Jemima Reduced Calorie Pancake Mix
¾ cup fresh blueberries

Reserve ½ cup strawberries. Mash remaining strawberries with a fork. In a medium saucepan, combine mashed strawberries, ¼ cup water, and dry pudding mix. Cook over medium heat until mixture thickens and starts to boil, stirring often. Lower heat and simmer while preparing pancakes. In a medium bowl, combine dry pancake mix and remaining ¾ cup water. Gently fold in blueberries. Using a ⅓-cup measure as a guide, pour batter onto a hot griddle or skillet sprayed with butter-flavored cooking spray to form 4 pancakes. Lightly brown on both sides. For each serving, place 1 pancake on a plate, spoon about ¼ cup warm strawberry mixture over pancake, and sprinkle 2 tablespoons reserved strawberries over top.

Each serving equals:
HE: 2 Bread, 1 Fruit, ¼ Slider

218 Calories, 2 gm Fat, 9 gm Protein, 41 gm Carbohydrate, 697 mg Sodium, 290 mg Calcium, 8 gm Fiber

DIABETIC: 2 Starch, 1 Fruit

Peach Melba Pancakes

■ ■ ■

I often order pancakes when Cliff and I have breakfast out, and I frequently top them with fresh fruit instead of the usual butter and heavy syrup. I like to think of it as my "breakfast dessert sundae"! Here's a recipe for a luscious way to start the day at home, maybe on a morning when you've got visiting grandkids. (That's what I do!)

Serves 4

> 1 cup (one 8-ounce can) sliced peaches, packed in fruit juice, drained, and ¼ cup liquid reserved
> ¾ cup Bisquick Reduced Fat Baking Mix
> ¼ cup pourable Sugar Twin ☆
>
> ⅓ cup Carnation Nonfat Dry Milk Powder
> ¼ cup water
> 1½ cups frozen unsweetened raspberries, thawed, and undrained
> ¼ cup Cool Whip Lite

Coarsely chop peaches and set aside. In a medium bowl, combine baking mix, 2 tablespoons Sugar Twin, and dry milk powder. Add reserved peach liquid and water. Mix well to combine. Gently stir in chopped peaches. Using a ¼-cup measure as a guide, pour batter onto a hot griddle or skillet sprayed with butter-flavored cooking spray to form 4 pancakes. Brown lightly on both sides. In a small bowl, combine undrained raspberries and remaining 2 tablespoons Sugar Twin. For each serving, place 1 pancake on a plate, spoon about ⅓ cup raspberry mixture over top, and garnish with 1 tablespoon Cool Whip Lite.

Each serving equals:
HE: 1 Bread, 1 Fruit, ¼ Skim Milk, 16 Optional Calories

162 Calories, 2 gm Fat, 4 gm Protein, 32 gm Carbohydrate, 295 mg Sodium, 101 mg Calcium, 3 gm Fiber

DIABETIC: 1 Starch/Carbohydrate, 1 Fruit

Italian Tomato-Cheese Muffins

If you're tired of dull and dreary "healthy" muffins that have absolutely no taste, here's the antidote! These are so festive and flavorful, you'll want to invite the neighbors over to share the excitement. They also freeze beautifully, and you can make larger batches for parties. *Serves 8*

1½ cups all-purpose flour
1½ teaspoons baking powder
½ teaspoon baking soda
1 tablespoon pourable Sugar Twin
¼ cup finely chopped onion
3 tablespoons (¾ ounce) shredded Kraft reduced-fat mozzarella cheese

⅓ cup (1½ ounces) shredded Kraft reduced-fat Cheddar cheese
¾ cup Healthy Request tomato juice or any reduced-sodium tomato juice
¼ cup Kraft Fat Free Italian Dressing
1 egg or equivalent in egg substitute

Preheat oven to 400 degrees. Spray 8 wells of a 12-hole muffin pan with butter-flavored cooking spray or line with paper liners. In a large bowl, combine flour, baking powder, baking soda, and Sugar Twin. Stir in onion, mozzarella cheese, and Cheddar cheese. In a small bowl, combine tomato juice, Italian dressing, and egg. Add liquid mixture to flour mixture. Mix gently just to combine. Evenly spoon batter into prepared muffin wells. Bake for 23 to 26 minutes or until a toothpick inserted in center comes out clean. Place muffin pan on a wire rack and let set 5 minutes. Remove muffins from pan and continue cooling on wire rack.

HINT: Fill unused muffin wells with water. It protects the muffin tin and ensures even baking.

Each serving equals:
HE: 1 Bread, ½ Protein, ¼ Vegetable, 5 Optional Calories

126 Calories, 2 gm Fat, 6 gm Protein, 21 gm Carbohydrate, 331 mg Sodium, 112 mg Calcium, 1 gm Fiber

DIABETIC: 1 Starch, ½ Meat

Pumpkin Chocolate Chip Muffins

Here's another terrific use for canned pumpkin, that oft-forgotten veggie sitting patiently in the pantry, just waiting for you to make it a star! You'll be delighted at how the tiny chocolate chips melt beautifully and deliver an astonishing amount of yumminess.

Serves 12

2¼ cups all-purpose flour
1 (4-serving) package JELL-O sugar-free instant vanilla pudding mix
¼ cup Brown Sugar Twin
2 tablespoons pourable Sugar Twin
⅔ cup Carnation Nonfat Dry Milk Powder
1 tablespoon pumpkin pie spice
1 teaspoon baking powder
½ teaspoon baking soda

¼ cup (1 ounce) mini chocolate chips
¼ cup (1 ounce) chopped walnuts
2 cups (one 15-ounce can) pumpkin
1 egg or equivalent in egg substitute
¾ cup Yoplait plain fat-free yogurt
1 tablespoon + 1 teaspoon vegetable oil

Preheat oven to 350 degrees. Spray a 12-hole muffin pan with butter-flavored cooking spray or line with paper liners. In a large bowl, combine flour, dry pudding mix, Brown Sugar Twin, Sugar Twin, dry milk powder, pumpkin pie spice, baking powder, and baking soda. Stir in chocolate chips and walnuts. In a small bowl, combine pumpkin, egg, and yogurt. Mix gently to combine. Add pumpkin mixture to flour mixture. Mix just until combined. Evenly divide batter among prepared muffin wells. Bake for 25 to 35 minutes or until a toothpick inserted in center comes out clean. Place muffin pan on a wire rack and let set 5 minutes. Remove muffins from pan and continue cooling on wire rack.

Each serving equals:
HE: 1 Bread, ½ Fat, ⅓ Vegetable, ¼ Skim Milk, ¼ Slider, 4 Optional Calories
172 Calories, 4 gm Fat, 6 gm Protein, 28 gm Carbohydrate, 243 mg Sodium, 116 mg Calcium, 2 gm Fiber *3*
DIABETIC: 2 Starch/Carbohydrate

Three-Way Apple Raisin Bread

■ ✳ ■

If you enjoy baking for the holidays and giving your breads and cookies as gifts, I hope you'll give this wonderful apple bread a try. The scent of apples and spice filling your kitchen creates such a happy atmosphere, you'll probably end up making more than you can possibly give away! Lucky for you, this bread freezes well and tastes even better the next day.   *Serves 8 (1 thick or 2 thin slices)*

1½ cups all-purpose flour
1 (4-serving) package JELL-O sugar-free instant vanilla pudding mix
¼ cup Brown Sugar Twin
1 teaspoon baking powder
½ teaspoon baking soda
1 teaspoon apple pie spice
¼ cup raisins

1 cup (2 small) cored, peeled, and finely chopped cooking apples
¾ cup unsweetened apple juice
¼ cup unsweetened applesauce
1 egg or equivalent in egg substitute
1 teaspoon vanilla extract

Preheat oven to 325 degrees. Spray a 9-by-5-inch loaf pan with butter-flavored cooking spray. In a large bowl, combine flour, dry pudding mix, Brown Sugar Twin, baking powder, baking soda, and apple pie spice. Stir in apples and raisins. In a small bowl, combine apple juice, applesauce, egg, and vanilla extract. Add liquid mixture to dry mixture. Mix gently just to combine. Spoon batter into prepared loaf pan. Bake for 50 to 60 minutes or until a toothpick inserted in center comes out clean. Place loaf pan on a wire rack and let set for 10 minutes. Remove bread from pan and continue cooling on a wire rack. Cut into 8 thick or 16 thin slices.

Each serving equals:
HE: 1 Bread, ¾ Fruit, ¼ Slider, 3 Optional Calories
141 Calories, 1 gm Fat, 3 gm Protein, 30 gm Carbohydrate, 253 mg Sodium, 12 mg Calcium, 1 gm Fiber
DIABETIC: 1 Starch, 1 Fruit

Sour Cream Blueberry Banana Bread

Banana bread is an American classic, from sea to shining sea, but wherever I've traveled, I've run into delightful variations on this recipe. Cliff particularly loved this version that I stirred up when we had a few extra pints of fresh blueberries sitting in the cooler one Sunday afternoon. This is a great way to use up those blackened, oh-so-ripe bananas!   *Serves 8 (1 thick or 2 thin slices)*

1½ cups Bisquick Reduced Fat Baking Mix
1 (4-serving) package JELL-O sugar-free instant banana cream pudding mix
⅓ cup (1 ripe medium) mashed banana

½ cup unsweetened applesauce
¼ cup Land O Lakes no-fat sour cream
1 tablespoon skim milk
¾ cup fresh blueberries

Preheat oven to 350 degrees. Spray a 9-by-5-inch loaf pan with butter-flavored cooking spray. In a large bowl, combine baking mix and dry pudding mix. In a small bowl, combine banana, applesauce, sour cream, and skim milk. Add banana mixture to flour mixture. Mix gently just to combine. Gently fold in blueberries. Spread batter into prepared loaf pan. Bake for 1 hour or until a toothpick inserted in center comes out clean. Place loaf pan on a wire rack and let set for 5 minutes. Remove bread from pan and continue cooling on wire rack. Cut into 8 thick or 16 thin slices.

Each serving equals:
HE: 1 Bread, ½ Fruit, ¼ Protein, ¼ Fat, ½ Slider, 1 Optional Calorie

126 Calories, 2 gm Fat, 2 gm Protein, 25 gm Carbohydrate, 445 mg Sodium, 33 mg Calcium, 1 gm Fiber

DIABETIC: 1½ Starch, ½ Fruit

Chocolate Zucchini Bread

■ ❄ ■

I know, I know, it SOUNDS very strange, but you've trusted me so far, so give this unusual blend a shot. Zucchini has the wonderful ability to take on the flavors of the bread's other ingredients and, in this case, blends quite remarkably with the cocoa and yogurt. Maybe when you serve this to guests, you'll want to wait until after they've tried it and are singing its praises before you confess what's in it!

Serves 8 (1 thick or 2 thin slices)

1½ cups all-purpose flour
¼ cup unsweetened cocoa
½ teaspoon ground cinnamon
2 teaspoons baking powder
¼ teaspoon baking soda
¾ cup pourable Sugar Twin
1 cup shredded unpeeled zucchini

¼ cup (1 ounce) chopped walnuts
½ cup unsweetened applesauce
2 teaspoons vegetable oil
1 egg or equivalent in egg substitute
1 teaspoon vanilla extract

Preheat oven to 350 degrees. Spray a 9-by-5-inch loaf pan with butter-flavored cooking spray. In a large bowl, combine flour, cocoa, cinnamon, baking powder, baking soda, and Sugar Twin. Stir in zucchini and walnuts. In a medium bowl, combine applesauce, oil, egg, and vanilla extract. Add applesauce mixture to flour mixture. Mix well to combine. Spread batter into prepared loaf pan. Bake for 50 to 55 minutes or until a toothpick inserted in center comes out clean. Place loaf pan on a wire rack and cool for 10 minutes. Remove bread from pan and continue cooling on wire rack. Cut into 8 thick or 16 thin slices.

Each serving equals:

HE: 1 Bread, ½ Fat, ¼ Protein, ¼ Vegetable, ¼ Slider, 4 Optional Calories
171 Calories, 7 gm Fat, 4 gm Protein, 23 gm Carbohydrate, 171 mg Sodium, 86 mg Calcium, 2 gm Fiber
DIABETIC: 1½ Starch/Carbohydrate, ½ Fat

Cranberry-Orange Bread

■ ❊ ■

This is a spectacular combination of flavors in a wonderfully moist quick bread. The orange is sweet and tangy, the cranberries tart and crunchy, and together they'll surely tango their way into your heart! Be sure to check that the apple-sauce label says no sugar has been added.   *Serves 8 (1 thick or 2 thin slices)*

1½ cups all-purpose flour
1 (4-serving) package JELL-O
   sugar-free instant vanilla pudding mix
1 teaspoon baking powder
½ teaspoon baking soda
½ cup pourable Sugar Twin
1 cup coarsely chopped fresh or
   frozen cranberries

¼ cup (1 ounce) chopped walnuts
½ cup unsweetened orange juice
1 egg, beaten, or equivalent in
   egg substitute
¼ cup + 1 tablespoon unsweetened applesauce

Preheat oven to 350 degrees. Spray a 9-by-5-inch loaf pan with butter-flavored cooking spray. In a large bowl, combine flour, dry pudding mix, baking powder, baking soda, and Sugar Twin. Stir in cranberries and walnuts. In a small bowl, combine orange juice, egg, and applesauce. Add orange juice mixture to flour mixture. Mix just to combine. Spread batter into prepared loaf pan. Bake for 50 to 60 minutes or until a toothpick inserted in center comes out clean. Place loaf pan on a wire rack and let set for 5 minutes. Remove bread from pan and continue cooling on wire rack. Cut into 8 thick or 16 thin slices.

Each serving equals:

HE: 1 Bread, ⅓ Fruit, ¼ Protein, ¼ Fat, 19 Optional Calories

147 Calories, 3 gm Fat, 4 gm Protein, 26 gm Carbohydrate, 314 mg Sodium, 46 mg Calcium, 1 gm Fiber 3

DIABETIC: 1½ Starch/Carbohydrate, ½ Fat

Nutty Chicken Dip

■ ■ ■

If you're stumped about what to serve with cut-up veggies at your next gathering, this dip will definitely please your guests! The tiny bits of red give it extra sparkle, and the nuts provide added texture. You may want to double the recipe if you're expecting a crowd!

Serves 6 (⅓ cup)

½ cup Land O Lakes no-fat sour cream
½ cup Kraft fat-free mayonnaise
1 teaspoon dried onion flakes
1 teaspoon dried parsley flakes

¼ cup (one 2-ounce jar) chopped pimiento, drained
1 cup (5 ounces) finely diced cooked chicken breast
¼ cup (1 ounce) chopped walnuts

In a medium bowl, combine sour cream and mayonnaise. Stir in onion flakes, parsley flakes, and pimiento. Add chicken and walnuts. Mix well to combine. Cover and refrigerate for at least 1 hour. Gently stir again just before serving. Great with veggies or crackers.

HINT: If you don't have leftovers, purchase a chunk of cooked chicken breast from your local deli.

Each serving equals:

HE: 1 Protein, ⅓ Fat, ¼ Slider, 13 Optional Calories

100 Calories, 4 gm Fat, 8 gm Protein, 8 gm Carbohydrate, 219 mg Sodium, 30 mg Calcium, 1 gm Fiber

DIABETIC: 1 Meat, ½ Starch/Carbohydrate, ½ Fat

Calico Ham Dip

■ ■ ■

Here's another savory dip that's great for hearty appetites at your next Super Bowl party. It's creamy and colorful, but best of all it'll fill you up and satisfy your urge for creamy munchies!   *Serves 8 (¼ cup)*

1 (8-ounce) package
   Philadelphia fat-free cream
   cheese
¼ cup Kraft fat-free mayonnaise
2 teaspoons prepared mustard
2 teaspoons dried onion flakes
2 teaspoons dried parsley flakes

¾ cup (3 ounces) shredded Kraft
   reduced-fat Cheddar cheese
1 full cup (6 ounces) ground
   Dubuque 97% fat-free ham or
   any extra-lean ham
2 tablespoons sweet pickle relish

In a medium bowl, stir cream cheese with a spoon until soft. Stir in mayonnaise, mustard, onion flakes, and parsley flakes. Add Cheddar cheese, ham, and pickle relish. Mix well to combine. Cover and refrigerate for at least 1 hour. Gently stir again just before serving. Good with crackers and celery sticks.

Each serving equals:
HE: 1¼ Protein, 12 Optional Calories
87 Calories, 3 gm Fat, 10 gm Protein, 5 gm Carbohydrate, 548 mg Sodium, 74 mg Calcium, 0 gm Fiber
DIABETIC: 1 Meat

Carrot-Stuffed Celery

■ ■ ■

No, you didn't read the recipe title wrong, although it might seem a bit strange. This is a great way to serve hors d'oeuvres that are colorful and tasty—and that also provide a substantial serving of vegetables! This is my favorite kind of finger food: crunchy and rich, but with surprisingly few calories and NO FAT!

Serves 8 (4 pieces)

1 (8-ounce) package Philadelphia fat-free cream cheese	1 teaspoon Italian seasoning
¼ cup Kraft fat-free mayonnaise	½ cup grated carrots
	16 (4-inch) pieces crisp celery

In a medium bowl, stir cream cheese with a spoon until soft. Add mayonnaise and Italian seasoning. Mix well to combine. Stir in carrots. Pack grooves of celery with cream cheese mixture. Cut celery crosswise into 2-inch pieces. Cover and refrigerate for at least 30 minutes.

Each serving equals:
HE: ½ Protein, ½ Vegetable, 5 Optional Calories
28 Calories, 0 gm Fat, 4 gm Protein, 3 gm Carbohydrate, 250 mg Sodium, 8 mg Calcium, 0 gm Fiber
DIABETIC: ½ Meat, 1 Free Food

Italian Baked Onion Rings

■ ■ ■

Love onion rings, but you've given them up in your quest to lose some weight and feel better? Now you can do both—isn't that good news? These turned out so delectably good, I had to grab a couple to taste-test before my kitchen visitors gobbled them all down.

Serves 4

1 egg or equivalent in egg substitute

1 tablespoon skim milk

6 tablespoons (1½ ounces) dried fine bread crumbs

1 teaspoon Italian seasoning

1 large onion, sliced and separated into rings

Preheat oven to 350 degrees. Spray a large baking sheet with butter-flavored cooking spray. In a small bowl, combine egg and skim milk. In another small bowl, combine bread crumbs and Italian seasoning. Dip onion rings first into egg mixture, then into crumb mixture. Arrange coated rings on prepared baking sheet. Bake for 15 minutes. Turn onion rings over and continue baking for additional 20 minutes. Lightly spray with butter-flavored cooking spray. Divide into 4 equal servings. Serve at once.

Each serving equals:

HE: ½ Bread, ½ Vegetable, ¼ Protein (limited), 2 Optional Calories

70 Calories, 2 gm Fat, 3 gm Protein, 10 gm Carbohydrate, 100 mg Sodium, 40 mg Calcium, 1 gm Fiber

DIABETIC: ½ Starch, ½ Vegetable

Dilly Deviled Eggs

■ ■ ■

What's summer without deviled eggs, I ask you? Especially out here in Iowa, where deviled eggs are one of the state foods—or they should be! Every grandma has her own family favorite recipe, but why not give this new one a chance to win your heart? (Cliff loves deviled eggs, so he quickly carried a couple of these off to the print shop when they were ready to taste!)

Serves 8 (2 halves each)

8 hard-boiled eggs
¼ cup Kraft Fat Free Ranch
*   Dressing*

¼ cup Kraft fat-free mayonnaise
¼ teaspoon dried dill weed

Cut eggs in half lengthwise. Remove yolks and place in a medium bowl. Mash yolks with a fork. Add Ranch dressing, mayonnaise, and dill weed. Mix well to combine. Evenly fill egg-white halves with yolk mixture. Cover and refrigerate for at least 30 minutes.

Each serving equals:

HE: 1 Protein (limited), 18 Optional Calories

89 Calories, 5 gm Fat, 6 gm Protein, 5 gm Carbohydrate, 207 mg Sodium, 26 mg Calcium, 0 gm Fiber

DIABETIC: 1 Meat

Heartland Deviled Eggs

■ ■ ■

If one deviled egg recipe isn't enough to serve at your next picnic, here's a second one to delight your family and friends! I think you'll be pleasantly surprised at how special these taste because of the tiny amount of lemon pepper you've stirred in. Come, join me in America's heartland, where people love their traditional foods—and they particularly love deviled eggs!

Serves 6 (2 halves each)

6 hard-boiled eggs
¼ cup Kraft fat-free mayonnaise
2 tablespoons prepared mustard
2 tablespoons Hormel Bacon
   Bits

¼ teaspoon lemon pepper
1 teaspoon dried parsley flakes
Paprika (optional)

Cut eggs in half lengthwise. Remove yolks and place in a medium bowl. Mash yolks with a fork. Add mayonnaise, mustard, bacon bits, lemon pepper, and parsley flakes. Mix until well blended. Evenly fill egg-white halves with yolk mixture. Lightly sprinkle paprika over top, if desired. Cover and refrigerate for at least 30 minutes.

Each serving equals:

HE: 1 Protein (limited), 15 Optional Calories

94 Calories, 6 gm Fat, 7 gm Protein, 3 gm Carbohydrate, 298 mg Sodium, 30 mg Calcium, 0 gm Fiber

DIABETIC: 1 Meat

Easy Refrigerator Shake Pickles

■ ■ ■

I included this recipe just for fun, and because homemade pickles are a delight-fully old-fashioned treat that ought to be revived as we near the millennium! If you've never even imagined making your own pickles in the fridge, it's way past time to try 'em! You should be able to find the spices you need in your super-market, even alum, which sounds a bit exotic but really isn't.

Serves 40 (¼ cup)

8 cups sliced unpeeled cucumbers	*1 teaspoon celery seed*
2 cups sliced onion	*1 teaspoon turmeric*
3 cups white vinegar	*1 teaspoon dry mustard*
3½ cups pourable Sugar Twin	*¼ cup salt*
1 teaspoon alum	

In a 1-gallon covered container, combine cucumbers and onion. In an 8-cup glass measuring bowl, combine vinegar, Sugar Twin, alum, celery seed, turmeric, dry mustard, and salt. Pour vinegar mixture over cucumber mixture. Cover and shake well. Place in refrigerator. Shake well once a day for 7 days. Ready to eat after 7 days. Store in refrigerator and shake well before serving each time.

Each serving equals:
HE: ½ Vegetable, 4 Optional Calories

8 Calories, 0 gm Fat, 0 gm Protein, 2 gm Carbohydrate, 640 mg Sodium, 7 mg Calcium, 0 gm Fiber

DIABETIC: 1 Free Food

Munch Mix

■ ■ ■

Tommy and Angie kept dipping their hands into a bowl of this the last time they were home, so I guess it was a hit! It's easy to eat too much of this, so I do recommend premeasuring the servings, at least the first time you prepare it, so you'll know how to judge the amount. It's great to take a self-seal bag of this in the car on a road trip, so keep it in mind when you're packing for your next vacation.

Serves 8 (⅔ cup)

3½ cups (6 ounces) Nabisco bite-size shredded wheat
½ cup (2 ounces) dry-roasted peanuts
1 cup raisins

¼ cup Peter Pan reduced-fat creamy peanut butter
¼ cup Cary's Sugar Free Maple Syrup

Preheat oven to 350 degrees. In a 10-by-15-inch rimmed baking sheet, combine shredded wheat, peanuts, and raisins. Set aside. In a small saucepan, combine peanut butter and maple syrup. Cook over medium heat until hot, stirring often. Drizzle hot mixture evenly over cereal mixture, tossing to coat. Bake for 10 minutes, stirring after 5 minutes. Place baking sheet on a wire rack and allow to cool for 10 minutes. Store in airtight container.

Each serving equals:
HE: 1 Fruit, 1 Bread, 1 Fat, ¾ Protein, 5 Optional Calories

226 Calories, 6 gm Fat, 6 gm Protein, 37 gm Carbohydrate, 59 mg Sodium, 21 mg Calcium, 4 gm Fiber

DIABETIC: 1 Fruit, 1 Starch, 1 Fat, 1 Meat

Maple Peanut Brittle

■ ■ ■

Peanut brittle in a healthy cookbook? Am I *nuts?* Well, peanuts, actually! This sweet treat is wonderfully easy to make in your microwave, and it's a great lunch-box surprise for your kids! Be sure to let it cool all the way or it'll be harder to break into pieces.

Serves 8

1 cup pourable Sugar Twin
½ cup Cary's Sugar Free Maple Syrup
1 cup (4 ounces) salted dry-roasted peanuts

1 teaspoon reduced-calorie margarine
1 teaspoon vanilla extract
1 teaspoon baking soda

Spray a 10-by-15-inch rimmed baking sheet with butter-flavored cooking spray. In an 8-cup glass measuring bowl, combine Sugar Twin and maple syrup. Microwave on HIGH (100% power) for 4 minutes. Stir in peanuts. Continue microwaving on HIGH for 4 minutes. Add margarine and vanilla extract. Mix well to combine. Microwave on HIGH for an additional 1½ minutes. Stir in baking soda and continue stirring until light and foamy. Pour mixture onto prepared baking sheet. Place baking sheet on a wire rack and allow to cool for 1 hour. When cooled, break into small pieces and divide into 8 servings. Store in an airtight container.

Each serving equals:
HE: 1 Fat, ½ Protein, ½ Slider, 5 Optional Calories
123 Calories, 7 gm Fat, 3 gm Protein, 5 gm Carbohydrate, 194 mg Sodium, 8 mg Calcium, 1 gm Fiber
DIABETIC: 1 Fat, ½ Meat

Cinnamon-Orange Maple Syrup

■ ■ ■

One of my favorite healthy cooking tips is taking a store-bought product and adding a bit of this or that to make it even better. I'm a big fan of sugar-free maple syrup and have used it in lots of recipes. But, good as it is, I knew it could be better, and so I stirred in a few goodies to test my theory. The end result—scrumptious!

Serves 4 (full ⅓ cup)

*1 cup Cary's Sugar Free Maple
    Syrup*
1 teaspoon ground cinnamon

½ cup unsweetened orange juice
1 tablespoon cornstarch
½ teaspoon vanilla extract

In a medium saucepan, combine maple syrup and cinnamon. In a covered jar, combine orange juice and cornstarch. Shake well to blend. Pour orange juice mixture into syrup mixture. Cook over medium heat until mixture thickens and starts to boil, stirring often. Remove from heat. Stir in vanilla extract. Serve warm over pancakes, French toast, or vanilla sugar- and fat-free ice cream.

Each serving equals:
HE: ¼ Fruit, ½ Slider, 8 Optional Calories

56 Calories, 0 gm Fat, 0 gm Protein, 14 gm Carbohydrate, 136 mg Sodium, 9 mg Calcium, 0 gm Fiber

DIABETIC: 1 Starch/Carbohydrate

Plymouth Rock Floats

■ ■ ■

The Pilgrims weren't exactly party people, according to the history books, but I bet if they'd had some Diet Dew and this recipe, they might have smiled a whole lot more! This is such a pretty drink, you might want to save it for company, but why not treat yourself like company, and serve it tonight?   *Serves 4*

2 cups Ocean Spray reduced-
   calorie cranberry juice cocktail
2 cups Wells' Blue Bunny sugar-
   and fat-free vanilla ice cream

or any sugar- and fat-free ice
   cream
1 cup Diet Mountain Dew

For each float, pour ½ cup cranberry juice cocktail into a tall glass, add ½ cup ice cream, then slowly pour ¼ cup Diet Mountain Dew over top. Serve at once.

Each serving equals:
HE: ½ Fruit, ¾ Slider

112 Calories, 0 gm Fat, 4 gm Protein, 24 gm Carbohydrate, 74 mg Sodium, 120 mg Calcium, 0 gm Fiber

DIABETIC: 1 Starch/Carbohydrate, ½ Fruit

Mexican Mocha Float

■ ■ ■

It's rumored that the Aztecs were the first to figure out the wonderful combination of chocolate and coffee, but I'm sure Montezuma and the gang would happily hand over some gold in exchange for this festive dessert drink! The cinnamon adds extra sizzle to a winning blend.　　　　　　　*Serves 4*

> *2 cups cold skim milk*
> *¼ cup Nestlé Quik sugar-free chocolate milk mix*
> *½ teaspoon ground cinnamon*
> *1 teaspoon instant coffee crystals*

> *2 cups Wells' Blue Bunny sugar- and fat-free vanilla ice cream or any sugar- and fat-free ice cream*
> *¼ cup Cool Whip Lite*

In a 4-cup glass measuring cup, combine skim milk, chocolate milk mix, cinnamon, and coffee crystals. Mix well using a wire whisk. For each serving, place ½ cup ice cream into a float glass or tall glass, pour ½ cup milk mixture over ice cream, and top with 1 tablespoon Cool Whip Lite. Serve at once.

Each serving equals:

HE: ½ Skim Milk, 1 Slider, 10 Optional Calories

153 Calories, 1 gm Fat, 8 gm Protein, 28 gm Carbohydrate, 136 mg Sodium, 274 mg Calcium, 1 gm Fiber

DIABETIC: 1½ Starch/Carbohydrate, ½ Skim Milk

Berry Bash Slush

■ ❋ ■

You know what I really like to do some nights before I head for bed? I fill the blender with these ingredients, pour myself a tall glass, and watch my favorite TV talk show. Now, doesn't Geraldo Rivera look like a man who'd enjoy this version of a frozen strawberry daiquiri? *Hmm . . .*   *Serves 4*

1 cup unsweetened orange juice
½ cup water
2 cups frozen unsweetened whole
    strawberries
¼ cup chopped lemon, including
    peel and seeds

1 (4-serving) package JELL-O
    sugar-free strawberry gelatin
6 ice cubes
1 cup Diet Mountain Dew

In a blender container, combine orange juice, water, strawberries, lemon, and dry gelatin. Cover and process on BLEND until mixture is smooth. Add ice cubes one at a time. Continue processing until mixture is smooth. For each serving, pour about ¾ cup mixture into a tall glass and add ¼ cup Diet Mountain Dew.

Each serving equals:
HE: 1 Fruit, 10 Optional Calories
56 Calories, 0 gm Fat, 1 gm Protein, 13 gm Carbohydrate, 8 mg Sodium,
16 mg Calcium, 1 gm Fiber
DIABETIC: 1 Fruit

Chocolate Brandy Alexander

■ ❄ ■

I've always enjoyed creating nonalcoholic party drinks. I know so many people who just love to celebrate but choose not to drink alcohol, and I keep them in mind when I'm fixing these cool and frothy beverages that make any gathering a joyful one.

Serves 2

1 cup cold water
⅔ cup Carnation Nonfat Dry Milk Powder
¼ cup Nestlé Quik sugar-free chocolate milk mix

1 teaspoon vanilla extract
1 teaspoon brandy extract
6 to 8 ice cubes

In a blender container, combine water, dry milk powder, chocolate milk mix, vanilla extract, and brandy extract. Cover and process on BLEND for 10 seconds. Add ice cubes, one at a time. Continue processing on BLEND until mixture is smooth. Evenly pour mixture into 2 small brandy snifters or beverage glasses. Serve at once.

Each serving equals:

HE: 1 Skim Milk, ½ Slider

117 Calories, 1 gm Fat, 9 gm Protein, 18 gm Carbohydrate, 168 mg Sodium, 276 mg Calcium, 2 gm Fiber 2

DIABETIC: 1 Skim Milk, ½ Starch/Carbohydrate

MAKING HEALTHY EXCHANGES WORK FOR YOU

■ ■ ■

You're ready now to begin a wonderful journey to better health. In the preceding pages, you've discovered the remarkable variety of good food available to you when you begin eating the Healthy Exchanges way. You've stocked your pantry and learned many of my food preparation "secrets" that will point you on the way to delicious success.

But before I let you go, I'd like to share a few tips that I've learned while traveling toward healthier eating habits. It took me a long time to learn how to eat *smarter*. In fact, I'm still working on it. But I am getting better. For years, I could *inhale* a five-course meal in five minutes flat—and still make room for a second helping of dessert!

Now I follow certain signposts on the road that help me stay on the right path. I hope these ideas will help point you in the right direction as well.

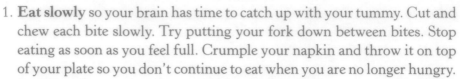

1. **Eat slowly** so your brain has time to catch up with your tummy. Cut and chew each bite slowly. Try putting your fork down between bites. Stop eating as soon as you feel full. Crumple your napkin and throw it on top of your plate so you don't continue to eat when you are no longer hungry.

2. **Smaller plates** may help you feel more satisfied by your food portions *and* limit the amount you can put on the plate.

3. **Watch portion size.** If you are *truly* hungry, you can always add more food to your plate once you've finished your initial serving. But remember to count the additional food accordingly.

4. **Always eat at your dining-room or kitchen table.** You deserve better than nibbling from an open refrigerator or over the sink. Make an attractive place setting, even if you're eating alone. Feed your eyes as well as your stomach. By always eating at a table, you will become much more aware of your true food intake. For some reason, many of us conveniently "forget" the food we swallow while standing over the stove or munching in the car or on the run.

5. **Avoid doing anything else while you are eating.** If you read the paper or watch television while you eat, it's easy to consume too much food without realizing it, because you are concentrating on something else besides what you're eating. Then, when you look down at your plate and see that it's empty, you wonder where all the food went and why you still feel hungry.

Day by day, as you travel the path to good health, it will become easier to make the right choices, to eat *smarter*. But don't ever fool yourself into thinking that you'll be able to put your eating habits on cruise control and forget about them. Making a commitment to eat good healthy food and sticking to it takes some effort. But with all the good-tasting recipes in this Healthy Exchanges cookbook, just think how well you're going to eat—and enjoy it—from now on!

Healthy Lean *Bon Appétit!*

INDEX

■ ■ ■

I WANT TO HEAR FROM YOU . . .

■ ■ ■

Besides my family, the love of my life is creating "common folk" healthy recipes and solving everyday cooking questions in *The Healthy Exchanges Way.* Everyone who uses my recipes is considered part of the Healthy Exchanges Family, so please write to me if you have any questions, comments, or suggestions. I will do my best to answer. With your support, I'll continue to stir up even more recipes and cooking tips for the Family in the years to come.

Write to: JoAnna M. Lund
c/o Healthy Exchanges, Inc.
P.O. Box 124
DeWitt, IA 52742

If you prefer, you can fax me at 1-319-659-2126 or contact me via e-mail by writing to HealthyJo@aol.com. Or visit my Healthy Exchanges Internet Web site at: http://www.healthyexchanges.com.

Healthy Exchanges recipes are a great way to begin—
but if your goal is living healthy for a lifetime,

You Need HELP!

JoAnna M. Lund's
Healthy Exchanges Lifetime Plan

"I lost 130 pounds and reclaimed my health by following a Four-Part Plan that emphasizes not only Healthy Eating but also Moderate Exercise, Lifestyle Changes, and Goal Setting, and most important of all, a Positive Attitude."

- If you've lost weight before but failed to keep it off . . .
- If you've got diabetes, high blood pressure, high cholesterol, or heart disease—and you need to reinvent your lifestyle . . .
- If you want to raise a healthy family and encourage good lifelong habits in your kids . . .

HELP is on the way!

The Support You Need

■

The Motivation You Want

■

A Program That Works

HELP: Healthy Exchanges Lifetime Plan
is available at your favorite bookstore.

Ever since I began stirring up Healthy Exchanges recipes, I wanted every dish to be rich in flavor and lively in taste. As part of my pursuit of satisfying eating and healthy living for a lifetime, I decided to create my own line of spices.

JO's Spices are salt-, sugar-, wheat-, and MSG-free, and you can substitute them in any of the recipes calling for traditional spice mixes. If you're interested in hearing more about my special blends, please call Healthy Exchanges at 1-319-659-8234 for more information or to order. If you prefer, write to JO's Spices, c/o Healthy Exchanges, P.O. Box 124, DeWitt, IA 52742.

JO'S SPICES . . . A Healthy Way to Spice Up Your Life™

Now That You've Seen
Make a Joyful Table, Why Not Order *The Healthy Exchanges Food Newsletter?*

If you enjoyed the recipes in this cookbook and would like to cook up even more of these "common folk" healthy dishes, you may want to subscribe to *The Healthy Exchanges Food Newsletter.*

This monthly 12-page newsletter contains 30-plus new recipes *every month* in such columns as: Reader Exchange • Reader Requests• Recipe Makeover • Micro Corner • Dinner for Two • Crock Pot Luck • Meatless Main Dishes • Rise & Shine • Our Small World • Brown Bagging It • Snack Attack • Side Dishes • Main Dishes • Desserts

In addition to all the recipes, other regular features include:

• The Editor's Motivational Corner
• Dining Out Question & Answer
• Cooking Question & Answer
• New Product Alert
• Success Profiles of Winners in the Losing Game
• Exercise Advice from a Cardiac Rehab Specialist
• Nutrition Advice from a Registered Dietitian
• Positive Thought for the Month

Just as in this cookbook, all *Healthy Exchanges Food Newsletter* recipes are calculated in three distinct ways: 1) Weight Loss Choices, 2) Calories with Fat and Fiber Grams, and 3) Diabetic Exchanges.

The cost for a one-year (12-issue) subscription is $22.50. To order, simply complete the form and mail to us, *or* call our toll-free number and pay with your VISA or MasterCard.

_____ Yes, I want to subscribe to *The Healthy Exchanges Food Newsletter*
$22.50 Yearly Subscription Cost .... $_____

_____ Foreign orders please add $6.00 for money exchange and
extra postage.. $_____

_____ I'm not sure, so please send me a sample copy at $2.50.......... $_____

Please make check payable to HEALTHY EXCHANGES, or pay by
VISA/MasterCard

CARD NUMBER:_____ EXPIRATION DATE: _____
SIGNATURE:_____

Signature required for all credit card orders.

Or Order Toll-Free, using your credit card, at 1-800-766-8961

NAME:_____
ADDRESS:_____
CITY: _____ STATE: _____ ZIP: _____
TELEPHONE: (___)_____

*If additional orders for the newsletter are to be sent to an address other than
the one listed above, please use a separate sheet and attach to this form.*

MAIL TO: HEALTHY EXCHANGES
P.O. BOX 124
DEWITT, IA 52742-0124

1-800-766-8961 For Customer Orders
1-319-659-8234 For Customer Service

Thank you for your order, and for choosing to become a part of the
Healthy Exchanges Family!

ABOUT THE AUTHORS

■ ■ ■

JoAnna Lund, a graduate of the University of Western Illinois, worked as a commercial insurance underwriter for eighteen years before starting her own business, Healthy Exchanges, Inc., which publishes cookbooks, a monthly newsletter, motivational booklets, and inspirational audiotapes. Her first book, *Healthy Exchanges Cookbook,* has more than 250,000 copies in print. Her second book, *HELP: Healthy Exchanges Lifetime Plan,* was published in 1996. A popular speaker with hospitals, support groups for heart patients and diabetics, and service and volunteer organizations, she has appeared on QVC, on hundreds of regional television and radio shows, and has been featured in newspapers and magazines across the country.

The recipient of numerous business awards, JoAnna was an Iowa delegate to the national White House Conference on Small Business. She is a member of the International Association of Culinary Professionals, the Society for Nutrition Education, and other professional publishing and marketing associations. She lives with her husband, Clifford, in DeWitt, Iowa.

Barbara Alpert is the author of *Child of My Heart, The Love of Friends,* and *No Friend Like a Sister,* and the co-author of many other books, including *Cooking Healthy with a Man in Mind, Dessert Every Night!,* and *HELP: Healthy Exchanges Lifetime Plan,* with JoAnna M. Lund. A former executive editor at Bantam Books, she has published articles in *Cosmopolitan, Hemispheres, New York Runner,* and *ParentSource* magazines. She teaches book editing as an Adjunct Associate Professor at Hofstra University in New York.